Working with Groups

John Wiley & Sons, Inc., New York · London

Working with Groups

GROUP PROCESS AND INDIVIDUAL GROWTH

Walter M. Lifton

DIRECTOR OF GUIDANCE PUBLICATIONS AND SERVICES
SCIENCE RESEARCH ASSOCIATES

formerly ASSOCIATE PROFESSOR OF EDUCATION
UNIVERSITY OF ILLINOIS

L7221

Preface

I have written this book in the hope that it will be helpful to people who find themselves working with groups. There is a growing tendency in the various professions to try to isolate the areas which they consider their own special provinces. I feel very strongly that group-work skills are a necessary part of several professional groups and as such should be considered on an interdisciplinary basis. It is my goal in this book to be useful to teachers, social workers, counselors, psychologists, and laymen who are seeking to acquire the skills and knowledge that are prerequisite to working with groups.

It is unfortunate that certain terms in this area have become loaded with feeling. The idea of group therapy tends to scare the teacher, and the social worker may reject being associated with a classroom setting. To facilitate communication, there has been a deliberate attempt to use terms that are less emotional so that students from different disciplines can relate to the concepts involved.

Because of my own background, there is a predominance of illustrations from the educational setting. Usually, however, I discuss the application to other situations of the concepts being explored. This is a personal book. It represents one man's point of view and way of functioning. As such, its value depends on the reader's critical evaluation of the ideas in terms of the way they fit his skills, values, and philosophical orientation.

As the material will reveal, it is virtually impossible to designate the people who have been involved in developing this book. Every student I have taught and every teacher with whom I have studied has made a contribution.

I am very lucky to have had the assistance of Mr. George Amsbary, and Professors Ray Simpson, Merle Ohlsen, and C. H. Patterson. Each of these men critically reviewed parts of this book and provided helpful suggestions.

I am also grateful to the editors of the *Review of Educational Research, Human Relations, Progressive Education,* and *Educational Administration and Supervision* for their permission to quote from their journals.

To my wife and children I owe a special debt. They are the ones who always provide love and support when I need it most.

WALTER M. LIFTON

Champaign, Illinois
October 1960

Contents

1 Group Process and Individual Growth   1

WHY THIS BOOK WAS WRITTEN, 3
DISCUSSION, 7
BIBLIOGRAPHY, 7

2 Theories, Professional Jargon, and Definitions   9

EDUCATION AND THERAPY, 12
A GROUP VERSUS A MASS, 15
THE GROUP DYNAMIC APPROVAL, 16
THE COMMON DENOMINATORS, 19
RESTATEMENT OF THE PHILOSOPHY EXPRESSED IN THE TEXT, 21
DISCUSSION, 22
BIBLIOGRAPHY, 23

3 The Tools and Techniques
Involved in the Helping Process   26

CLARIFYING OPERATIONS, 30
THE SHOW-HOW OPERATIONS, 32
SECURITY-GIVING OPERATIONS, 35
DISCUSSION, 38
BIBLIOGRAPHY, 40

vii

4 A Group in Action 42

DISCUSSION, 86

BIBLIOGRAPHY, 91

5 Typical Problems in Group Process 93

THE INITIAL LEADER, 93

VOLUNTARY AND INVOLUNTARY GROUPS, 102

GROUP COMPOSITION, 105

OUT-OF-GROUP SESSIONS, 108

GROUP SIZE, 110

LENGTH OF GROUP LIFE—FIXED AND CONTINUOUS GROUPS, 110

ADMITTING NEW MEMBERS, 111

THE SILENT MEMBER, 112

SILENCE IN THE GROUP, 114

THE MISSING MEMBER, 115

THE MISSING LEADER, 115

THE MONOPOLIST, 116

RESISTANCE, 117

CATHARSIS, 117

THE ROLE OF STEREOTYPES, 118

DECISION MAKING—TO VOTE OR NOT TO VOTE, 119

RESPONSIBILITY IN A GROUP, 122

OTHER TOOLS AND TECHNIQUES, 125

SUMMARY, 126

BIBLIOGRAPHY, 126

6 Group Techniques Applied 130

ORIENTATION, 130

GROUP GUIDANCE PROGRAMS, 135

GROUP TECHNIQUES IN THE SUBJECT MATTER CLASSROOM, 140

IDENTIFYING GROUP GOALS, 143

USING RECORDS FOR SELF-EVALUATIVE PURPOSES, 144

EFFECT OF COURSE UPON THE AUTHOR, 147

AS APPLIED TO A WORKSHOP, 148

STUDIES ON WORK WITH FAILING AND UNDERACHIEVING
STUDENTS, 150

STUDENT COUNCILS, 151
MORAL AND SPIRITUAL VALUES, 156
GROUP TECHNIQUES IN DEVELOPING A PROGRAM, 158
DISCUSSION, 160
BIBLIOGRAPHY, 161

7 *Evaluation and Research* **164**

Evaluation, 164
GROUP GROWTH, 164
INDIVIDUAL GROWTH, 165
A COMPARISON OF SELF WITH OTHERS, 166

Research, 170
SUMMARY, 174
BIBLIOGRAPHY, 175
BIBLIOGRAPHY OF DOCTORAL DISSERTATIONS, 176

8 *Conclusion* **180**

TERMINATING GROUPS, 180
THE TRAINING OF THE EFFECTIVE GROUP WORKER, 181
SUMMARY, 182

*Appendix: A Diary Report of the Complete Life
of a Group* **184**

Index **233**

1

Group Process and
Individual Growth

Let's face it. The values we cher-
ish in our society are apparently
contradictory. On the one hand, we value our heritage of rugged
individualism; on the other, we are proud of the picture of ourselves
as the champions of democracy.

Contradictions provoke controversies. We need but to glance at
some major controversies in our society—labor-management-govern-
ment interrelations, integration-segregation problems, national defense
needs, the role of government in health, education, welfare, and science—and we see that they stem from this common contradiction of
values.

Is this apparent contradiction of values real? Is the point at which
the rights of the individual end and society's rights begin a Never
Never Land of inevitable conflict? It seems unlikely. A major pre-
mise of this book is that there is no necessary contradiction between
individual growth and societal, or group, process. And it follows that
as the speed of communication increases and the complexity of our
problems increase, so also it becomes increasingly imperative that we
find a way to communicate how group action can be a source and a
means of freeing the individual rather than enslaving him.[1]

For example, clichés sometimes give clues to current concerns of
society. Is the frequent use of the terms "togetherness" and being
"other directed" just another way of demonstrating concern in the
public's mind over conformity?

The role of the group in politics represents a major present concern.

1

Equal concern is being expressed over the use of groups to help individuals secure their maximum growth potential. We all know there is a current shortage of counselors, psychologists, and social workers. The estimates vary, but all demonstrate how impossible it is to train enough professional workers to provide all the help needed for individuals in our society. Such shortages influence the redefinition of the role of the personnel worker. Here is one example:

Recently the College of Education of the University of Illinois wished to assess the effectiveness and appropriateness of its counselor training program. Administrators from all over the state were invited to the campus. During the day they were presented with a detailed description of the kinds of skills and abilities being developed in students who were in training to be counselors. At the end of the day, the administrators were asked to comment on their impressions and to provide suggestions for revision in the program.

Almost to a man, the group placed major priority on group work and group therapy skills. Recognizing that they could not hire enough counselors to work with all students individually, they wanted the counselors to work with groups of teachers. In groups they felt counselors would provide teachers with skills and insights which might enable teachers to help some of the youngsters now being referred to the counselors. The administrators also wanted the counselors to help students in their group activities, whether it be the student council or such groups as those organized to help failing students. And, recognizing the importance of parent understanding, they sought help from the counselors in working with P.T.A.'s and child study groups. Over and over again the cry was for people trained to work in group settings—people with the skills to transform group settings into effective learning experiences.

This demand for group work skills does not stem purely from a desire for economy of effort or a desire to relieve staff shortages. The demand also stems from a growing awareness—an awareness that there are some peculiar growth experiences available to individuals in groups that are not present in a one-to-one relationship.

One cannot train people to help others with just a book. The process is too complicated. A counselor not only has to try to understand one person, but, as is more vital in a group, he must also be aware of the interplay between several people. Obviously the demands on the counselor are for an extremely high level of skill and sensitivity.

But every day, whether anyone likes it or not, laymen and professionals alike find themselves thrust into group environments. And they have to do the best job they can under the circumstances. Increasingly they call for help in understanding the problems involved in group process. They want also a clear statement of appropriate techniques to employ. Therefore, this book is intended both to provide some immediate help for the beginner and to help potential group workers to recognize their need for formal professional training.

Why This Book Was Written

Every teacher experiences the day when he is asked by his students "How did you do that?" or "Why did you do it that way?" Although he may be successful in presenting a rationale for his behavior, the day arrives when the student says, "Teach me how to do it." When the subject to be taught involves human relationships, it soon becomes obvious to us all that what helps one person just doesn't work with the next person. The initial limitation of this book, if the book is to be useful, is that it can present some ideas and ways of relating that have proved useful to at least one person—the author.

To avoid the cookbook concept of teaching, this book will be organized in the following way. First, is a summary of issues involved in group process, which is followed by definitions of some of the terms to be employed in the text. Chapters 4, 5, and 6 offer descriptions of several group situations that are instructional. Each of these situations is presented as completely as possible to allow the reader to come to his own conclusions. And further to stimulate the reader in the development of his individual philosophy, each chapter concludes with a résumé of writings by people who would interpret differently than I would the concepts being explored. In this way the lay reader may find concepts presented that are within his present experience, whereas the professionally-trained person can go beyond this text to the controversial interpretations that are always present in such a young and multidisciplined area. Chapters 7 and 8 are designed to help the reader evaluate himself and the groups with which he works.

Roles Need to Be Defined.* Teachers and counselors are human beings. To be effective they must be secure. They must have a clear

* A restatement of excerpts from W. Lifton, "The Teacher's Role in Mental Hygiene, Therapy, and Social Reconstruction," *Progressive Education*, May 1955, pp. 65–67.

idea not only of their own values but also of the skills and abilities they possess which will enable them to do the jobs that are important to them. These facts we all recognize. But we apparently fail to see that it is equally important to understand clearly the job itself. The threats or rewards offered by society have a very real effect upon the productiveness and originality that a person exhibits. This is especially true when what society really wants is in question.

Years ago people used to say that every teacher did guidance—indeed, that education *was* guidance.[2] This saying probably meant that no matter what the teacher did his actions affected and influenced the behavior of the people with whom he worked. Today, when we conceive of the teacher's role in its therapeutic aspects, we tend to say that the teacher helps people learn through doing. We now imply, correctly, that youngsters are more sensitive to our actions than to the things we say.

The educator's role and the learning process are at heart psychological problems. For the educator to function adequately, it is important for him to know the philosophy of the agency within which he works, the limits of behavior which will be tolerated by the community, his own ability to tolerate differences with his own value system, and probably most crucial of all, the kind of behavior he exhibits as contrasted with the things he would like to be doing. Therefore, we need to look to the field of psychology and draw from it a better understanding of the counselor's job. In industrial psychology we learned a long time ago that the efficiency of an organization is vastly increased when the jobs for each individual within the organization are clearly defined. Then each individual not only knows what he is responsible for, but also clearly perceives the authority he has and the freedom that he possesses to act within the job limits that have been described.

But society's policies, limits, and definitions are not as clear as a corporation's. Whereas a corporation employee can know what ideas he should try because he knows the purposes, attitudes, and values of his organization, a teacher or group leader cannot. Differing concepts in society about the nature of man and differing criteria to employ in determining appropriate life goals make the job more difficult.

If man is perceived as having needs which are basically evil or does not have needs he ought to have, we cannot then comfortably develop an educational setting which will permit the needs of the individual to become an instrumental part in the learning process. Feeling the necessity for being our brother's keeper, we must develop every idea and technique within our power which will keep man from hurting himself. By every known device we must institute situations which will require behavior that will provide a more effective way of living.

For some, man is seen as initially rather neuter in quality. Through experiences and learned reactions he develops gradually a repertoire of typical responses. People most comfortable with this concept of man still cannot avoid value judgments in deciding what responses ought to be reinforced or led to extinction.

An opposite viewpoint to those presented has its philosophical root in the idea that man is basically good and that he is striving constantly toward a more effective kind of life. It also assumes that he has within him the desire, which is ever growing, to achieve a more satisfactory way of life. Holding this point of view, every effort is made to provide the individual opportunities to recognize his needs and to test ways in which he can achieve satisfaction. This viewpoint holds that as the individual searches for a more satisfying life, he will, of his own volition, seek information about how others before him have solved his problem. Implicit is the idea that if the eternal truths are really eternal and vital to living, there need be no fear that the individual will discover them for himself. It is only when we are not sure that our answer is best that we fear having a person seek his own best solution.

One of the problems associated with this self-actualizing concept of man is the fear that the individual will develop into an antisocial, anarchistic kind of being. Initially the individual may start out with a selfish, egocentric point of view. He quickly discovers as he tests out his needs in a group, that he can only get from others the things he wants when he has developed a relationship with them which will cause them to want to give to him what he seeks. When you help an individual face the world in which he finds himself, you also help him discover how his needs must be modified in order for him to get from society the security and rewards he desires.

The nature of the group atmosphere is basic to how people develop their security patterns. If we assume a democratic framework, an individual learns that his ability to gratify his needs can only come through developing in the group itself a climate and relationship with others which will cause them to feel responsible to and dependent upon him to secure the kind of life they desire together.

It should become quickly apparent that I have accepted as my concept of man a philosophy based upon man's positive growth potential. With this point of view, it is possible to start with the society we now have, including its many faults, and to try to help the individual realistically perceive what he can get from his environment. But of greater importance for social change, this point of view helps the counselor assist the individual in developing the security that he needs when he begins to investigate the ways in which he can modify his own environment. Under a democratic educational setting, youngsters learn to be responsible for their own behavior. As they grow to be more responsible, however, they also begin to recognize the ways in which the society which their parents have developed does not necessarily represent their own needs and goals. Probably the greatest failure of this democratic framework is that in it teachers have not also helped people learn a new kind of security that will go along with the changing environment which is now being created. A rather interesting illustration of this might be seen in the furor over the new methods of teaching reading or writing. Parents generally want their children to see them as wise and helpful. When a system is introduced that makes them unable to help their children, because of their own ignorance of the procedure, parents resent being put in that position. Teachers who have discussed with parents the reasons for changes in teaching methods prior to their introduction have helped the parents prepare themselves for a new role, before their security is threatened. In such schools new methods are rarely the focus of public hostility.

George Sharp in his book entitled, *Curriculum Development as Re-education of the Teacher*, Teachers College Bureau of Publications, 1951,[3] stated rather well the ethical and social problems within this point of view. On page 38 he states, ". . . he must realize that he is embarking on a program aimed at the deliberate change of society and individuals, and as he has no sanction to do either, he must work to develop the insights of others instead of imposing his own views. He must have a working knowledge of the dynamics of behavioral change not only in terms of theory but in terms of human behavior. Finally, he must understand the ethical and psychological requirements of the role he is to play and be able to control his own behavior in accordance with these requirements."

This chapter has tried to demonstrate that the teacher's or group leader's role is deeply rooted in philosophical and religious concepts. Because as a nation we have prided ourselves in our heterogeneity, we have not always been willing to face the need to homogenize our views when we define the teacher or educator's job. In Chapter 2 these differing value systems will be related to theories of personality and terms commonly used in group settings.

Discussion

In subsequent chapters, frequent reference is made to the thinking of different psychological schools as they apply to group situations. To prepare for this material, the following readings are suggested.

Good summaries of the positions of the Freudians can be found in Samuel Slavson's *The Practice of Group Therapy*,[4] and Saul Scheidlinger, *Psychoanalysis and Group Behavior: A Study in Freudian Group Psychology*.[5]

Rudolph Dreikurs has described "Group Psychotherapy from the Viewpoint of the Adlerian Psychology" in the *International Journal of Group Psychotherapy*.[6]

The nondirective point of view is clearly presented by Thomas Gordon in *Group-Centered Leadership*.[7]

Those readers seeking to relate psychological theory to classroom practice will find *Guidance in Groups* by Margaret Bennett [8] and *Group Work in Education* by Ruth Strang[9] helpful.

A good definition of the activities of the social group worker are presented in the 1954 and 1957 Social Work Yearbooks.[10,11] Also helpful is Trecker's *Social Group Work*.[12]

BIBLIOGRAPHY

1. DeHuzar, George B. *Practical Applications of Democracy.* New York: Harper, 1945.
2. Association for Supervision and Curriculum Development, 1955 Yearbook. *Guidance in the Curriculum.* Washington, D. C.: ASCD, 1955.
3. Sharp, George. *Curriculum Development as Re-education of the Teacher.* New York: Teachers College Bureau of Publications, 1951.
4. Slavson, Samuel. *The Practice of Group Therapy.* New York: International Press, 1951.
5. Scheidlinger, Saul. *Psychoanalysis and Group Behavior: A Study in Freudian Group Psychology.* New York: Norton, 1952.
6. Dreikurs, Rudolph. "Group Psychotherapy from the Viewpoint of the Adlerian Psychology." *Intern. J. Group Psychother.*, Vol. VII, No. 4, 363–375, October 1957.
7. Gordon, Thomas. *Group-Centered Leadership.* Boston: Houghton Mifflin, 1955.
8. Bennett, Margaret. *Guidance in Groups.* New York: McGraw-Hill, 1955.
9. Strang, Ruth. *Group Work in Education.* New York: Harper, 1958.

10. Coyle, Grace. "Social Group Work." *Social Work Yearbook, 1954.* New York: Stratford Press, pp. 480–486.
11. Luck, Juanita M. "Social Group Work." *Social Work Yearbook, 1957.* New York: Stratford Press, pp. 531–537.
12. Trecker, Harleigh. *Social Group Work.* New York: Whiteside, 1955.

2

Theories, Professional Jargon, and Definitions

Words and labels are very important to people. For the practitioner who desires to help others grow in a group, it is vital that he think through his concept of the way personality develops, and subsequently, what is necessary to effect change. Because the theories of personality are based on such varied assumptions, the same terms have come to have different meanings in different psychological systems.

Hall and Lindsay[1] in the beginning of their book exploring various theories of personality set forth the attributes that serve to differentiate one theory of personality from the next. Included are the following.

1. Is man purposeful in his life or are his actions just mechanical reactions based upon learned patterns acquired early in life?

2. Is man's behavior determined by conscious or unconscious motives? Or as a third possibility, is normality really a function of the degree to which man is aware of his needs and motives?

3. To what degree is man's behavior a function of seeking rewards? A corollary of this question is the concept that the only responses that will be learned are those accompanied by a reward or reinforcement.

4. Does the theory focus on the outcomes of learnings rather than on the learning process itself?

5. How critical are the effects of early childhood experiences? Is personality an ever changing thing or is it jelled early in life?

6. Is there an objective reality that we all can perceive or is a person's perception a unique subjective experience?

There are many theories about what personality is. They involve an infinite combination of the factors listed previously, along with many others. Because any extensive discussion of this problem would detract from the major purpose of this text, the material which follows admittedly represents an oversimplification of the relationship of theory to the professional labels commonly employed.

Probably the most popular concept of personality structure is that personality has a basic core that is developed early in life. Personality is effected by specific major experiences, and to be changed it requires a reliving of these critical experiences. Such terms as "Oedipal situation," describing the child's experiences in coping with his parents, and "exploration of libidinal development," referring to the child's learning to express sex drives, are common to this point of view. With this concept also comes the idea of *depth* in effecting personality change. *Psychotherapy* is the term reserved for helping relationships that will require dealing with these basic experiences to help the person. The term *psychotherapy* refers only to those processes directed by a skilled, professional individual toward improvement of a client who needs help to remedy a defined pathological condition. The treatment is specifically focused toward this situation, and the therapist is concerned with the client's "basic" or "core" personality.[2,3] This group separates psychotherapy from counseling on two major counts: (*a*) the degree of pathology, and (*b*) the focus of the therapist toward personality change instead of solely attitude change. Problems dealing with attitudes or situational factors are considered amenable to counseling. Because the situational factors are more superficial, different techniques may be employed to provide help. Commonly the Freudian philosophy and its descendents operate within this framework.

Another major group of theories does not differentiate between psychotherapy and counseling. Advocates of this point of view perceive as therapeutic any relationship which enables the individual more clearly to perceive his needs and to modify his behavior. Although all past experiences affect present behavior, any present experience can cause the past to have new meaning. Since it then becomes possible to help a person by dealing with his present perceptions, the concept of depth becomes meaningless. Counseling and psychotherapy become interchangeable terms. No special experiences become the focus of attention, since any problem of relationship or of needs which have persisted, can be found and expressed in present behavior.

Treatment is oriented toward enabling the client to clarify his self-concept and toward enabling him to practice new methods of adjustment in a protected setting. Any change in the client's attitude toward himself is considered to change the client's total personality. Rogers, Rank, Taft, and the Gestaltists fall within this frame of reference.

As indicated in the preface, I titled the book in general terms to avoid the confusion that presently exists over the meaning of such words as group guidance, group therapy, group dynamics, group work, etc. For many authors these terms have been differentiated by alluding either to the primary purpose of the group or the way in which different groups approach their goal. In an earlier article[4] I tried to develop definitions that would reflect current concepts of the meanings of terms commonly used to describe group process.

In this article reviewing research on "Group Therapy in Educational Institutions" * I said any review of research pertaining to group therapy in educational institutions is predicated on the belief that this area represents a defined body of common knowledge. It also assumes that the term "group therapy" is commonly understood and interpreted by the profession. Unfortunately, the limits of the field and an understanding of what can properly be called group therapy is interpreted in markedly different fashions by members of the profession. It is, for example, a clear commentary of the confusion of the profession— or more correctly, the lack of agreement as to the acceptable limits for purposes of definition—that in Combs' recent attempt[5] to define psychotherapy for legislative purposes, he found it impossible to differentiate definitively what might be termed "counseling" from "psychotherapy," or "group therapy" from "education."

To quote further a section of my article which states the basic assumptions also made in this book—the school involves working with essentially normal people. It has also been assumed that the focus of the therapeutic situation in educational institutions arises through the relationship of a client's problem to his educational adjustment. Finally, . . . to differentiate . . . the term "group guidance" from "group therapy," group therapy in an educational setting is here considered to be operating in any group where the *emphasis* is upon providing group members with opportunities to explore their own feelings and attitudes, rather than upon the imparting of information.

* Excerpts in this chapter are quoted from W. Lifton, "Group Therapy in Educational Institutions," *Rev. Educ. Res.*, Vol. XXIV, April 1954, pp. 156–158.

\plified way of making the differentiation between guid-
\py might be in terms of the difference between a
\tered as contrasted to a pupil-centered type of classroom
\n. However, the differentiation between guidance and therapy
\tot quite as clear-cut as that; for the student-centered classroom, in
order to be therapeutic, needs to incorporate certain other characteristics beyond providing students with opportunities to meet their own
needs. For therapy to exist, students must not only feel secure within
the situation but must also experience some anxiety about a problem
which they wish to resolve. The view taken here is that for *group
therapy* to function in a classroom, there must be a sharing of these
concerns.

It is not, however, the purpose of this text to discuss the nature of
the classroom and the factors within a class which would militate
against the security necessary for a therapeutic experience. Suffice it
to say that where the teacher's role represents that of an evaluative
authority figure, and where the individual will lose status within the
group or within the community by exploring negative feelings or ideas,
it is impossible for therapeutic growth to take place.[6,7,8] Wieder, for
example,[9] has supplied evidence which suggests that this difference
is a genuine one. He compared a classroom group led according to
nondirective group-therapy procedures with another group taught according to traditional lecture methods. His results indicated that the
"therapy group" measurably modified attitudes associated with racial,
religious, and ethnic prejudice; the group taught according to traditional methods did not significantly modify these same attitudes.

Therapy and Counseling: Further Distinctions. Defining these
boundaries helps clarify the area for discussion, but it does not heal
the basic rift between two major opposing conceptions of the nature of
psychotherapy and counseling. . . .

The following selected fragments from letters received will point up,
in terms of current practices in the field, the alternative conceptions
of psychotherapy and counseling. The first two quotations are representative of the group which regards psychotherapy as dealing with
basic personality change; the third quotation represents the philosophy
of those who do not distinguish between psychotherapy and counseling.

> *Group therapy* is a therapist working with more than one client having
> difficulties in areas with much communality. Prerequisite to operations,
> there must be individual assessment (diagnosis). Individual therapy is
> usually necessary either in the same time-span, or following group therapy.
> "They say" (and I believe) that group interaction speeds anxiety reduc-

tion but does not eliminate the need for individual attention. . . . Personally, I much prefer to think of "group preparation for counseling therapy" since, in my experience, good therapy tends to come ultimately from the one-to-one relationship.

. . . interested in the group-therapy approach to work with emotional problems of college students. He feels that it is a particularly suitable form of therapy for students in the educational setting since it sets limits on the identification with the individual therapist on the part of the patients. This makes the break at summers and vacation times much easier. . . . He finds that new students are more readily fitted into the group-therapy situation who would, in the individual situation, find identification with the therapist difficult. Many students give up their physical symptoms very quickly in this setting. The patients are clients of the clinic for whom group therapy is prescribed by the psychiatrist in charge.

Certainly there is evidence year after year of increased self-insights and altered behavior. . . . At times I am confused as to the relative importance of the two directions—content, and exploration of feelings—as well as with my own ability to handle the latter experience. . . . I am hesitant even to use the word "therapy" in relation to any group experience. Perhaps "education" is more accurate for what I am describing, but it is education of feelings and emotions rather than an amassing of knowledge and concepts.

Education and Therapy

Symonds[10] makes the distinction between education and therapy in the following way:

Education is concerned with helping an individual to adjust to his environment and to form the habits and skills which enable him to do so most effectively. Therapy, on the other hand, is concerned with helping an individual to work out for himself a personal reorganization, and to achieve new points of view, new attitudes, new courage and self-assurance, so that he may find it possible to become educated, that is, to adjust to the situation with which he is faced.

This definition of education seems to hinge on the role of information and skill development. To a degree it suggests dichotomy between mind and body. Perception and behavior are seen as discrete.

Although it is certainly true that the individual who is preoccupied with his own difficulties finds it very hard to consider new ideas, it is equally true that learning appears to take place when the individual is aware of how an idea or skill meets his needs and is relevant to his goals and aims in life.[11,12,13,14] The conditions necessary for a good learning situation appear to be similar for both education and therapy. Both require that the student or client:

1. See a need to achieve something beyond his present status. (Unless a person has some discomfort with his present situation he has no motivation for change.)

2. Is secure enough in the situation to feel able to look at ideas or feelings which are threatening him. (The youngster who can't spell, like the man who feels inadequate, cannot explore his inadequacy in a setting where to admit weakness is to make himself vulnerable.)

3. The setting provides a basis for the person to check the reality of his perception of himself. (Do others see me as I really am, and if they do, what do they think of me? Also, if others see me differently, whose estimate of me is correct?)

4. Based upon a perceived need for new skills in relating or performing, he receives help in discovering (information) new ways of acting.

5. Have an opportunity to rehearse and practice these new skills or ideas until the person feels equally competent in their use to the ones he had before. This practice must be in a setting which is protected so that his mistakes will not hurt him. (The boy who is learning to dance starts with his sister who may tease him, but whom he basically knows is interested in helping him. He then moves on to his sister's girl friend. Only after he feels he has passed the grade here is he ready to consider asking *the* girl for a dance.)

Group Dynamics. Dissension about the definition of group process also has come from representatives of the group-dynamics movement who object to classifying every attempt to change attitudes in an educational setting as "group therapy." The point has been made in numerous studies[15,16,17,18] that it is important to differentiate therapy groups from "problem solving" and "action" groups. The significance of this distinction is registered in the observations by researchers in those studies, focused toward therapy and using the group-dynamics devices of process-observer and the like, that the presence of a nonparticipating, judgmental person limits the security that individuals need in a therapeutic situation before they can afford to face the threat within them.

One solution to the semantic difficulties involved in distinctions between "group dynamics" and "group therapy" might be to reserve the former term for those processes employed to assist a group to achieve goals outside the group itself. In this setting, the needs of individuals become subservient to the goals of the group.[19] "Group therapy" would then cover those groups which are designed as a means through which people's needs and attitudes could be expressed. The therapy group would serve only as a vehicle for an individual's clarification of his own ideas and values as he tries them out on his peers.

For those who are disturbed by what would appear to be a dilution of differences between the needs of the disturbed individual and the normal person, or between the content needs of our society and its affective needs, it is important that there be a brief discussion of the role of limits. It has been stressed that true learning takes place only when a person feels secure in the setting. One of the first things that any group seeks to discover is the dividing line between what is acceptable and what is not. There are two kinds of limits. Those imposed by society and those internal ones we impose on ourselves. Society has the responsibility continually of determining which of its rules are unyielding and those that require change. The setting in which the group meets, the question of voluntary or forced membership, the societal expectations of the purpose of a group all will influence where the limit is set and how it is interpreted. People need security to see how the group can be useful to them and they to it. The group has the responsibility of setting limits to what it can offer. Some needs ought to be met elsewhere.

A Group versus a Mass

For many people any grouping of people carries with it the concept of the loss of individual responsibility and identity. Freud [20] in describing the effect of group behavior on people was particularly concerned with the tendency for people to reinforce in each other the needs of an antisocial nature that could be expressed since a person's identity in a group was lost from view. This concept is not unlike that which we see in a lynch mob. The concept of a "group mind" as a unique entity that is the sum of the people involved but responsible to no one certainly has not become obsolete in popular thinking.

The definition of the characteristics of a group described by Loeser[21] is of interest in the light of our desire in some way to differentiate the labels we apply to numbers of people. Loeser states that groups have:

1. Dynamic interaction among members.
2. A common goal.

3. A relationship between size and function.
4. Volition and consent.
5. A capacity for self-direction.

Applying these concepts to a group of theatergoers one could possibly find every defined characteristic except the group's capacity for self-direction. As long as they were all reacting on an individual basis to the show they are watching, even if they are aware of other people, they more aptly could be called a crowd or a mass. They do not become a group until there is an awareness of their dependence on each other to accomplish a goal and an acceptance of their responsibility to each other in the process. An educative or therapeutic group demands that there is continual awareness of each person's behavior in the group and the acceptance of each person of responsibility for his own actions. Fundamental in a democracy to the use of any group technique is a concern over the rights and needs of the individual.

There can be little question that group processes such as those employed in the concentration camps can modify behavior and attitudes. When, however, the pressures for achievement need to arise from within each individual, it becomes very relevant that these motivating needs reflect the intrinsic values of each group member as he shares in developing group goals. Within this context, each term describing group techniques has to be considered as it relates to the way it facilitates or hinders individual growth. Within such a context, for example, group guidance is evaluated in terms of the conditions under which people develop the need for information and the environment which best facilitates the incorporation of the desired information.

The Group Dynamic Approach

The articles and research in the area of group process reflect ideas about alternative roles available to members of a group. One body of publications seems to be focused primarily on how to help groups become more effective in achieving their goals.[22] This pragmatic orientation partially reflects the feeling that for democracy to prove its worth it must do so by demonstrating the results of group effort. For many, the yardstick becomes the speed with which a group achieves a goal external to the group. An illustration of this kind of concern can be seen in the writings of such people as Benne and Sheats.[23] The following table is an adaptation of the concept of group roles developed by them.

MEMBER ROLES IN GROUPS ATTEMPTING TO IDENTIFY,
SELECT, AND SOLVE COMMON PROBLEMS

A. Group Task Roles. Facilitation and coordination of group problem solving activities.

1. *Initiator contributor.* Offers new ideas or changed ways of regarding group problem or goal. Suggests solutions. How to handle group difficulty. New procedure for group. New organization for group.
2. *Information seeker.* Seeks clarification of suggestions in terms of factual adequacy and/or authoritative information and pertinent facts.
3. *Opinion seeker.* Seeks clarification of values pertinent to what group is undertaking or values involved in suggestions made.
4. *Information giver.* Offers facts or generalizations which are "authoritative" or relates own experience *pertinently* to group problem.
5. *Opinion giver.* States belief or opinion pertinently to suggestions. Emphasis on his proposal of what should become group's views of pertinent values.
6. *Elaborator.* Gives examples or develops meanings, offers rationale for suggestions made before, and tries to deduce how ideas might work out.
7. *Coordinator.* Clarifies relationships among ideas and suggestions, pulls ideas and suggestions together, or tries to coordinate activities of members of sub-groups.
8. *Orienter.* Defines position of group with respect to goals. Summarizes. Shows departures from agreed directions or goals. Questions direction of discussion.
9. *Evaluator.* Subjects accomplishment of group to "standards" of group functioning. May evaluate or question "practicability," "logic," "facts," or "procedure" of a suggestion or of some unit of group discussion.
10. *Energizer.* Prods group to action or decision. Tries to stimulate group to "greater" or "higher quality" activity.
11. *Procedural technician.* Performs routine tasks (distributes materials, etc.) or manipulates objects for group (rearranging chairs, etc.)
12. *Recorder.* Writes down suggestions, group decision, or products of discussion. "Group memory."

B. Group Growing and Vitalizing Roles. Building group-centered attitudes and orientation.

13. *Encourager.* Praises, agrees with, and accepts others' ideas. Indicates warmth and solidarity in his attitude toward members.
14. *Harmonizer.* Mediates intra-group scraps. Relieves tensions.
15. *Compromiser.* Operates from within a conflict in which his idea or

position is involved. May yield status, admit error, discipline himself, "come half-way."

16. *Gatekeeper and expediter.* Encourages and facilitates participation of others. Let's hear. . . . Why not limit length of contributions so all can react to problem?

17. *Standard setter or ego ideal.* Expresses standards for group to attempt to achieve in its functioning or applies standards in evaluating the quality of group processes.

18. *Group observer and commentator.* Keeps records of group processes and contributes these data with proposed interpretations into group's evaluation of its own procedures.

19. *Follower.* Goes along somewhat passively. Is friendly audience.

C. Antigroup Roles.   Tries to meet felt individual needs at expense of group health rather than through cooperation with group.

20. *Aggressor.* Deflates status of others. Expresses disapproval of values, acts, or feelings of others. Attacks group or problem. Jokes aggressively, shows envy by trying to take credit for other's idea.

21. *Blocker.* Negativistic. Stubbornly and unreasoningly resistant. Tries to bring back issue group intentionally rejected or by-passed.

22. *Recognition-seeker.* Tries to call attention to himself. May boast, report on personal achievements, and in unusual ways, struggle to prevent being placed in "inferior" position, etc.

23. *Self-confessor.* Uses group to express personal, non-group oriented, "feeling," "insight," "ideology," etc.

24. *Playboy.* Displays lack of involvement in group's work. Actions may take form of cynicism, nonchalance, horseplay, or other more or less studied out of "field behavior."

25. *Dominator.* Tries to assert authority in manipulating group or some individuals in group. May be flattery, assertion of superior status or right to attention, giving of directions authoritatively, interrupting contributions of others, etc.

26. *Help-seeker.* Tries to get "sympathy" response from others through expressions of insecurity, personal confusion or depreciation of himself beyond "reason."

27. *Special interest pleader.* Verbally for "small business man," "grass roots" community, "housewife," "labor," etc. Actually cloaking own prejudices or biases on stereotype which best fits his individual need.

A rapid survey of these labels quickly illustrates that the needs and personalities of the group members are judged by the way they facilitate the rapid movement of the group toward the predetermined goal. Let's see how this type of group might function.

The newspapers announce that there will be a meeting of all citizens interested in helping promote the local bond issue. Mrs. Smith decides that this is just the kind of volunteer work she would like to do. She is tired of being-cooped up in the house and aches for someone to talk to. At the meeting that night Mrs. Smith pitches in with enthusiasm. She has found that to understand an idea she must put it in her own words. Since she isn't too clear about the issue, and since she likes to talk, she unwittingly monopolizes the meeting. At the end of the session, the group process observer points up the way in which her behavior slowed down the group. Since Mrs. Smith really wants friends, and since she is concerned over the group goal she sits quietly through the next couple of meetings.

How can we evaluate what happened? The group has exercised control over its members to insure maximum movement. Mrs. Smith has learned what not to do, but no longer knows how to participate since her normal method of functioning brings group disapproval. The group has achieved conformity at the expense of a member's individual growth.

Much of what has been presented so far reflects the philosophy of some members of the "group dynamics" movement. The term Group Dynamics actually covers all studies of group process and group roles.[24] There have been, however, a series of individuals who have developed techniques which they feel provide optimum group control for efficient problem solving. These techniques have been popularly labeled as the group dynamics approach. There is one other basic concept associated with this group. Stated simply it would be that man, through the use of logic and cognitive processes, can alter his behavior. Feelings and needs are subordinate.

The Common Denominators

Common in most therapeutic groups is the feeling that basic to the development of any meaningful decisions or changes in behavior is the awareness and acceptance by group members of the needs or feelings which motivate their actions. Although groups may differ in the techniques they employ to facilitate self-understanding, all would accept the following concepts.

1. People need security in the group before they can afford to look at the underlying bases for their actions.
2. Topics form the basis for the group to pull together, but it is a

vehicle rather than an end in itself. Therefore "digressions" are not seen as such, but rather an attempt is made to see what need the new topic is representing, and how it relates to the one it followed.

3. The group strives to put across the feeling which indicates a continued acceptance of the individual despite possible rejection of his behavior or idea. This concept reflects the epitome of the successful group. When group members can feel the continued interest and concern in them as people and not feel rejected when others disagree with their idea, the group has achieved the kind of security which maximizes spontaneity and puts the premium on individual difference. Jung[25] has stated the basic concept here in clear terms:

> I fully approve of the integration of the individual into society. However, I want to defend the inalienable rights of the individual; for individuality alone is the bearer of life and is, in these times, gravely threatened by degradation. Even in the smallest group the individual is acceptable only if he appears acceptable to the majority. He has to be content with toleration. But mere toleration does not improve the individual; on the contrary, toleration causes a sense of insecurity, by which the lonely individual who has something to champion may be seriously hindered. Without intrinsic value social relations have no importance.

4. The group is a place to test the reality of an idea and it is the role of the leader or other members to react honestly.

5. Group members will present their feelings not only through the words they use but also by physical behavior.

6. The more a member participates in a group the more he gets out of it.

7. The group is strengthened by recognizing individual differences rather than merely focusing on the bases of similarity or consensus.

8. People react in terms of their present perception of a situation. This perception, however, is based on past experiences. To the degree that present perceptions can be related to the past, it is possible for the person to determine if he wishes to continue in the same direction for the future.

These are but a few of the common denominators to be found among groups that see the major reason for group life as being the means for most effectively recognizing and gratifying the needs of the individual. Like it or not, none of us lives in a vacuum. The ultimate lesson we have to learn is that we can find ourselves only as we relate to others.

Restatement of the Philosophy Expressed in the Text

It should be clear that my philosophy is biased toward describing personality as an ever-changing thing and holding that in dealing with an individual it is impossible to divide your relationship into levels. Accordingly, it is possible to use terms like teaching, counseling, or psychotherapy interchangeably without doing violence to the kinds of relationships that need to be developed in a group to achieve the goal of individual growth.[26] With this point of view it is possible to draw from both the fields of education and psychology in our attempts to explore the problems and skills associated with group leadership skills.

The values I use as a counselor place me squarely in the camp of those who take a phenomenological and client-centered point of view. The following hypotheses about the nature of personality and way to achieve behavior change represent my theoretical position.

1. To help people we need to start with their perception of a situation.
2. Help is most useful if it is initially directed toward the problem causing an individual (or group) the most immediate concern.
3. Individuals (groups) have an innate capacity to heal themselves, if they are provided a setting where they can feel secure enough to examine their problems.
4. As an individual (group) is helped to feel more secure, his need to shut out unwanted bits of information decreases. As he broadens his perception of the problem he must by necessity include the values and attitudes expressed by society. Particularly in a group setting, this means that the solution to a problem although it starts out as egocentric, must ultimately resolve the paradox that man can only get his needs met through others. The following sequence may explain this concept.

I want you to meet my needs.
For you to be willing to do so, I must give you
    a reason for doing so.
It therefore follows that I can only meet my needs
    after I have first considered yours.
I have learned then that I can start out being
    as selfish as I like, but I cannot achieve
    my goal without considering how others will respond.

5. A change in any part of an individual's life affects all other aspects of his being. A new perception today can cause all past experiences to have a new and different meaning.

Certainly these assumptions are not original. As indicated earlier they can be traced back to the works of such people as Rogers, Wertheimer, Rank, Taft, Bergson, and Rousseau.

Since any belief is manifest only by the way it employs tools and techniques, the following chapter will consider just how people can be helped in group situations.

Discussion

This chapter provided many ethical and philosophical concepts worthy of further study. For the reader who is intrigued by the question of the appropriate role of the therapist or educator in our society, two books are especially recommended. Both Lindner's *Prescription For Rebellion*[27] and DeGrazia's *Common Errors in Psychotherapy*[28] will force you to examine your own beliefs.

If you find yourself somewhat confused by the brief survey of psychological theories, reading *Individual Behavior* by Snygg and Combs[29] will be helpful. Some may be disappointed by the absence of any specific discussion of learning theory. Its absence is not due to any question of the technical help learning theory has offered to practitioners. As a philosophy, however, except for the Pavlovian mechanistic approach to people, learning theory has made its greatest contribution when it has been used to explain phenomena within differing psychological systems. The symposium by Shoben,[30] Shaw,[31] and Combs[32] as well as the works of Dollard and Miller[33] provide examples of how these relationships are conceived from different frames of reference.

The question of where education ends and where therapy begins is highly controversial. An entire issue of *Progressive Education* (May 1955) has been devoted to this topic. Included are articles by philosophers, psychiatrists, group workers, educators, and psychologists. Also in this area, and presenting differing points of view, is the Volume VII, January 1957, No. I issue of the *International Journal of Group Psychotherapy* covering Group Dynamics and Group Psychotherapy.

Although not discussed in this chapter, the question of the need for adopting a theoretical position rather than developing a smorgasbord of techniques conveniently labeled an eclectic approach, deserves the careful attention of the serious student in the area. To help in an understanding of the difference between a philosophical stand which reflects personal consistency rather than rigidity, Carl Rogers' *Client-Centered Therapy* is highly recommended.[34] On the question of a philosophical eclecticism, the article the author wrote in *Occupations* (now the *Personnel and Guidance Journal*) entitled "A Reply to a Plague on Both Your Houses,"[35] may amplify why eclecticism of philosophies is considered impossible.

Common to both of the last two references is the work by Lecky on the importance of self-consistency. Also helpful is the discussion by Corsini[36] on the relationship of a leader's personality and the methods he will employ.

For teachers, Arthur T. Jersild's *When Teachers Face Themselves*[37] carries out the same themes in the classroom setting.

A good historical summary of writings defining group work, group therapy, and group organization can be found in a book of readings edited by Dorothea F. Sullivan entitled *Readings in Group Work*.[38] It contains articles printed in a journal entitled *The Group* which is now out of print (New York Associated Press, 1952).

Particular violence was done in the extremely brief presentation of the activities of members of the group dynamics movement. It is suggested that the more mature reader will enjoy browsing through *Group Dynamics* by Dorwin Cartwright and Alvin Zander.[39] This book and *Dynamics of Groups at Work* by Herbert Thelen,[40] present excellent descriptions of the philosophy and techniques employed by people operating from that theoretical position.

BIBLIOGRAPHY

1. Hall, Calvin, and Gardner, Lindsay. *Theories of Personality.* New York: Wiley, 1957.
2. Scheidlinger, Saul. "Group factors in Promoting School Children's Mental Health." *Amer. J. Orthopsychiat.*, 22, 394–404, April 1952.
3. Slavson, Samuel R. "Common Sources of Error and Confusion in Group Psychotherapy." *Intern. J. Group Psychother.*, 3, 3–28, January 1953.
4. Lifton, Walter M. "Group Therapy in Educational Institutions." *Rev. Educ. Res.*, Vol. XXIV, No. 2, 156–158, April 1954.
5. Combs, Arthur W. "Problems and Definitions in Legislation." *Amer. Psychologist*, 8, 554–564, October 1953.
6. Laycock, Samuel R. "Mental Hygiene of Classroom Teaching." *Understanding the Child*, 16, 39–43, April 1947.

7. Lifton, Walter M. "Group Classroom Techniques." *Progressive Education,* 30, 210–213, May 1953.

8. Super, Donald E. "Group Techniques in the Guidance Program." *Educ. psychol. Measmt.,* 9, 496–510, Autumn 1949.

9. Wieder, Gerald S. *A Comparative Study of the Relative Effectiveness of Two Methods of Teaching a Thirty-Hour Course in Psychology in Modifying Attitudes Associated with Racial, Religious, and Ethnic Prejudice.* New York: New York University, 1951. 192 p. (Doctor's thesis). Abstract: *Dissertation Abstracts,* 12, 163, No. 2, 1952.

10. Symonds, Percival. "Supervision as Counseling." *Teachers College Record,* Vol. 43, 49–56, October 1941.

11. Alpert, A. "Education as Therapy." *Psychoanal. Quart.,* 10, 469–474, 1941.

12. Baruch, Dorothy W. "Therapeutic Procedures as Part of the Educative Process." *J. consult. Psychol.,* 4, 165–172, 1940.

13. Ojemann, Ralph. "Basic Approaches to Mental Health: The Human Relations Program at the State University of Iowa." *Pers. & Guid. J.,* Vol. XXXVII, No. 3, 199–206, November 1958.

14. Zlatchin, Philip. "Round Table: Education and Psychotherapy." *Amer. J. Orthopsychiat.,* Vol. XXIV, No. 1, 133–140, January 1954.

15. Gordon, Ira J. "The Class as a Group: The Teacher as Leader—Some Comments and Questions." *Educational Administration and Supervision,* 37, 108–118, February 1951.

16. Gordon, Ira J. *The Creation of an Effective Faculty Adviser Training Program Through Group Procedures.* New York: Teachers College, Columbia University, November 1950, 224 p. (Doctor's thesis).

17. Pepinsky, Harold B. "An Experimental Approach to Group Therapy in a Counseling Center." *Occupations,* 28, 35–40, October 1949.

18. Trow, William C., and others. "Psychology of Group Behavior: The Class as a Group." *J. educ. Psychol.,* 41, 322–338, October 1950.

19. Herrold, Kenneth F. "Evaluation and Research in Group Dynamics." *Educ. psychol. Measmt.,* 10, 492–504, Autumn 1950 (Part II).

20. Freud, S. *Group Psychology and the Analysis of the Ego.* London: International Psychoanalytic Press, 1922.

21. Loeser, Lewis. *Intern. J. Group Psychother.,* Vol. VII, No. 1, 5–19, January 1957.

22. Lippitt, Ronald, Kenneth Benne, and Leland Bradford. "The Promise of Group Dynamics for Education." *J. Nat. Educ. Assoc.,* 37, 350–352, 1948.

23. Benne, Kenneth, and P. Sheats. "Functional Roles of Group Members." *J. soc. Issues,* Vol. 4, 2, 42–47, Spring 1948.

24. Jenkins, David H. "What Is Group Dynamics?" *Adult Educ. J.,* 9, 2, 54–60, 1950.

25. Illing, H. A. "C. G. Jung on the Present Trends in Group Psychotherapy." *Human Relations,* 10, 77–84, 1957.

26. *Journal of the National Association of Deans of Women.* "Counseling and Group Work," Vol. X, No. 3, 99–124, March 1947.

27. Lindner, Robert. *Prescription for Rebellion.* New York: Rinehart, 1952.

28. DeGrazia, Sebastian. *Errors in Psychotherapy and Religion,* Garden City, New York: Doubleday, 1952.

29. Snygg, Donald, and Arthur Combs. *Individual Behavior.* New York: Harper, Revised Edition, 1958.

30. Shoben, Edward J.   "Counseling and the Learning of Integrative Behavior," *J. counsel. Psychol.*, Vol. 1, No. 1, 42–48, Winter 1954.
31. Shaw, Franklin J.   "Counseling from the Standpoint of an 'Interactive Conceptualist.'"   *J. counsel. Psychol.*, Vol. 1, No. 1, 36–42, Winter 1954.
32. Combs, Arthur W.   "Counseling as a Learning Process."   *J. counsel. Psychol.*, Vol. 1, No. 1, 31–36, Winter 1954.
33. Dollard, John, and Neal E. Miller.   *Personality and Psychotherapy.*   New York: McGraw-Hill, 1950.
34. Rogers, Carl.   *Client-Centered Therapy.*   Boston: Houghton Mifflin, 1951, p. 9.
35. Lifton, Walter M.   "A Reply to a Plague on Both Your Houses," *Occupations,* Vol. XXX, No. 6, 434–437, March 1952.
36. Corsini, Raymond.   *Methods of Group Psychotherapy.*   New York: McGraw-Hill, 1957, pp. 125–127.
37. Jersild, Arthur.   *When Teachers Face Themselves.*   New York: Bureau of Publications, Teachers College, Columbia University, 1955.
38. Sullivan, Dorothea F.   *Readings in Group Work.*   New York: Association Press, 1952.
39. Cartwright, Dorwin, and Alvin Zander.   *Group Dynamics.*   Evanston, Illinois: Row Peterson, 1956.
40. Thelen, Herbert.   *Dynamics of Groups at Work.*   Chicago: University of Chicago Press, 1954.

"No man can reveal to you aught but that which already lies half asleep in the dawning of your knowledge."

From The Prophet by Kahlil Gibran.*

3

The Tools and Techniques Involved in the Helping Process

Differences in philosophy, as described in Chapter 2 (Freudian, Rogerian, etc.), affect the frequency with which some techniques are used over others, and certainly affect the manner in which the practitioner plays his role, interprets process, and plans for the future. But in the minute-to-minute operation it would be difficult to distinguish one philosophy from another. Since in the material which follows it will be helpful for the reader to be able to analyze the interactions described, a look at a few specific techniques is in order. These techniques are the same as those found in a one-to-one learning situation, although, as we will see, the group setting permits different ways in which they can be employed.

Before examining some of the more basic techniques it is important to have a prior understanding of the way communication provides the key to the helping process. Essentially the major problem in our society is a breakdown in communication. Not only do people have trouble understanding each other, but frequently a person is not sure of himself. Actually this book, itself, is limited to only that help which can be provided through the use of words. The first and hardest lesson for the beginner to learn is that you cannot assume that the other person meant what *you* assumed his words to mean. Not only do words frequently have a variety of meanings, but the way in which they were said can vastly alter their intent. Shakespeare understood this well when he had one of his characters say, "The lady doth protest too much, methinks." One of the skills most desired by maturing youth is to know whether a girl really means no, when she says it. To review then, words are defined with a variety of meanings in the dictionary, they change meaning according to the setting, and they can reflect the exact reverse of their stated meanings. To further complicate the issue, people use ideas to express feelings that are important to them. It is almost as if words were a car, with the feelings being its passenger, and with the passenger being more vital than the car itself. The major problem, then, is to see how one can learn what the other person is trying to convey. Until you understand the feelings you cannot begin to help him (or them) face the issue to be solved.

The first place anyone can start is with his own experience. "What could the words I hear possibly mean?" Having explored the range of possible alternatives, a person next tries to examine the context in which the words occurred to select the most likely meaning. He still cannot be sure that his own needs are not causing him to distort what he has heard so that ultimately all he can do is to check if his idea is what the other person actually meant.

This attempt at precision of meaning is really the very heart of the helping process in which several things are going on at once. To clarify the relationship in the helping process, the person being helped will be called the client. For the client who hears from another his idea exactly as he meant it, there is the wonderful feeling of being understood, of not being alone in the world, and of having someone else available who can help him see if he is getting across to others the things he desires. For the client who sees someone else trying to understand, but who finds that his words do not seem to convey the exact meaning he desires, there is still the opportunity to try to redefine himself. In this process of redefinition—this attempt to clear away ambiguity—frequently the speaker becomes clearer not only in what he wants to say, but also in what his true feelings really are.

The skilled group worker needs more than a text to train his sensitivities to hearing and responding to others. The group leader not only needs to have knowledge of others, but also has to be sure his own house is in order. We do not hear others say things which, if we recognize them in others, would force us to see unacceptable things in ourselves. The more we need to block out from hearing, the less we can help others. Although this chapter can discuss techniques, no true learning can take place for the reader until he has a chance to see if he can use the ideas himself. He also needs help from others who can call his attention to the things he typically doesn't hear or respond to.

Thus, the primary goal in the helping process is to assist others in examining their words or behavior to see if they represented what the client wished to communicate. With this as our goal let's explore some tools which help people clarify their thoughts. The process of reflecting back to the client the literal dictionary meaning of what he says is called *"reflection of content."*

When we reflect back to the person what he is *trying* to say, or the latent desires in his words, the process is called *"reflection of feeling."* Reflection of feeling is particularly tricky. If we can help put into words a feeling of which the person was dimly aware, but had not found a clear way to state, he will be helped by this clarifying process. If, however, we pick up feelings which we feel are there but which the client is either not ready to examine or which represent our distortion of his feelings, we may be in for trouble. The attempt to reflect these unconscious needs or to link up past experiences with present behavior is called *"interpretation."* Since any linking of past with present or any predicting of future behavior has to come from the perceiver's own experiences or logic, the success of this technique will be vitally dependent upon its accuracy and the concurrent help given to the person to face frightening or unacceptable ideas. Since interpretation is so dependent upon a vast experience and an ability to judge a person's readiness for threatening material, it is a device best reserved for only the most skilled person.

Since most helping relationships demand ways of relating that are not part of the typical social situation, a technique called *"structuring"* is used. In essence, "structuring" involves either a statement of the rules of the helping process or the development of an understanding of such rules by the way the therapist or group leader does or does not act in specific situations. In a group setting, the initial group leader may take the responsibility of indicating to the group the limits to be imposed on the group by the setting in which they are meeting or by the nature of the group. In other words, he is indicating the outside limits imposed by society. Rules developed inside the group reflect a philosophy along with its concept of how the leader can be most helpful. In this book, the leader's role in "structuring" is seen as that of assisting the group to become aware of problems they need to solve and helping them learn to work together in setting up the rules by which they will function together.

Because many people coming into a helping situation expect the expert to take over, it is important that the initial leader make clear early in the sessions what the group can or cannot expect from him. Since the group will be more responsive to his behavior than his words, it is vital that there be consistency between what he says and does. The leader or therapist has been referred to as the initial leader because as early as possible it is the leader's objective to have members of the group assume responsibility for directing and assisting their fellow members.

In the initial sessions of a group, structuring will include, among many others, such questions as, "What is the group going to do?" "What is the leader's role?" "How are people treated here?" "What are the acceptable things to talk about?" "How confidential will the contents of group sessions be?" "Isn't it a sign of weakness to admit confusion over ideas or goals?"

Although most of the structuring occurs early in the group's life, structuring can continue as long as the group needs to develop ways of handling new situations.

Other more common tools that all of us have had a chance to experience include *questioning, supplying information, clarifying an idea* (summarizing all the points raised that bear on each other), and (probably most important of all) the use of *silence* to allow the other person to think his own thoughts in his own way. These are but a few of the techniques available. At the end of this chapter the reader will find references that can help fill in needed knowledge on the counseling process and tools involved.

Recently there has been a tendency in the field of counseling to believe that probably none of these tools is in itself of great importance. The touchstone of the helping process is, now more than ever, felt to lie in the way the person who is trying to help indicates to another that he really cares about him. It is a relationship that cannot be faked. One way to let others know that you feel what they say is really important is to constantly look at them. To actually understand them you need to see their facial expressions and gestures that go along with their words. For example, try the following experiment yourself.

Knowing that constant eye contact is helpful, try this on a friend: Tell him that you wish to have him help you learn how to convey interest in a client. Ask him to let you know when he feels you are with him and when he feels you are wool-gathering. For the first few moments try your hardest to listen to the feelings the client is expressing. Then, while still focusing your eyes on the client's face imagine a scene taking place behind him, and in a sense look right through him to the scene beyond. Return again to a real attempt to listen. This time, however, spend your time thinking of how you would like to answer him. In other words, although you are concerned with his problem, your major attention is on what it means to you. If you are successful in playing these roles you will discover to your dismay that when you are not really listening to what he is trying to express, you are fooling no one but yourself.

Part of the purpose of this chapter is to introduce you to the jargon used by professionals in the fields of counseling and therapy. Since the remainder of the book will focus on psychological skills coming from these professional fields let us take a look at the teaching process so that we can recognize its similarity to the material which follows. The following analysis of what teaching is represents a summary of an excellent article on this subject by Louis Raths.[2] The comments on each heading, however, are the author's interpretation of their applicability to the helping process.

Raths has divided teaching into separate operations. We will specifically examine what he has called the "Clarifying Operations, the Show-How Operations, and the Security-Giving Operations."

Clarifying Operations

I.1. *Clarifying through reflection.* This has been partially covered by the preceding section.

I.2. *Clarifying through use of a definition or illustration.* For a person to understand an idea fully he must be able to communicate its meaning to others. Clarification is frequently best achieved by describing an applicable concrete situation. The group seeks to facilitate its understanding by requesting the person to illustrate his idea.

I.3. *Clarifying by pointing up what appear to be apparent inconsistencies.* Notice the word "apparent." What does not make sense to the hearer initially may be seen as related when the speaker draws up the relationship as he sees it. One good illustration of this comes in the popular refrain, "you always hate the one you love." A moment's thought will reveal the fact that it is hard to feel strongly about someone who is unimportant to you.

I.4. *Clarifying similarities and differences.* Particularly in a group where there may be a tendency to get support by either forcing a single stand or by the operation of cliques, this approach is very important. As a pressure group forces opinion by presenting a united front, helping members of this subgroup examine their stand and pointing up both areas of hidden disagreement as well as consensus, within their group, causes the clique to disintegrate and join the total group. It also points up that the strength of the group can come from difference as well as agreement.

I.5. *Clarifying through questioning underlying assumptions.* This can be a dangerous tool. If the group by this device rejects any assumptions but those the majority believes in, it can have a threatening and restricting effect. If, however, it is used to help the person or total group define the assumptions they are making so that they can decide if these are beliefs they can really accept, then the approach has positive implications for growth.

I.6. *Clarifying through anticipation of consequences.* Since the response of others to our actions is a major concern, the degree to which the group helps provide possible results enables the person to determine his course of action. One rather popular way that is used to think through this situation is by having group members act out with a person a scene in which he tries his idea. The others, by their behavior, give him concrete evidence of what the future effects of his approach might be.

I.7. *Clarifying through questioning meaning.* Is this what you mean? or, Do I understand you to say . . . ? The latter implies that the hearer could be misperceiving but wants to understand.

I.8. *Clarifying by examining points of difficulty.* This could apply not only to an idea but also to helping the group examine their own group process. For example, sometimes a group seems at a loss as to what they want to do. Helping them examine the feelings or ideas that seem to be causing trouble is the first step in removing this road block. What's getting in our way? Why are we so upset?

I.9. *Clarifying if a personal statement was meant to show a personal feeling or one that the individual feels all people must hold.* This is one way of helping the group see demands that individual members are making on them. It also points up to the individual demands he is making on others.

I.10. *Clarifying by relating feelings to behavior.* By calling attention to the feelings others are getting from a person's behavior, it helps the person accept responsibility for the way he expresses his emotion. "We all seem to be so angry at each other that we seem unable to let the other person talk."

I.11. *Clarifying through a review of the steps in a person's logic.* This concept is somewhat like I.5. Implicit is the idea that a review of the steps will help a person see the fallacy of the logic involved. Although this approach can sometimes work, it cannot help failing if the motivation for his reasoning will not be more effectively met by an alternative logic which is presently in the client's available repertoire of responses. For example, the group points out to a member that the client is tired when he stays out late with the boys and his health and school work are suffering. The client recognizes the truth of the group's statement, but the logic does not meet his need for peer group approval or the satisfactions he gets when he is out with the fellows.

I.12. *Raising questions of purpose.* What are you trying to prove? This is an attempt to help the person search for and recognize the underlying motivation for his activity. To the degree that he is secure in the group and has a motivation to get an answer, this approach may be helpful. Also, the question must reflect an attempt to help the person rather than being a belligerent challenge of his rights or goals.

I.13. *Seeking origins of an expression or idea.* Since nothing we think or do is unrelated to our past experiences, to the degree that we can integrate a present idea with the concepts that led to its creation, we achieve a fuller realization of the meaning of the idea to us.

The Show-How Operations

II.1. *Through demonstrations.* Although copying movements to learn skills can be a helpful way of learning, the motivation to succeed through being like someone else is really a double-edged sword. The more the individual sees happiness as being achieved by emulating someone else, the more he will try to be like the other person. In the process he will tend to overlook the things that make him different from his idol. He will assume an equivalence in their interests, skills, personality, and goals. Since he can never be the other person, he never achieves a sense of accomplishment that he feels really reflects what he could achieve on his own two feet. Especially in a democracy we seek to preserve the individual's right to his own life. The issue therefore really is: How do we help people incorporate into their own lives the values *we* feel are important? The answer to this is not a simple one. The author takes the stand that society has the responsibility of providing young people with many samples of roles to examine and try. It must then provide a setting in which each person can examine how the parts of each role will be consistent with his unique abilities and goals. The group with its different members and opportunities for trial behavior is particularly suited for this job.

II.2. *Use of resource persons and teaching aids.* The use of resource people and materials is closely tied to the meaningfulness of these sources of help to the goals of the group. The resource person who comes in to tell others what they should be doing will be useful only to the extent that he is supplying information that the group needs, wants, and is ready to use. The fundamental concept here is the difference between *information* and *advice*. Although many people ask for advice as one way of avoiding responsibility ("He told me to do it, it wasn't really my idea"); advice rarely works. If the adviser tells people exactly what they want to hear, it is experienced as reassuring. At the same time, people then react with the feeling that they already knew the answer and that the resource person had added nothing. If, however, the adviser suggests ideas that clients cannot accept, a dilemma arises. In the event that they take advice that they basically cannot go along with, they experience the feeling that they are not very worthwhile people if anyone can persuade them to actions that violate their own beliefs. There is then a resulting decrease in feelings of personal worth and in their ability to be responsible for their own behavior. On the other hand, if the group decides to ignore the advice of the resource person it makes it difficult for them to again seek his help since by their actions they have demonstrated a lack of faith in the correctness of his advice.

Information as contrasted from advice, then, is provided only when the people seeking a solution which clarifies their problem see need for knowing alternative ways to reach their goal and are willing to accept responsibility for both implementing their decisions and accepting the fruits of their action.

The timing, then, when information is sought by the group, is vitally dependent on what has preceded their request and the clients' security in accepting responsibility for their behavior. Information, volunteered before a group perceives a need for it, actually works as advice, since it implies the direction in which the adviser thinks they ought to be going and his feeling that they ought to be ready to accept responsibility.

II.3. *Exploring alternative methods or ways to solve the problem.* Our security in feeling able to cope with our environment certainly is a function of the range of techniques we have learned to use in coping with a variety of situations. We facilitate security and growth of the individual when we provide both a secure setting and opportunity for trial behavior. In this type of group setting the client can dare to experiment with new methods since the price of failure is not the same as society imposes.

An example here might be helpful: Little Billy Smith comes home from school crying. He has been beaten up by another youngster.

We could solve (?) the problem by taking action against the other child, but Billy will not have learned how he can cope with the next bully. He will have learned that if you go to someone else he will solve your problem for you. Suppose, as just an alternative solution, Billy had discussed this with the coach, and the coach had offered to teach Billy to use judo. Let's imagine that Billy receives one lesson and on his way home he again meets the bully. How will he fight? The way he did in the past. He will use his judo lessons only when he feels he can get results that are equal to or better than what he already knew. Incidentally, Billy was willing to try to develop his skills with the coach because he knew that while he was learning the coach would not hurt him. In his lessons he could make mistakes without suffering irreparable damage. The role of the school or therapeutic group is to offer the same opportunities to make mistakes without irreparable damage to the person.

Also involved in this area is the concept of failure. Typically failure has come to mean that the person has not measured up to a preconceived standard. This is but one way of looking at the inability to achieve beyond a certain point. A more helpful way of conceiving failure is that the point of failure provides a concrete measure of all the person has achieved to that point. For example, how can a person discover how high he is able to jump? He keeps raising the cross bar until he reaches the point where he can no longer clear it. This point of failure is both the measure of how high he *can* jump and a concrete point against which to compare his hoped for goal. Too often in our competitive society, we spend so much time in measuring the distance between where we are and where we feel we must go, that we lose sight of what we have already accomplished. If our goal in society is to help each person feel a sense of personal worth, at some point they need to be helped to examine where they are, where they have been, and where they feel they need to go. It is in helping a person reconcile what he is and the bases he has used to decide where he must go, that we are simultaneously providing motivation for learning while we are improving his mental health.

Actually, in a true learning situation the goal of the people or person providing help is to help the individual discover what he possesses as personal tools he can use to solve problems. The ultimate goal of any therapeutic situation is *not* the resolution of the problem. Rather it is an attempt to teach problem-solving techniques.

Security-Giving Operations

III.1. *Meeting the need for belonging.* It has been said that all of us determine our personal worth through the eyes of others. Essentially we recognize that since each person wants to feel worthwhile, to the degree that we share things in common, we are sure of mutual acceptance. The fly in the ointment is, however, that while we can achieve acceptance by being a carbon copy of the stereotype, this role does not enable us to be recognized as a unique person. This need for group acceptance is strongest in the adolescent. Picture the typical high school girl of our day dressed in the uniform of the day. It may be leotards, bobby socks, or whatever the group has decided. Suppose this young lady should overhear two boys trying to decide whom to take to a dance. "I don't see what the problem is, Tom, these gals spend so much time together you can't tell one from the other." Young Miss walks away in confusion. What do you have to do and be, not to be considered a square? How different does she dare let herself be without risking group rejection as a queer? Although the example chosen was that of an adolescent, these questions are common to people at all age levels. What are the limits of our society? How can I meet my needs within these limits? And for the mature adult there is added the more difficult question, how can I help others see that the status quo needs changing without losing group membership?

III.2. *Meeting the need for achievement and personal growth.* One way we prove to ourselves that we are worthwhile is by examining our day-to-day accomplishments. If we keep repeating what we could do yesterday, the glow of accomplishment fades. Personal growth then involves a constant reassessment of the reality of the new goals we are setting up for tomorrow. Since we do not achieve in a vacuum, part and parcel of this assessment process is the reaction and support we get from the reactions of others. One of the rather unique characteristics of the group setting is that as we observe other people solve problems and grow, it gives us courage to try solving problems ourselves. Part of it might be from the feeling that if the other person, whom we feel is weaker, can achieve—we can, too. Along with this is the support that comes from knowing that other people are facing similar problems. We are not alone.

III.3. *The need for economic security.* Although a group does not meet this specific need it can be very helpful in assisting the person in sharpening his skills in achieving economic self-sufficiency. Job security in our society is more than just having needed skills. One of the major reasons people lose jobs is their inability to get along with fellow workers and to accept responsibility. Job security rests also on the degree to which the job gratifies basic needs. For some, job satisfaction depends purely on the money they earn. This is not only a status symbol but also a means to gratify needs that cannot be met through their jobs. For other people the conditions under which they work are more vital. A group can be helpful in assisting a person in defining what he seeks from a job so he can decide if the job he wants will meet these needs. For many, the group can provide a setting in which to practice job-getting or interpersonal skills. The group frequently can help a person think through more effective ways of solving problems on the job. Not least of all, it can help a person examine what he needs in the way of economic security to meet his present needs for effective living in his society.

III.4. *Need to be free from fear.* Although the group can within its own limits set up rules that will protect the individual from physical and other threats, there is a real question as to whether freedom from fear itself is a good thing. Fear can be a motivating force to solve a problem. It can also be the basis for avoiding situations which realistically are dangerous and beyond the control of an individual. Rather than freedom from fear there ought to be substituted help in facing fear. For example, many of us are aware of the fact that any day some trigger-happy person could fire a bomb which might precipitate the end of the world as we know it. This is a very real possibility. There are many things an individual can do to attempt to modify society so that this no longer will be possible. Immediate solutions are not likely. Living in daily fear could make a person unable to do even those small things which on a combined group basis might solve the problem. In other words, at some point we need to help people live in a society where security and the absence of fear can become a possibility. We need to build up individual security that comes from knowing that each person has used the full extent of his capacity. No more can be demanded of any man.

III.5. *The need for love and affection.* Raths has described this as showing others you are hurt when they are hurt. There is a real question if this is a helpful thing. To the extent that you are truly hurt each time another suffers, the trials and tribulations of the world can soon overwhelm you. As an alternative the development of an empathic attitude might be considered. Instead of sympathizing and

.

identifying with each pain of the other person, you attempt to let him know that you understand how he feels and that you want to help. In your own mind you recognize that *he* is feeling the pain, not you. Unless you are free of the pain you cannot be objective enough to provide him help in looking at his feelings. When the counselor identifies with his client we have two clients instead of one. This augments the problem rather than lessens it.

There are many kinds of love. Many of you are familiar with what has been termed "sMother Love," or the possessive kind of attention that robs the person of his rights and personality. All of us tend to be suspicious of other people. A rather frequent question is "Why are you being so nice to me?" People basically recognize that all behavior is motivated by some need of the individual. Understanding the needs the "loving" person is trying to meet helps the recipient decide if this is helping or hindering his own desires. The more honestly we express our motivations for being concerned about others, the more secure both they and we will feel. In the group this problem is somewhat simplified. Very quickly groups come to realize that they will sink or swim together. The growing awareness of how interdependent they are on each other makes very clear that from what may appear as a selfish basis, each person wants the others well and happy. This is so that the other people can meet your needs which they couldn't do if their abilities were impaired.

Feeling important to others in and of itself demonstrates your value. The security of love works two ways. It proves that there are others who care while at the same time increasing your esteem in your own eyes.

III.6. *The need to be free from guilt.* Feelings of guilt can so immobilize a person that any positive action is impossible. Guilt feelings can be alleviated in several ways. One common method is for an authority to remove guilt by providing you with punishment which will pay for the action that is causing guilt feelings. A common example of this is the little boy who confesses to misbehavior and feels relief when he is spanked since he then considers the score has been settled. A group sometimes acts this way, but generally they do not want to sit in judgment. In the group setting there is a more effective method to deal with guilt feelings. As members of the group feel able to share their feelings with each other, frequently members of the group discover that they are not alone in their perceived misbehavior or guilty thoughts. Part of the weight of guilt feelings comes from the sense of being different in one's behavior or problems. Each person feels alone. As he discovers others facing the same situation, although his feelings haven't changed, each person feels better able to cope with his problem. Realizing that others have faced and solved the problem gives support. Knowing there are others with whom you can feel free to discuss the situation also is a source of security. You are free to talk with them because you feel they are no better than you, and you do not lose group acceptance by admitting your feelings.

III.7. *Need for acceptance of the other person.* A group soon learns that each person in his turn will ask questions that are very naive in the eyes of others. Accepting the "naive" person's need for information and his right to use the group to clarify his own thinking causes the group members to examine questions, not in terms of their sophistication, but rather in terms of what it means to the person asking.

III.8. *Ways of controlling conflict situations.* Groups develop a sixth sense in judging when a group member is being pressed beyond his ability to cope with the situation. Since taking a problem out of someone else's hands implies a lack of faith in their capacity to handle the problem, group members hesitate to take overt action. Rather than have the person retreat from danger, or remove the danger, group members provide support to the person under attack so that he has additional strength in facing the situation. It is not uncommon for the group to take overt action toward a member who seems to be unfairly treating another. Learning that the way that he treats other group members will affect how the rest of the group will treat him causes each person to carefully consider his effect on others.

These are a few of the characteristics that Raths covers in his article. Although there are many other aspects of teaching, those presented should demonstrate the communal focus of teaching and therapy.

Discussion

In the chapter which will follow, the reader will have an opportunity to get the feel of a group in action. To get the most out of the protocol and marginal comments it would be wise for the newcomers to the field of counseling to do some outside reading to improve both their technical skills and depth of understanding.

To gain insight into the counseling process, texts like Arbuckle,[3] Porter,[4] Tyler,[5] Thorne,[6] and Rogers[7] are recommended reading.

The books mentioned above plus Wittenberg's[8] *So You Want to Help People* will describe the nature of the helping relationship.

These books also will help in preparing the student in identifying different techniques.

A rather delightful way of broadening a student's cultural experiences along with an increased understanding of people having different problems can be achieved through leisure reading. The following books are just a few that can provide enjoyment along with increased sensitivity.

Algren, Nelson. *The Man with the Golden Arm.* Garden City, New York: Doubleday, 1949.

Baruch, Dorothy W. *How to Live with Your Teen-Ager.* New York: McGraw-Hill, 1953.

Baruch, Dorothy W. *One Little Boy.* New York: Julian Press, 1952.

Baruch, Dorothy. *New Ways in Discipline.* New York: Whittlesey House, 1949.

Beers, Clifford. *A Mind that Found Itself: An Autobiography.* Garden City, New York: Doubleday, 1935.

Bettelheim, Bruno. *Love Is Not Enough.* Glencoe, Illinois: Free Press, 1950.

Bisch, Louis E. *Be Glad You're Neurotic.* New York: McGraw-Hill, 1936.

Cozzens, James G. *By Love Possessed.* New York: Harcourt, Brace, 1957.

Davis, W. A., and R. J. Havighurst. *Father of the Man.* Boston: Houghton Mifflin, 1947.

Deutsch, Helen. *Psychology of Women* (Volume 1—describes development to maturity and Volume 2—deals with salient phases of adult life). New York: Grune and Stratton, 1944.

Dunbar, H. Flanders. *Mind and Body.* New York: Random House, 1947.

Engstrand, Stuart. *The Sling and the Arrow.* New York: Creative Age Press, 1947.

Eysenck, Hans J. *Uses and Abuses of Psychology.* Baltimore: Pelican Books, 1953.

Freeman, Lucy. *Fight Against Fears.* New York: Crown Publishers, 1951.

Fromm, Erich. *Forgotten Language: An Introduction to the Understanding of Dreams, Fairy Tales, and Myths.* New York: Rinehart, 1952.

Gerber, I. J. *Man on a Pendulum: A Case History of an Invert.* New York: American Press, 1956.

Jersild, Arthur T. *In Search of Self.* New York: Bureau of Publication: Teachers College, Columbia University, 1952.

Josselyn, Irene. *The Adolescent and His World.* New York: Family Service Association of America, 1952.

Levy, John, and Ruth Monroe. *The Happy Family.* New York: Knopf, 1938.

Maslow, Abraham H. *Motivation and Personality.* New York: Harper, 1954.

Menninger, Karl A. *Man Against Himself.* New York: Harcourt, Brace, 1938.

May, Rollo. *Man's Search for Himself.* New York: Norton, 1953.

Packard, Vance. *The Hidden Persuaders.* New York: McKay, 1957.

Peters, Arthur A. *The World Next Door.* New York: Farrar, Straus, 1949.

Redl, Fritz. *Children Who Hate.* Glencoe, Illinois: Free Press, 1951.

Redl, Fritz. *Youth in Conflict.* Glencoe, Illinois: Free Press, 1955.

Reik, Theodor. *A Psychologist Looks at Love.* New York: Rinehart, 1948.

Reik, Theodor. *The Secret Self: Psychoanalytic Experiences in Life and Literature.* New York: Farrar, Straus, and Young, 1952.

Schulberg, Bud Wilson. *What Makes Sammy Run?* New York: Random House, 1941.

Selye, Hans. *The Stress of Life.* New York: Macmillan, 1956.

Steiner, Mrs. Lee. *Where Do People Take Their Troubles?* Boston: Houghton Mifflin, 1945.

White, Robert W. *Lives in Progress.* New York: Dryden, 1952.

Wolfe, Thomas. *You Can't Go Home Again.* New York: Harper, 1940.

Wright, Richard. *Black Boy.* Cleveland: World, 1950.

Wright, Richard. *Native Son.* New York: Harper, 1940.

Implicit in the description of the teaching operations is the question of the role of the group leader. Questions of identification of members with the leader certainly carry overtones of the problems associated with the transference relationship. Although the nature of the leader's role will be covered in detail later, reading material on transference now will enable the reader to have a more fundamental conception of the variety of relationships that are occurring simultaneously in the group. The term transference covers feeling and behavior directed toward another person which may be due to the effects of earlier experiences. Specifically, the chapters dealing with transference and countertransference in Patterson's[9] text will provide a summary of the literature in this area and a résumé of the issues involved.

Although I have not always agreed with the categories suggested by Raths as appropriate to the teaching process, basically I hope that this chapter provided the last needed bridge to demonstrate the essential similarity in the various aspects of the helping process.

BIBLIOGRAPHY

1. Bordin, Edward. *Psychological Counseling* (chapters dealing with concept of the role of ambiguity in counseling). New York: Appleton-Century-Crofts, 1950.

2. Raths, Louis. "What Is Teaching?" *Sociatry,* Vol. II, No. 3, 4, 197–206, 1948.

3. Arbuckle, Dugald. *Teacher Counseling.* Reading, Mass.: Addison-Wesley Press, 1950.

4. Porter, E. H. *An Introduction to Therapeutic Counseling.* Boston: Houghton Mifflin, 1950.

5. Tyler, Leona. *The Work of the Counselor.* New York: Appleton-Century-Crofts, 1953.
6. Thorne, Frederick. *Principles of Personality Counseling.* Brandon, Vermont: *J. clin. Psychol.*, 1951.
7. Rogers, Carl. *Client-Centered Therapy.* Boston: Houghton Mifflin, 1951.
8. Wittenberg, R. M. *So You Want to Help People.* Association Press, 1947.
9. Patterson, Cecil. *Counseling and Psychotherapy: Theory and Practice.* New York: Harper, 1959, chapter 9, "Transference and Countertransference."

4

A Group in Action

In any training program there are
several ways of helping the par-
ticipants become involved on a more intelligent basis. The whole area
of group process is so involved that it appears helpful to give the
reader the feel of what a group such as we will discuss sounds like.
Specifically, this chapter will be devoted to a transcription of an actual
demonstration presented at the American Personnel and Guidance
Association Convention in April 1955. This group, although artificially
assembled for demonstration purposes, goes through many of the
typical growth pains of any new group trying to jell. In addition, the
group raises issues and problems that form the basis for the major por-
tion of this book. To assist the reader, the actual protocol is on the
left-hand side of the page. To the right are comments on process,
pinpointing of issues, and discussion of controversial issues raised.

The session described was held in a large ballroom in a hotel. To
facilitate observation and to assist the audience in feeling a part of the
group, the demonstration took place around a table set in the center of
the room. This meant that the group was surrounded by people, some
of whom they could not see. It also meant, however, that they had
cut the distance between the group and the audience. The material
that follows is taken from a tape recording and has been edited
for greater ease of reading.

One of the problems that we will be facing here today as you may
very well guess is the fact that if we are to be able to try to have some

fun, and at the same time relax, we have to make this as natural as we possibly can. We have our mikes down on the table and although people will try to talk to each other so that you can hear us, if we're not talking loud enough, I'm afraid that the responsibility will have to be yours to move up. Our ability to try to do what we are attempting depends upon our relaxing, and believe me, we're pretty anxious right now. Let me try to describe to you what we think we are doing, and then maybe, when we get into the discussion section you can help us know if we achieved our objective.

Some of you have been at sessions recently where we've been talking about counselor training, and how counselors find their own values get in the way of doing the things that are important. We have also discussed how counselors use different techniques to avoid facing clients. At the U. of I. we have felt very strongly that we must spend considerable time during counselor training in helping the person who is to be the counselor get a chance to see what some of his needs are, and to begin to understand what it feels like to be in the roles which he will be holding later on. When the trainees have clients, their ability to empathize will partially depend upon their understanding of what it feels like to be in the client's role. We believe that the way you learn group techniques is not by hearing about them, through lectures or in books, but by seeing what it feels like right down here. Our course is, therefore, structured in the following way. When the students arrive at the very beginning of the course they are greeted by my smiling face, welcoming them. The class is limited to 12 people, that's a luxury that I know many of you cannot afford. But this makes a very real difference in what we can hope to accomplish.

The group is told that the purpose of the course is to help them learn how to work with groups, what they want to do in groups, and what it feels like to be in a group. They are also told that the contents of the course and the way the group will achieve its goal is left completely for the group to work out, with whatever help from me they want to have. The net result is, as we will try to help you see, a relationship which becomes fairly informal and also one where we begin to look at each other as people and begin to tie in some of our experiences that are quite beyond the classroom.

The people seated around this table were all students in courses in group guidance.

Now I'd like to go around the table and let you know who we've got here—some of these folks are looking for jobs, so I surely want you to know who they are—starting to my left is Elizabeth Mullins. She is a director and counselor trainer at Indiana University in the Residence Halls. Across from me is Mary Ann Pelican; it's kind of hard describing what her job is. She works for the Chicago Council on Foreign Relationships. She was trying to describe her job to me before. She said when people come from other countries, she takes them around and shows them the Wrigley Building. (*Laughter.*) Mary Ann is also a person who has had considerable training in counseling, and she'll be glad to talk to any of you afterwards, since she is interested in a new job. (*Laughter.*)

Curt Stafford is at the U. of I. as a research assistant, working at the Office of Teacher Placement in charge of the follow-up studies where we attempt to see how effective we've been in helping people in our Teacher-Training program. Bill Lewis is a counseling psychologist working at the Danville V. A. Hospital, while he is completing his work on his doctorate at the University of Illinois. Dorothy Farris has got some interesting things going on, and I hope she shares some of them with us. She's the YWCA program director in Alton, Illinois.

Bill Carlson is a teacher and counselor working with junior high and high school students at Weldon, Illinois. Louise Sharpe, Dean of Women at Central Michigan State Teachers College, is our recorder for today. She will have a rough time because this won't go according to protocol.* Dominick Mazzitelli formerly was a psychologist at Manteno State Hospital. He now is on the campus at the U. of I. While he is taking his work there, he is working as a counselor in the Elementary Education Teacher Training Program. Last of all, Rita Newton, whose field is Art Education. So as you see, we've got quite a diversified group.

I might indicate that this is something that we want. Unlike some people who see group therapy as being most effective when you have a homogeneous group, we strive for heterogeneity. If this group is to reflect the world of reality, it ought to contain different people with different needs, interests, and different ways of expressing themselves. If we can learn to communicate among each other in the group, then we've learned something that will be a skill that we can use in other groups where we will have as great a diversity as we have here.

I think at this point I will not say any more—except just to indicate this: that we will try here to have what is rather a typical session for us. How typical it may be of the usual classroom is something we would like to discuss with you later. There is just one other thing I'd like to mention to you: I indicated to you that the goal of the course

* Dean Sharpe was assigned by the convention to cover our session. She was not part of the group, although she was seated with them.

is indicated to the students at registration and at the initial class session. There are only two other limits imposed in the course. One is that every session, like this one, is to be tape recorded; after every session students are required to listen to the recording so they can have a chance to hear what went on in the group that they didn't hear, because they were so personally involved. We have one other gimmick. Right after each session the students write logs on their impression of what's been going on in the group. They then have a chance when they listen back to the recording to discover what they failed to perceive in their initial impressions.

Generally, when we listen back to a tape, we do it in a group so that we can all share our perceptions of what's going on. It gives us a chance to compare what one person is seeing and the other is not. At this point I'm just going to leave it to the group to carry on. I might tell you that we did not plan this session before and so have no idea of what's coming up. (To the group)

Comments

1. Where do you want to start?

1. An open-ended question indicating immediately to the group that the responsibility is theirs.

2. CURT: Well, we noticed one thing right off, Walt; as soon as you stood up, way back, you notice how the group kind of quieted down. Boy, they perceive you as an authority figure. Well that's your last chance.

2. Continuing of structuring by group redefining initial leader's role.

3. LIZ: I, uh, I don't like the recorder (pointing to Louise Sharpe) down there at the end of the group.

3–17. Group sets about task of developing security with each other. The presence of a nonparticipating and nonvulnerable observer has to be resolved. The group recognizes that Dean Sharpe's presence has both positive and negative effects. They examine ways to incorporate this person so she will not be a source of threat.

4. DOM: If she was not down there then I'll have to be down there, and I don't like being at the end of the group.

Comments

5. CURT: You mean this is something different from what we've had before?

6. LIZ: We've never had a member in the group before that wasn't a part of the group.

7. DEAN SHARPE: Well, the recorder doesn't write legibly, so maybe that will help.

8. WALT: Dorothy. Are you trying to say something?

9. DOROTHY: I was uh, well, when you were talking about the recorder down here, I thought that maybe we could pull her in and make her be a part of us. Or did you mean that you just don't, you don't like anyone writing stuff as we . . .

10. LIZ: Oh no, it's not the writing, 'cause we write ourselves.

11. SHARPE: This is something personal, between you and me. (*Laughter*)

12. DOM: The role, huh?

13. LIZ: I'll see you after class . . .

14. DOM: You leave her here 'cause I need some support on this.

15. BILL L: I think it's the role that she's not comfortable with, not the personality.

16. BILL C: Is it a matter of her being up here with us physically, but not being with us as part of the group?

17. LIZ: That's right.

18. DOM: I have a different idea on this. I think we're going to take out on Dean Sharpe what we would like to take out on the rest of the group watching because we're scared, 'specially the ones behind me. Real paranoid. (*Laughter*) (To Dean Sharpe) So don't take it personally. (*Laughter*)

18. An interpretation of underlying hostility coming from being in a threatening situation. Attempt to help Dean Sharpe see the hostility is not directed toward her, but rather what she represents.

19. CURT: This is certainly something unique from the way we've been used to functioning in class. We haven't had all these externals to try to get over with. . . . I hope we get over them in a little bit. (*Laughter*)

20. MARY ANN: Have you noticed how we are deferring getting started?

21. BILL: Yeah!

22. CURT: Yeah, we're very much aware of their presence.

23. WALT: We haven't gotten started?

24. LIZ: We've started, but we're ahead of ourselves. (*Laughter*)

25. BILL L: All this laughing shows some tension.

26. DOM: That's an understatement!

27. MARY ANN: (*Jumble of voices*) We got started awfully quickly for a beginning session. It usually takes us quite some time. I think one of the reasons is that I don't think I could stand much silence with so many people around, where I would be comfortable with about 30 seconds of silence in the classroom. No more than 30 seconds.

28. WALT: Then it's not only the person who is using writing differently, but also silence has taken on a different meaning for us in *this* group.

29. MARY ANN: The thing is that I've often found silence to be

19. Having faced the underlying feeling, the desire is expressed to move on.

20–22. Awareness of the fact that this topic is also serving the purpose of delaying the group from having to face the threats from within the group.

23. Question designed to point up that (20–22) are really subterfuges since they, too, are part and parcel of the steps a group goes through to achieve security.

24–26. Another reflection of the underlying anxiety and tension.

27. After recognizing feeling, group is again able to examine reasons for tension. Definition of how silence in this context is a source of threat.

28. Reflection of two feelings recognized as sources of threat.

29–34. With acceptance of feeling, they move on to see

a very comfortable thing . . .
and here, all of a sudden, it
scares me to death!

what these feelings really
represent.

30. BILL C: I wonder if we had
only the people at the table we
could comfortably be silent, but
we feel some other pressures.

31. BILL L: Well, we're supposed
to be up here to show something, to prove something, and
we feel that the silence won't
prove anything.

32. RITA: In radio the worst crime
is over 5 seconds of silence.

33. DOROTHY: Yeah, and we also
realize that we won't have too
much time to do it in, so we try
to make the best use of the time
that we do have.

34. MARY ANN: I feel a terrific pressure to perform . . . and say
something.

35. CURT: And we've all gone
through the experience in the
actual class setting. You can't
hurry the thing along. That's
what really makes it bad.

35. Recognition of the limits
of time along with an ac-
ceptance of limits of hu-
man abilities.

36. WALT: Sort of a conflict for us.
On the one hand we see that we
can't speed it up . . . and yet
we feel that we've got to put
across a point.

36. Reflects ambivalent needs
that are in conflict.

37. DOM: What are we trying to
put across? We're trying to
condense in a half hour the experiences we've felt, and I believe it's very close to all of us,
a whole term's work or a whole
year's work in a half hour and
show these people that we've
got something *good* here! How
can we do this in a half hour?
I feel defeated before I start.

37–38. Sees a need to define problem prior to an attempt at
resolution.

38. LIZ: Dom, that's a big problem
I've run into in my work . . . I
want to convince them that
here's something good . . . and
words can't describe it. You al-

most have to go through the
session to do it, but if you have
to go to Illinois and take this
course to start using it, it's not
going to go very far, very fast.

39. Liz: It's a frustrating situation!

                    39. Reflects tension and frustration in problem solving.

40. Dom: Yeah, this is something
similar to this meeting I was sitting in on yesterday . . . where
we were talking about something, and the thing that they
seemed to be talking about was:
how do you convey, or how do
you describe, how do you *tell*
a person about what he feels in
a client-counselor relationship?
No one seemed to know how to
say it. This is the problem we
have now, how do we show what
we're feeling? How could we
describe this? How can we tell
them that when we were in this
particular class—and I'm using
this because there was security
there—how can we tell them
that this was a good thing? You
just don't describe it . . . the
words that we use, I forgot the
topics we talked about, except
the sex life of the Eskimo.
(*Laughter*)

                    40. Sees problem as difficulty
in communication of personal feelings, along with
a recognition that the content of the words used
may be very foreign to
the feelings they are communicating.

41. Mary Ann: That was a good
discussion!

       41–44. Awareness that content
cannot serve as easily as
feelings as a basis for providing a common denominator. Also present is the
right of the individual to
help the group see the
effect of its behavior on
him.

42. Curt: You're excluding me from
the group now. (*Mixed voices*)

43. Curt: How many different
classes do we have represented
here now?

44. Walt: Yeah, I think that's one
point that we might clarify and

that is that the people here were
not all in a group together and
that we have several groups represented. The people at the table
today represent a new group
that has never really worked together. We are going through
some of the growing pains of being a group even at this time.

45. Liz: Wait a minute Walt, hold
on.

45. Leader made the mistake
of trying to speak for the
group without either being
so delegated or being sure
he represented their position.

46. Bill C: I think we are simply
saying that the security we get
can be gotten from the groups
that we were once in, but we
have to get it from the group we
have here.

46–56. Group recognizes need to
find security. Initially
they seek security in past
experiences. From this
grows the recognition that
whatever the basis of past
security, to be really useful it must be used to help
develop a new basis for
security in this new set-
ting.

47. Dom: Until I get it here, I'm
going to use my other group as
a basis. (*Laughter*)

48. Mary Ann: The only thing is,
though, that the support that
we once had . . . for example,
the four of us . . . pardon me,
Walt, the five of us . . .
(*laughter*) and the security that
we had together, can be a basis
to begin reaching out to these
folks that we don't know as well.

49. Bill L: Yeah, but why
can't . . .

50. Liz: If they feel left out, what
then? How do you pull them
in?

51. Dom: What you're saying is that
we should pull them into our
group. Why shouldn't they pull
us into their group?

52. Bill L: Why don't we just
realize this is a different group?

53. Dorothy: Yes!

54. Dom: O.K.

Comments

55. BILL C: But it's this group here that we're working with now.

56. DOROTHY: Uh huh.

57. Walt: This is kind of hard for us to face at this time.

58. BILL C: It's nice to look back, but our problem isn't in looking back . . . it's looking here.

59. DOM: I think one thing we can do, though, although they are different groups . . . there were similar types of experiences in the sense that the structures were similar, and we are trying to understand each other and ourselves through this structure, and I think one of the ways in both groups or the three groups that are represented here, is that we are looking for some kind of support so that we could feel less threatened and talk about ourselves. I think we could start in terms of that. If I know what I'm talking about. (*Laughter*) I'm not sure.

60. MARY ANN: It's hard to talk. Will you try again?

61. DOM: Yeah, I think that one thing we've experienced, is that when we did get a group going . . . ah . . . we had enough support from each other so that we could deal with problems that we wanted to deal with, that were pressing, whether they were . . . ah . . . manifested in the group. Or . . . ah . . . seemed peculiar to the group, or they were really something we brought in from outside. We had something we wanted

57. Reflection of difficulty in facing present threat rather than past security.

58. Acceptance of these feelings.

59. Having faced threat, the group now tries to seek a solution. The idea being confused, the words reflect ambiguity. A good example of an attempt through words to search for the idea.

60. First overt effort of a group member to provide specific support to another person. Support is offered through acceptance of the feeling plus an offer of continued acceptance.

61. Recognition of effect of group support on enabling a person to think through an idea.

to talk about to somebody. Ah
. . . however, we did this didn't
make any difference to me. I
got a good feeling going . . . I
felt that somebody was understanding what I was saying.

62. CURT: The thing that still bothers me about this, Dom, is the
thing that was brought up a little
earlier, this time pressure. Ah
. . . I'm in the class right now
. . . and uh . . . we've had
something like 12 sessions, 12
2-hour sessions, and just *now*
we're getting around to the point
where we're dealing with some
things that have really been
bothering a lot of people. Well
that's 24 hours of work. Here
we are pushing on this 15 minutes to ½ hour and it still bothers
me.

62. A return to a previous
strong feeling which, at
least for this person has
not been resolved. Group,
however, accepts the right
of the person to return to
an idea he has not worked
out for himself.

63. RITA: But some of it transfers
from one of the 427 (number of
group guidance course) groups
to another, because one of the
people in your group happens
to be the minister at our church;
and he thinks . . . because he
knows I took the course, he's
able to say . . . just one sen-
tence . . . "Rita, we've become
a group!" (*Laughter*)

63–67. The group returns to an
issue which will be a ma-
jor issue for some time.
The question is whether
transfer of experiences to
new situations is possible.
This ability to see the abstract ideas which are common to both old and new
situations is the height of
mature understanding and
learning.

64. LIZ: You understand what he
means . . .

65. RITA: Yeah, and so he singles
me out to tell this to. So that
in a way, if you were in 427,
there are a lot of things like
that I could say to you, and
I'd know you'd understand.

66. DOM: I have the same experience with one of the girls . . .
this girl in your class now . . .
she looked at me and said she
was taking 427 . . . and I said
"Uh huh" . . . (*laughter*) I
didn't have to say a word.

67. DOROTHY: But you know, on the other hand, uh . . . there can also be some people who maybe . . . haven't had 427 . . . that you can be talking about some of these things to, and they, too, can understand. And they can know the thing you're trying to do and even be helpful.

68. MARY ANN: I think the thing that's so hard to in any way demonstrate to people is the kind of relationships we establish with each other, that are so abnormal . . . in the college community, in the graduate school . . .

69. RITA: 427 makes us abnormal? (*Laughter*)

70. MARY ANN: No, I mean the ways we acted toward each other were different in the ways we could talk and feel . . .

71. BILL L: Such an in-group feeling.

72. LIZ: But is this necessarily the result of the college community . . . or can you do this anytime you put a collection of people together in the proper atmosphere and create a group?

73. DOROTHY: We are trying to understand something together.

74. LIZ: That's right, you can do this anywhere, whether it's on a college campus or (*group adds names of other settings*).

75. MARY ANN: What I mean though, Liz, let me try to clarify this, is . . . in the business world, or in the academic world, people *don't* act toward each other the way you and I act toward each other in our groups. It's a stripping of a lot of things.

76. DOM: It's a real different structure.

77. MARY ANN: That we carry around all the time.

68–69. Beginning of acceptance of underlying sex components of feelings and the difference between the appropriateness of expressing these feelings in different settings.

70–77. An exploration of the limits and relationships which distinguish this type of group from others.

78. Dom: When we walk into an or-
    dinary classroom we usually
    have someone standing up at
    the front of the room. We don't
    look at each other, but we look
    at someone standing there who
    is going to give.

79. Curt: Even if it isn't this situa-
    tion, Dom, even if you've got a
    group sitting around a circle in
    the classroom, you don't neces-
    sarily have the kind of thing we
    have here. You're not baring
    your soul to your neighbor, nec-
    essarily.

80. Mary Ann: Let me throw this
    in, if I may, if it means any-
    thing. I was talking to an ad-
    vertising executive the other
    day. He was . . . Oh, all in-
    terested in this kind of attitude
    . . . and he said, "Well, of
    course we have people seated
    around in a circle!" As if this
    was the thing that made for the
    kind of attitude to relate one per-
    son to the other. You can set
    up the vehicle but . . .

81. Liz: You mean the physical
    setup without the feeling?

82. Mary Ann: He was still "Boss,"
    and people were still cautious
    about what they were saying.

83. Liz: Are you saying that what
    we've got here is an unreal situa-
    tion, as far as reality goes, with
    the barriers down and security
    present?

84. Mary Ann: It's real, very much
    real.

85. Liz: For us . . . but I mean
    . . . take it up to the Wrigley
    Building, if you will. (*Laugh-
    ter*) Then what you get from the
    group we can carry with us, but
    you can't go up there and have
    the same thing talking to "Joe
    Blow" in the advertising game.

78–85. Examination of differences
       between past group expe-
       riences   and   present.
       Group looks at physical
       organization, role of ini-
       tial status leader, security
       needs, and problems of
       communication.

Comments

86. Dom: Oh let me get a word in. (*Laughter*)

86. Upset, needs to verbalize his feelings.

87. Walt: You're real upset about this.

87. Acceptance of feelings as reflected in his behavior rather than words.

88. Dom: Ah . . . ah . . . what I hear you saying is that first of all we had a completely different structure. One of the things that's very important is that when you're not set for this kind of structure, it's hard to see it. How long did it take us to realize what this guy's role was? (*Pointing to Walt Lifton*)

88. As before with Dom, idea presented by person who provided help is incorporated in Dom's thinking. Specifically he focuses on the differences in perception that are gained through words versus behavior. Emphasis is on importance of behavior.

89. Mary Ann: A long time.

90. Dom: He told us point-blank we could take care of the marks, the grades, important. Every class we go for grades. They go up to the Teacher Placement Office and they are on our records, and if we're looking for jobs someone's going to look at them. We think. Sometimes they don't. How long did it take us to work out the idea that he wasn't suddenly going to snatch away this function that he was handing us, and leave us high and dry?

91. Mary Ann: What I'm *trying* to say is that in a normal situation in business or somewhere else people don't have the security to do the things that we do here.

91. Recognition that ability to perceive is a function of perceptual defense. Concept of perceptual defense (you see what you can stand seeing) with increased security people see more of the world around them.

92. Bill L: That's right. It takes so long to get the feeling for the group. . . . Like we were talking about "we've got a group now." It took how many weeks to understand what it meant? Whereas, in the business world if things don't go like that (*snapping his fingers*) or in the class-

92. Again a repeat of an earlier theme of the inability of society to recognize the realities of both time and human ability.

room if things don't move right
along, well generally the instructor or the students are so insecure they can't stand it.

93. LIZ: Didn't we become a group
after we hit the wall, and when
we hit it and fell, they picked
us back up and that's when we
became a group?

93. This comment points up
the fact that the height of
group security is achieved
when the person falls in
his own eyes, yet contin-
ues to be accepted by others. It is the beginning of
the feeling that they are
accepted as people, not
just because of their ideas
or behavior.

94. DOM: I still have the scars.

95. DOROTHY: Mary Ann: are you
really trying to say that in groups
outside of this class this thing
can't happen?

95–100. Recapitulation of trans-
ferability concept now
combined with the role
security plays in under-
standing.

96. MARY ANN: No, I don't mean
that at all . . .

97. RITA: No, but you can't expect
it.   Sometimes you leave the
classroom with a sense of ex-
pectancy.   I would leave 427
and dash down to a very small
seminar group, and we all sat
around a table just the same size
and boy did I get into trouble
day after day!

98. MARY ANN: What I mean is this
. . . I'm not saying it's not possible; as a matter of fact it would
be fine if it were able to be put
into use.   I'm saying that people, in business or somewhere
else, can't say kind or nasty
things to each other, without
having a reaction that is negative. Here we can do both of
those things.

99. LIZ: Well, isn't that why you
created this kind of group for
teaching purposes?

100. BILL L: Well, it really doesn't
become a group until the anxiety gets so high about this sort

of thing and then there has to
be the cohesiveness.

101. WALT: You mean we became a
group because we were so
afraid of something else?

102. BILL L: We were so threatened
if nothing was going on, we'd
have to get together.

103. DOM: I think what we're saying here . . .

104. LIZ: Dom!

105. DOM: Wait a minute Liz—
(*laughter*). I think what we're
saying here is that people are
not used to perceiving each
other this way or reacting to
each other this way and what
it takes is a complete reorienta-
tion. Ordinarily, when anyone
walks into a classroom, he's set,
he's been trained, I remember
when I sat in elementary school,
this way, (*showed his hands
clasped in front of him*) every-
time the teacher walked down
the aisle, it was hard for me to
unseat myself this way . . .
and . . . outside of groups
that are planned this way . . .
it's a difficult thing to set up.
It takes time for people to realize and to become comfortable.
They're comfortable in a role
where someone gets up and
tells them something. They're
used to this, and it's very
threatening to take on the responsibility of a group member
and to be responsible for the
other person sitting on the other
side of the desk or the chair
. . . desk or the chair, I'm confused! (*Laughter*) . . . The
table, I'll get to it Liz. Ah
. . . it takes a lot of time to
take on this responsibility of
somebody else's needs and to
say if I'm going to get my own

101. Reflection that group is
perceived as a means of
dealing with threat.

103–105. Resurgence of former relationship where these two
people competed for lead-
ership. Although Dom
cuts Liz off, he indicates
his awareness of what he
has done, and his feelings
of responsibility to her.

needs satisfied, I'm going to have to help someone else! We just don't work that way ordinarily . . . it's hard to shift!

106. MARY ANN: But . . .

107. RITA: Wait! Liz, you had one oar in, this is the supreme sacrifice for me. (*Laughter*)

108. LIZ: I know! The thing that threw me now was when people use the word "group" they generally mean something entirely different from what we have here. And the same word being used on two things, and the only way I could differentiate was the way I felt in the two places, and this I couldn't explain. It was terrible.

109. CURT: This is what I was wondering about your group, Mary Ann, are you thinking of a group as setting out to do something . . . say get a certain job lined up in business?

110. MARY ANN: Well . . . I . . . certainly . . . people aren't going to group around nothing but, still, does that mean that there doesn't have to be some sort of relationship established?

111. WALT: There's something here that bothers me, as it must. Are you saying that when we are related on a feeling level, we got no tasks done?

112. MARY ANN: Thank you.

113. CURT: No, there's a difference between going specifically at a task as, say, the stereotype which I have, in which you might be doing something in business, as opposed to the way we approach it here.

114. LIZ: I think we ought to let Rita come in with what she has . . .

107–108. Very interesting by-play. Rita is indicating to the group not only how she has changed but is also demonstrating how "time" —time to talk or think— is now seen as "giving" rather than just submission. Liz is re-raising problems of semantics and communication.

109–111. Exploration of concept that goals of groups whether they be work or "people" oriented would effect group relationships. Raises the basic philosophical issue as to the reason for the existence of groups. As a means toward an end or as an end in itself.

112. Support obtained through identification.

114. Having been helped Liz now wants to help Rita use the group, too.

115. RITA: You know, this is a real change for me from last year. And it operated back in New York two weeks ago when I gave up the floor in the midst of twenty-five people, when I'd been trying to get in all morning! Ah . . . now I forgot what I was going to say! (*Laughter*).

116. CURT: You lose your thought when you wait.

116. Support through reflection of feeling while also indicating an interest in what she is trying to say.

117. RITA: If you've got the ability to structure this kind of thing in other groups, it can be done in other groups. It doesn't have to be a counseling department of a college for it to work. It can work in other groups, but it has to be planned for, and worked for, and wanted. The limits have to be set; it has to be explained. I lived with a minister for awhile, two years ago; this always floors people! She was a *girl* minister. (*Laughter*) . . . and she had a youth group, and it was in a church that was fairly authoritarian about its other relationships . . . at least didn't have this kind of orientation, and she was able to set up a group, of people which included me . . . and it was a church with which I had very little sympathy for. She included me as sort of "Devil's Advocate," and I got the warmest, most wonderful, secure feeling from that group! And they were people whose ideas I ordinarily could not tolerate.

117. People can be accepted for themselves not just their beliefs.

118. MARY ANN: I wanted to tell an experience. I didn't think I'd get a chance to say anything beyond the Wrigley

118. Mary Ann returns to her attempt to reconcile work groups and therapeutic groups.

Building. We designed study
groups to work in different geo-
graphical and political areas.
My pride and joy is the Latin
American group, who wanted
to study like crazy for weeks.
We started in September. We
are just getting to the point
now, when one of the ladies in
particular, who is only there
not to learn about Latin America, but to have some *friends,*
is making her friends. The
group leader is just becoming
aware of this. We've begun doing work, and we're learning
about *Latin America.* She's
not worrying about her friends
anymore, 'cause she has them.
She's gotten away from all this
other junk, which is no longer
important. And . . . what
I'm saying is . . . it took me
from September to April to get
this idea across. 'Cause this
was a man who's in the insur-
ance business who *told people
what to do!* (*Laughter*) And
no one seemed to realize . . .

119. Dom: You know, the funniest
thing just happened . . . I
didn't hear a word you said. I
was just so pleased to hear your
voice again. (*Laughter*)

119. Indicates support from relationships and strong
feelings of affection that
develop in groups. It was
remarks like these that
caused some members of
the audience to be con-
cerned about the possibility that group members
would "act out" their
needs with each other,
in out-of-group sessions.
Briefly, this problem was
faced by the group in class
and techniques developed
to deal with it. Actually
it has never represented
a problem since basically
a respect for the other person's need led group mem-

bers to be very careful about the effect of their behavior on others. Dom's comment also demonstrates that the relationships are effected by more than just the words used. Mannerisms and physical gestures became a language in themselves.

120. MARY ANN: You see this is what you can't explain to people.

121. LIZ: Aren't we trying to describe what exists here that doesn't exist many places, a climate that permits you to use this kind of group in any way you want to?

122. MARY ANN: Yes.

123. LIZ: We can use it to learn group dynamics, or counseling, or "basket weaving," or . . .

124. DOROTHY: (*Jumble of voices*) That we can take it out into groups that possibly are in situations or places where people have never heard of this type of thing before, and apply some of the principles that ah . . . that we have gained, that we have experienced eh . . . as you were talking a little while ago Dom . . . we actually experience these things in this group. Well, all right, we've experienced them, so we can go out in situations and . . . begin making these things *work*.

125. CURT: That was what was getting me. You were mentioning things like "basket weaving," and I got to thinking of that, and I didn't hear all of what you said Dorothy, so I had to pick up the tail end. It's more than what you learn about

125. Picks up idea of learning problem solving rather than the solution in a specific situation.

Latin America. It's well, "here's me," "here's how I function," "I'm learning some new things about how I function." "It gives me this greater freedom."

126. RITA: Here's something I thought about when you were saying "Go forth and do likewise." The thing I found in my sort of work was that I *couldn't* go forth and do likewise. And I'm still not capable of working with my Art Ed classes in the way that this group works . . . but I'm a different person, so I'm working differently with the classes.

127. CURT: Are you different, Rita, or are you seeing yourself differently?

128. RITA: Oh well, let's not go into that!

129. BILL C: Are we saying that we can't possibly jump from what we have in the security of a group like this immediately to other groups, but that we have to work for some kind of security with them? Sometimes we have to start quite a ways down the "totem pole" to work on up towards the top.

130. BILL L: It seems like you're expecting too *much*, if you're expecting every group to have this sort of feeling about it.

131. LIZ: It takes a long time to get it, but I think the big problem, at least I found it was going as a member of this group to a leader of another group. The thing that made us a group actually was getting rid of Walt as a leader and pulling him in as a member.

132. DOM: It's an interesting thing we are saying . . . how do

126. Understanding the concept frees the person to express his idea in his own way.

129–132. Here we have one of the major problems in a democracy. Having solved a problem once, it's hard to accept that each new group demands the right to develop in its own way, even if it involves making mistakes others have made before them. This is the eternal cry of the adolescent who resents parental domination and wants the right to shape his own life. As the group matures they are better able to use other's past experience as a basis for making their decisions. They cannot accept this information until they feel sure they are secure enough to not let the data itself guide them in directions they may not wish to go.

we tell people about this? Do we go in as a leader and try to describe this and yet when we came into the group and Walt described it to us, I thought he was talking Chinese! The conclusion I come to is wherever the specific places that we want to initiate this type of relationship, and you can't do it everywhere . . . it's not the panacea for relationships, it's specific. . . . The only way we can do it is by going out and living it, because you can't do it just by saying it. You have to go out and instead of explaining it, just like we didn't understand it, how do we expect them to understand it? It's a feeling, thing, it's a . . .

133. Liz: A big problem I ran into was . . . here I'm accustomed to saying what I'm feeling. You've clobbered me back down whenever I've gone too high, and I have . . . and I got into a group this year that when I *did* it, I scared some of the people and they backed away. And it really frustrated me because I wanted to say what I was feeling, but if I did it, I destroyed what grouping they had to begin with.

133. Just expressing feelings isn't enough. The setting where it is done, and the way it is done both will effect a person's relationship to a group.

134. Bill C: The group didn't have enough security to accept what you were doing.

135. Mary Ann: For the first time I found out the tricky problem Walt probably had, because first of all, here I am . . . I am the leader, and there were people there that were 30 years my senior! And yet they referred to me as an authority figure, and this isn't what I wanted! And then, I tried to "group it up" and be a member

135–136. Being a leader may put you in a conflict situation where what you want to be does not always coincide with a group's perception of your role. It's not comfortable to be misperceived.

(*laughter*) . . . and I felt rejected and I drove home with
my "tail between my legs" feeling "nobody likes me!"
(*Laughter*) You suddenly have
to try to find out where you
do fit in this group.

136. Liz: I think part of the problem is, we expect the other
members of the group to perceive what we're doing, and to
see what we're doing as we
are just expressing ourselves.
They take the common, ordinary way of perceiving it.
"They're directing this at me
personally."

137. Bill L: Well, one of the big
things that Mary Ann was talking about, seems to me, is that
when you're taking the course,
it's not until we're really *into*
the course that we really understand. We get real threatened in the middle, and that's
probably what's happened to
you . . . now . . . you're
right in the middle of it and
it's pretty hard.

138. Liz: But we held together so
we could get to the end.

139. Mary Ann: Yeah!

140. Bill L: Yeah.

141. Liz: Sometimes they collapse
around you when the first
threatening occurs. And then
they escape into an authoritarian setup.

142. Mary Ann: That's what they
did.

143. Liz: That's exactly what they
escape into . . . because it
holds security for them.

144. Bill L: Well, Mary Ann's going to have to have a pat
on the back once in awhile.
(*Laughter*)

137–143. Part of the group process
includes periods of threat.
The group can face the
threat only as they pro-
vide support to one an-
other. During threat peo-
ple regress to a more de-
pendent kind of role.

144–147. Until the group develops
an acceptance of the
leader, he needs a basic
personal security to accept

145. MARY ANN: Who's gonna give *me* security?

146. LIZ: You're kind of by yourself on it because you're the only one that's there!

147. WALT: Aren't we saying that a part of the problem of the leader's role is to help the group cope with him and give him the support to do the role that he wants to have?

148. DOROTHY: Yeah.

149. MARY ANN: Uh huh.

150. LIZ: That's the problem we keep having trouble with.

151. MARY ANN: Now the point is, how are we going to implement this? Solve my problem please! (*Laughter*) I can't stand another one of these Latin American sessions. (*Laughter*)

152. RITA: Well, you'd have to solve mine, too.

153. LIZ: Mine, too.

154. RITA: I have one group that just doesn't want to be a group. (*Laughter*) And uh . . . I am learning how to use myself in a different way from what I used to be. I think 427 didn't teach me how to use myself as a group leader the way 427 used a group leader. I have become a different kind of group leader, and it fits me, and I can do it that way.

155. BILL L: What . . . what's your concept of a group leader?

156. RITA: In one group I don't . . . this didn't work either and I haven't got any technique for it.

157. LIZ: What's a group leader?

158. BILL L: Look at the way Walt's leading this group. (*Laughter*)

159. LIZ: Yeah . . . but he's not leading it.

the hostility and rejection he may experience. Leader's role may be to help group learn how to deal with the leader.

148–153. In facing this problem group is providing each other support as they identify with each other. Feelings of guilt based on fear of personal inadequacy are alleviated as they are shared.

154–166. With an acceptance of problem group now is free to examine different ways members could solve problem.

160. BILL L: That's what I'm trying to say.

161. RITA: Can you picture me leading a group this way? (*Laughter*)

162. DOM: I think it is a bad comparison because Walt isn't leading this group and . . .

163. BILL L: Well, that's what I mean, she's saying . . .

164. DOM: We have already had other experiences with Walt. We have him sort of controlled in our own minds. (*Laughter*) However we did it, we did it, but Rita is talking about going in with a new group, and I think this is a different situation. I don't know . . .

165. WALT: Are we saying that there is no leadership in this group?

166. BILL L: No.

167. LIZ: No, we're saying no one person holds the role of leadership.

168. BILL L: But . . . apparently . . . it seems to me that she is perceiving it differently.

169. DOM: (*Everybody said no*) Why not . . .

170. LIZ: Because leadership is a quality of the group, and we shift it back and forth as we go. You had it a minute ago; I've got it now. Bill's gonna get it.

171. CURT: I think one thing we can . . . (*Jumble of voices*) (*laughter*)

172. CURT: Uh . . . this business of leadership I think it's been a group leadership on this one point. Now compare our

167–170. Group explores idea that leadership doesn't need to be the prerogative of only one person. Concept that leadership can include verbal passivity is examined.

171. Play on words "who's going to get it" reflects anxiety over hostility expressed by group members when a leadership role is assumed by a person.

172. Facing anxiety, group examines how with less tension their behavior is changing.

Comments

group here. We're a first . . . an initial group here. This is our first session, and you compare it with the first sessions you remember from 427 and . . . uh . . . boy! We went through a period here where everyone was trying to get into it so (*gesturing cutting each other off*). In the beginning it was fast and furious . . . but we have slowed down a little now. I am starting to recognize some of you as I normally know you outside . . . I . . . (*laughter*) I . . . we're talking a little more slowly and also we've moved off . . . uh . . . uh . . .

173. DOM: A good indicator of this is that we haven't bothered Dr. Sharpe here. (*Laughter*)

174. BILL L: Let Curt finish.

175. LIZ: Yes . . .

176. MARY ANN: Let's let Curt finish.

177. DOM: Well, I . . . if you insist . . . (*Laughter*)

178. CURT: The things we have been getting into here at the end of examining these things that have been happening to us since then. We have moved a good bit from the opening. I . . . I think we've grown.

179. DOM: I see what you're saying, what you are saying is that we have reached the level where people don't bother us as much as they did, and one of the indicators is that we didn't bother Mrs. Sharpe. She's sort of faded in the background.

180. MARY ANN: I only want to say one thing . . . uh . . . and that was what Rita said. I want to try to figure it out, if I can . . . uh . . . she was

174–178. Almost because of 170 and 171 group fights to protect the rights of the individual.

180–188. Growing awareness that new roles are possible, and that new behavior in some situations is valuable. Also present is the realiza-

giggling when she said, "Try to imagine me being quiet as Walt has been." Try to imagine *me* being quiet as Walt has been, but I have done it. And it's completely amazed me. I mean . . . under particular circumstances where the only thing you could do was to shut up, you shut up.

tion that real growth comes not from identifying with and copying someone else, but in developing one's own way of doing things.

181. CURT: You know, we're . . . we're loaded here in one thing. Now . . . looking around at the table. I don't know Dorothy and Bill too well from seeing them in class, but the rest of you I have seen in action. There isn't anyone here who is noted for his silence.

182. BILL L: Well, we can't all be talkers. (*Laughter*) We can't imitate Walt. We have to relate in the way we feel most comfortable.

183. MARY ANN: It depends on what at that point is the thing one must do.

184. LIZ: But . . .

185. BILL L: Uh hum.

186. RITA: Mary Ann, I can do what he does by being quiet, and I can do it by talking, too. I found this out just a few weeks ago. I was leading a group and uh . . . uh . . . I got the same kind of results, I think, in terms of people being able to come out with highly unacceptable opinions in a group that had never seen each other before and never would again.

187. DOROTHY: Are we saying in a sense that. . . .

188. RITA: Uh . . . but I did it by doing more talking than he would do. I did it Newtonian instead of Liftonian, I guess. (*Laughter*)

Comments

189. LIZ: Yes . . . but . . . no . . . there were times in our classes when Walt carried a large verbal part of the 2-hour session.

190. MARY ANN: Yes, but what always happened? He'd get slugged at the end.

191. CURT: Wait, wait, I'll tell you.

192. DOROTHY: Just a minute. I . . . I was wanting to say . . .

193. DOM: Bang the table, kids. (*Laughter*)

194. DOROTHY: Maybe there are many, many ways of being a group leader.

195. GROUP: Yes . . . sure.

196. BILL C: For example, uh . . . if we could go on long enough, we might guess that people who had been most aggressive here might find themselves in rather . . . find themselves in certain leader roles . . . that the group would react to. I remember this happening in our own group that uh . . . uh . . . after the group settled down after some of the beginning sessions, and then some of the individuals in the group began . . . began to pick up bumps because Walt . . . the group had . . . well, I guess Walt took it first, didn't you?

197. WALT: Uh huh . . .

198. BILL C: And then . . . then it got passed around to some of the others.

199. CURT: Walt, do you mind if I mention a little bit about . . . about the way you were using the group . . . uh . . . as a member yourself?

200. WALT: Uh huh.

201. CURT: You *would* mind?

202. WALT: No. (*Laughter*)

189–198. Repeat on theme that leadership carries with it possible group hostility and rejection. 196 may be in response to Dom's statement that to be recognized one needs to bang the table. The idea here is that the group has a mellowing effect. It subdues the too aggressive while encouraging the more subdued.

199–202. Reflects concern for concept of confidentiality.

203. CURT: Something that pointed out a lot to us . . . uh . . . Walt's wife has been sick, for those of you who have been away . . . she's been sick for 3–4 weeks in the hospital now and boy! We could . . . we could just see his behavior in class. He wasn't a leader at all. I mean, he was in there. . . . "I've got some problems." Boy, "my home is all shook up and all." I think everyone in the group was aware of this after a very short time. He was . . . he was just using the group to help himself out. And uh . . . this I think, is above all is the thing that . . . oh . . . which destroyed any ideas that anyone may have had that he was still an authority. He was just using us for himself.

204. WALT: It is a real question, now, Curt, as to whether that's a good thing. Certainly people differ on this.

205. LIZ: Isn't that the . . .

206. CURT: Well, I know that . . . oh . . . the way . . . we had been discussing his role so much, trying to find his role and all. Not the fact that it came out and here it was . . . uh . . . we were doing his role, I mean. It was defined by his actions.

207. BILL C: Is this suggesting that to the extent that the leader can himself get help from the group, he can then help other people?

208. LIZ: I think it's also saying that to the extent that the leader is seen as an authoritarian . . . uh . . . it's related to how much the group will become a group as we speak of it here.

204–218. Controversial issue as to whether initial group leader ought to allow personal needs to enter into group situation. The concept present here is that since initial leader provides, through group identification with him, clues as to ways to behave in a group, the more roles he is able to play with honesty, the larger the range of possibilities of behaviors are made available to the group. Group seems to react to behavior as described in 203 with the feeling "If it's all right for him to admit these feelings and weaknesses it surely ought to be O.K. for me to do the same." Along with this is the idea that if a group can accept a leader as having human

209. MARY ANN: Well . . .

210. BILL C: I think you are turning it upside down. To the extent that he's *not* an authority, he can be helpful.

211. LIZ: That's right.

212. MARY ANN: Yeah, the point is that . . . that he is not the only therapist, that each one of us, in our turn, we are equal to serve when we are able to be a therapist.

213. LIZ: But it is terrifically frustrating to people, and I know 'cause I was one of them . . . that have relied on an authority for security.

214. CURT: Uh hum.

215. LIZ: And to have it pulled away . . . why you hit hard. I bounced back up, though, fortunately.

216. DOM: That's an understatement.

217. BILL L: That's where the (*laughter*) where the group leader, the one who is initially the group leader, has to be very secure because the group members when they first start out say "where's the authority; where's the security," and they all start griping and complaining.

218. LIZ: And if you can't find it in him, you turn and look to each other for it, and the minute you get it or get a taste of it, why that's when the group rolls.

219. MARY ANN: Yeah.

220. BILL L: Yeah, that's when it's worth all the anxiety and frustration.

221. WALT: I have a problem at this point . . . I wonder how we want to solve it. We didn't set any finite limits on this group. Do we want to keep

weaknesses, rather than being perfect, they change their concept of what to expect from a leader. It also changes their concept of the ways in which they should relate to him. Concurrent with this changing concept which permits the leader to be imperfect, is the growing willingness on the part of group members to assume a role they feel they now can measure up to.

218. Awareness that group members, too, have potentiality for giving leadership and support provides the security that promotes group growth.

221. Setting of limits is a group function. Time is a major limit. In deciding on limit, group, as usual, examines its own needs as

rolling, or should we let the
other people have a chance?

the basis for making a decision.

222. LIZ: Let's let them have a
chance.

223. BILL C: Yeah.

224. WALT: How about it?

225. CURT: I think so . . . because
there's only so much that they
can get from listening.

226. DOM: I would like to let the
rest of the people in on it.

227. WALT: O.K.

228. DOM: They have been so *quiet.*
(*Laughter*)

229. WALT: Well, I am going to
stand up so at least I can see
people. Also, with the session
over, my authority role won't
get at me so badly. Thanks
a lot. I would welcome any
questions or comments that any
of you (to audience) would
like to raise. We would feel,
I am sure, much more comfortable if we could have a chance
to explain what we . . . yes?

From audience:

230. DR. MARGARET BENNETT: The
young lady directly across from
you . . .

231. WALT: Rita Newton.

232. BENNETT: A moment ago . . .
uh . . . made some statement
about a person expressing a
highly unacceptable opinion,
and I'd like to raise a question
and hear the group discuss.
Uh . . . whether in a real
group therapy class you can
ever say anything that is highly
unacceptable or whether what
you say may not be a means of
your helping to understand
yourself.

233. RITA: What . . . what . . .
what . . .

232. Question of the nonjudg-
mental nature of a thera-
peutic group.

234. BENNETT: Or . . .

235. RITA: I'd like to answer.

236. BENNETT: Or allowing the group to help you understand yourself. I wasn't quite sure what she meant.

237. WALT: Rita.

238. RITA: When I said unacceptable I meant . . . this was a human relations conference, and people went with the expectation that they would talk in favor of brotherhood. People . . .

239. BENNETT: Oh, I see, you were speaking about . . .

240. RITA: People came out saying things that sounded very . . . unorthodox as far as what one is supposed to believe about brotherhood if one comes to a brotherhood conference. (*Laughter*) There was a great deal of hostile feeling; there was a great deal of Chauvanistic type feeling, and it was getting expressed by people. People were saying . . . I noticed that the leader of the entire convention was sitting facing me and they had asked me to lead this particular small group. And when anyone said anything which was not part of the brotherhood party line, uh . . . uh . . . a frown would come over her face, whereas I was sort of saying, "No, keep going . . . I see what you mean. I see the frame of reference, I think, in which you're saying this. And even if you say it and no one agrees with you . . . they at least now know that there are people who think this." So that's what I meant when I . . .

240. Focus on acceptance of person rather than his idea or behavior.

241. BENNETT: Yes, but in a real group therapy class I wonder if you can ever say anything that is highly unacceptable.

242. WALT: Not in a value sense or judgmental sense. Whatever you say hasn't a value of being acceptable or unacceptable, but rather in societal terms, these are some of the things we don't usually talk about because they're threatening.

242. Attempt to distinguish between role of group in helping others see what "society" would reject, as contrasted with what the group will permit to be expressed.

243. WALT: Dr. Wrenn?

244. DR. WRENN: What is the so-called leader's role? Now, I grant you that this is a leader-less group (*laughter*) . . . leaderless group in the sense . . . in the fact that the leadership shifts . . . uh . . . as a teacher in a situation like this for instance . . . when somebody sticks their neck way out . . . and says something that others resent. Maybe it's a statement of hostility toward the so-called leader, you see. Then is it possible that it is the leader's role to try to relieve a little of this hostility against the one person or rather should we leave it to the group to take care of that over a period of time?

244. Therapist has responsibility for welfare of group members. Question raised as to if this does not include controlling experiences and threats the person faces in the group.

245. WALT: I think I can answer that. It's a function of the leader's own security and his feelings of confidence in the group. But . . . uh . . . for myself, I think that at the beginning I tend to be more anxious, wondering whether this group is really going to jell. And . . . I don't always have the confidence I ought to have. But my role then becomes not pulling the pressure off a per-

son, but trying to help clarify the feeling that we're facing. "We seem to be pretty mad about something here. I won-, der whether we can take a look at what's happening and what we can do about it." Uh . . . as a matter of fact, I had another kind of role that sometimes the group found helpful and sometimes not. It almost might be called didactic. "What's going on now?" I would say. "What are we doing?" "Do we like it?" So that we could all not only label what was going on and see it for what it was, but possibly begin to take a look at the way we wanted to deal with it. And this I did fairly actively. But, as I say, this is me and some other person might . . .

246. WRENN: In a well-jelled group somebody else might take over and try to fix the situation.

247. WALT: I think that there is something that's very important here . . . that uh . . . might be clarified. My role as a leader . . . uh . . . as I perceived it anyhow, was to help the group set up a structure with me in which they could work. It was not in terms of the *way* they would work. I would try to help them. But because folks like Liz and others had feelings about authority figures, I had to be destroyed as an authority figure before there *could* be other leaders in the group. That's what happened in the group that Dom was in . . . that after I was . . . chopped off . . . Dom was next. And after Dom, Liz was next. You see, we were all three author-

ity figures, and we had things in our personalities that made us this. And when the group disposed of some of our needs that were getting in their way and they learned how to cope with them, then things really rolled. I think there is one concept here I'd like to make clear. Uh . . . there are many weaknesses as a person that I am sure that I have. Uh . . . I'd like to live with them. I'd like to be aware of them. But I think that my ability to work with a group depends not upon being a perfect person, but trying to set up a setting where my weaknesses won't get in the group's way. And I recognize that I have some of these needs that aren't always helpful to the group. It, therefore, to me appears more important that I give the group a device to get me out of their way when I am not being helpful. But . . . just . . .

248. UNKNOWN MALE VOICE: Walt, I would like to get some ideas about the original problem that was brought up by the group here. That is, this business of getting some identification since they were more or less strangers from the three different groups. And I noticed some cohesion and some division here, one particular physical one which seems to be . . . uh . . . uh . . . by chance. That is, there is a brief case between two people, and they are seated apart. . . . (*Laughter*) This man here has had his back turned practically the whole time on one group member.

249. WALT: Uh hum.

248. Focuses on importance of group cohesiveness as relating to the degree members relate with one another. Demonstrates the way the physical setting can effect the nature of the relationships.

250. (As IN 248): She, in turn, has
been sitting on the opposite
side of her chair. Could we
get a poll of the people around
here to see how they feel identified with each other in this
group relationship between
each other?

251. WALT: How about it? Do you
want to speak to it?

252. GROUP: Yes! It's all right with
me. I . . .

253. LIZ: I . . . I feel quite well
identified with everybody. I
completely forgot the recorder.
(*Laughter*) Umm . . .

254. SHARPE: Is that a compliment?

255. LIZ: I have become identified
with Miss Farris (Dorothy)
and Bill on the end I have less
identity with. Now, I've never
met these two people before
10:30 today. Uh . . . I didn't
. . . I feel quite well identified
with both of these people, and
then the others I have known
from the group I was in and
so I automatically picked that
up, I think.

256. WALT: I think there is one
point I'd like to raise. I . . .
I feel a certain mission involved in this session. The
things that you are describing
are the things that came out in
the logs. These are the things
that people began to perceive
and recorded in their written
impressions of each class.

257. WALT (*to Mary Ann*): I . . .
do you remember one of the
things that you did? May I
tell about it?

258. MARY ANN: Sure, I don't care.
(*Laughter*)

259. WALT: In one session, Mary
Ann . . . for whatever her rea-

251. Group is still given responsibility of making decisions.

257. Vital that confidentiality
be preserved. It is the
member's right to decide
what can be shared with
people outside the group.

son was . . . (*laughter*) . . .
made a wall chart of how many
times people participated.
Boy, did the group clobber her
with that. She was raising the
question as to whether or not
we were worthwhile people.
If we weren't . . .

260. LIZ: It was how she presented
it.

261. DOM: Yeah.

262. MARY ANN: Yeah! It was the
manner in which I did it.

263. WALT: You carry on . . .
(*Laughter*)

264. MARY ANN: Well, it was . . .
uh . . . (*laughter*) . . . and . . .
the tapes, and I took down the
number of responses of each
party in the group. And . . .
uh . . . (*laughter*) . . . and
. . . uh . . . as I did this . . .
uh . . . I found . . . uh . . .
to some extent, the people who
I thought were not talking were
actually responding. Well, I
came into class on my white
horse (*laughter*) . . . and uh
. . . instead of . . . I certainly learned a lesson.
(*Laughter*) Uh . . . I put it
on the blackboard without saying anything to anyone in the
class. And 15 minutes of the
session went by and somebody,
I guess it was Liz, made some
crack about "What is this ba-
loney on the blackboard?" And
then they all climbed down my
throat, and I had to try to explain what it meant and I also
. . . the thing that was most
important in my regard is that
I realized the personal, emotional reason why I had done
it. And uh . . . it was a matter of terrific antagonism toward me. And yet it was fol-

260–264. Demonstrates again effect
of "consultant" or infor-
mation giver who volun-
teers data group has not
sought. It was not the
data itself that was re-
jected, but rather what the
presenting of the data implied about the group
members' capabilities of
recognizing problems on
their own.

lowed up by *so* much security and support afterwards that I was able to face it, and . . . uh . . . personally was almost raised rather than diminished.

265. WALT: What we're suggesting here is that through this action which threatened the group, the group became responsible for helping an individual see what it meant to them. And in doing this, the person who had been threatened got support.

266. MARY ANN: Uh huh.

267. WOMAN'S VOICE IN AUDIENCE: I'm interested in the language used here . . . and I would guess that perhaps you found this in the beginning sessions . . . uh . . . perhaps that such words as "threatened," "external security," or "insecurity" were quite frequently used in class discussion, and then began to drop out. Do you find this in the regular class session as a kind of barrier? How is that handled in your group?

268. WALT: Dom, I wonder if you want to talk on the question of jargon and what happens in the group when you do use jargon? (*Laughter*)

269. DOM: Uh . . . the question of jargon came up quite abruptly with me. I had a lot of clinical background, and in the class I used quite a bit of the specific terminology of the clinician. And . . . uh . . . for a while I threatened the group with this because they felt . . . first of all, they didn't understand, and second of all, they . . . uh hum . . . it sounded like I knew so much more than everyone else until

265. Despite hostile nature of the act, group accepts the person while rejecting the act.

267. Communication being a vital issue, part of a group's growth comes in developing a "language" which is commonly understood. Part of the role of slang in the adolescent is that this is a clearly understood language.

finally when they got a little
security, I started getting my
head banged in. Until . . . I
had to leave this realm, otherwise leave class bloody every
day.   Uh . . . but . . . the
jargon comes up not in terms
of this internal and external security and threat, it wasn't, I
would say, part of the vocabulary of the class . . . until we
would have sessions, part of
the sessions in which we would
try to find out . . . just as we
did here toward the end, we
were trying to say where have
we gone; what have we done.
And uh . . . these were the
best words we could find to
. . . uh . . . describe the process that had gone on previously,
if someone said, "I didn't like
what so-and-so said." Well, in
this session where we were trying to pull things together and
understand what went on,
someone said, "You might have
felt threatened." And this was
a good word to express the
feeling.   And this is how the
words developed, because actually when you come into the
class with jargon you have such
a diversified group, you tend
to run into the "wall." I developed the word "wall" because I felt I was running up
against it quite a bit. I kept
bouncing off it for a while until
the group felt secure with me.
And I was insecure with the
group, and this is why I was
using it, let's face it!

270. CURT: Uh . . . I would like
to speak on two points, one
right along with this and another that is somewhat new
here. We haven't brought it
in yet. I can't describe too

270. Demonstrates that this is
a common problem.

much about a similar instance going on in the class now, because there's a problem of confidence in this group and . . . uh . . . this is one of the things that you don't come out with in one session . . . about how sacred are the things that we say in here? How far should they be carried? One of the persons in the present group is sitting out in the audience now. And so . . . uh . . . I can be reported back on this by this other one in class. (*Laughter*) I'll be very careful about what I say, but I would say almost 100% the same problem has come up in the present class now, Dom. We have a person who is being accused of being a Freudian, and throwing his Freudian terms around. And . . . uh . . . boy, it wasn't about two sessions ago it happened.

271. DOM: I'd like to add another thing, by the way . . . that when the group felt secure with me and I felt secure with the group, they didn't hesitate to ask me when I did use a word that I was using as part of my ordinary vocabulary because of the setup I was in. It didn't . . . they didn't hesitate to ask me what I meant. They allowed me to use it after they understood what I was . . . my own problem, and they accepted me this way.

272. WALT: One of . . . I'm sorry. Go ahead.

273. DOM: Don't interrupt me! (*Laughter*) In fact, in fact, there were times when they asked me about different things that I have had in my own experience, which was related to

271–277. The group language is a growing thing. They will tend to try to share each person's unique language as long as they feel it will help both the person and the group.

this, which they had clobbered me for previous to this. So that it was strictly a matter of relationship and counter threat . . . and threat. That once we worked this out, it . . . this didn't constitute a threat any longer, so it was all right to do this.

274. CURT: There's something else that bothers me, Dom, this word clobber that you use. I think this is part of our jargon.

275. RITA: We made a new jargon.

276. DOM: Very descriptive term. I'll show you the bumps. (*Laughter*)

277. CURT: Clobbered is more than getting hit over the head with a baseball bat, but it is with soft pine because, after you have been hit over the head, there's security in this group so that you can take a hit over the head and you can grow from it.

278. WALT: Well, I think the thing we learned from it was that we get hit because people care enough about you to try to do something about it.

279. MARY ANN: Let me, let me say something about what Dom said in his use of jargon in our group. And that was . . . we certainly clobbered Dom, but good! And then he found out that he could be a man that could explain things to us. After the threat was gone to both Dom and to us, he could explain his words to us and help us understand. I think part of this was in my counting responses, this same thing happened to me. I found I could help people if we both felt well enough about it.

278. Repetition of theme that honest feeling reactions from group, rather than being seen as source of threat, provide comfort since they not only let the person know where he really stands but also show others' concern about him.

280. WALT: Part of what we're saying here is an important concept. "How can the group learn to use people as resource people, but not as advisors who will tell them what to do?" And I think that when anyone came in with jargon or anything similar to that which by implication said to the group "This is right, this is the way it is, this is your label," the group resented it. But when a person came in and provided something that the group needed and he had, the group was very, very accepting of him. And that was a hard lesson for us to learn.

281. RITA: I'd like to say something about the value of learning your vocabulary this way. If you . . . if you learn what the words mean by feeling them first, and then maybe using words like "clobber," "the wall," and all the slang we put into it, it isn't awfully hard to pick up the technical jargon when you start reading. Because when you read all of the technical words, you know how they feel inside. And somebody else could have been taught the vocabulary in a straight academic class and never know what the words really mean.

281. Words to be truly meaningful need to be incorporated into each person's personal frame of reference.

282. WALT: Yes? (*to woman seeking question*)

283. WOMAN'S VOICE: I noticed that these two people were sort of left out of the group (*referring to Bill C. and Dorothy F.*) What would you as a leader do about this?

284. WALT: Nothing, absolutely nothing. I want to explain something about that, because

284–286. Role of isolate is a common source of concern. Idea is presented that this

I think that's kind of interesting, too. In several groups now, I have had members who have said almost nothing, and as the group continues one of the things they discover is that their security with each other depends on knowing what the other person is feeling. Communication, incidentally, I might indicate, goes on in other than just a verbal level. People who are indicating their feeling by their affect, by their faces, by their movements or in any way, are accepted by the group, but the individual who seems to be isolated forms a threat to the group and the group takes it up as a problem. And then the individual who doesn't talk becomes quite anxious because his status in the group depends upon his . . . and his acceptance . . . depends upon his giving to the members what the group needs for security. And so the pressure is not my asking them to talk, but the person's seeing that they'd better talk if they want to use the setup.

285. WOMAN'S VOICE: Dorothy seemed to have a lot of the answers in her mind so she gave out this feeling to the rest of them so that's probably the reason she was accepted more by the others than he was and yet she didn't ever say very much. She perhaps could be frustrated in the group. Would you as a leader have shown this?

286. CURT: Walt, you wanna . . . (*Laughter*)

287. DOM: Wait a minute. I think one of the things that will explain this is a question that was

is both a problem for the person and for the group, rather than being solely the responsibility of the leader.

raised by this gentleman here.
We only have met for a half
hour. I am very close to the
girls because . . . (*Laughter*)

288. DOM: Good enough, maybe I
shouldn't say more. I have
been in class with them in particular situations. I could sit
here and I know what they're
talking about. Dorothy has
the same experience because
she's been in with this group.
Now Carlson . . . I don't
know whether Carlson . . .
I met Carlson here yesterday.
I don't know if Carlson has
been in a class with any one
of us here, you see. Curt I
know from around the campus,
but I haven't been in classes
with him so I didn't feel as
close or as understanding because I hadn't shared this experience with either Bill Lewis
or Curt.

289. CURT: One of the problems
here is the fact that I was
blocking you (to Mary Ann)
out because I was concerned.
I was picking this up. Most
of your talk was directed down
in this corner and Bill off in
this corner was getting sort of
shut out.

290. MARY ANN: Let me . . .

291. CURT: It was kind of hard to
get around to see him, so in
trying to pull him in I was
shutting Mary Ann off.

292. MARY ANN: Well, let me just
try and answer this lady's question. We had this occur in our
group . . . uh . . . and it was
a matter of sometimes there
would be a daddy who would
say, "All right now, Mary Ann
wants to talk." So I would always depend on Dom making

289. Indicates some of the
motivations for physical
"blocking behavior.

292–293. Comment provides illustrations of how people
learn to be responsible for
own behavior. On a sym-
bolic level it also shows
how a single person can
be perceived as representing to others, a variety of
important figures in their

Comments

room for me to talk. I took
no responsibility on my own.
But he mothered me along the
path.

293. WALT: (*to Dom*) Now you are
a mother too. We seem to
play many different roles for
each other.

life. To the degree that
one group member can
use another to work out
significant relationships,
and to the degree these
relationships are perceived
as being common to other
situations, to that degree,
incidents in the group,
have a major effect on the
person's total life.

Discussion

The protocol you have just read represents just one of many different
approaches using groups in the helping process. Corsini[1] has included
sample protocols in his text from each of several different philosophies.
Bach[2] demonstrates his approach in great detail while relating his
theory to psychological systems. Sample protocols involving groups
in educational settings can also be found in Hinkley and Hermann,[3]
Gordon,[4] Moreno,[5] and Hobbs.[6] If films are available to you, the
following titles are worth considering:

> Role Playing in Human Relations[7]
> Activity Group Therapy[8]
> Meeting in Session[9]
> Belonging to the Group[10]

Despite the differences a reader can find in the sources cited, there
are many group characteristics he will discover that are common to
almost all approaches. An examination of what happened in the group
we just explored may be helpful. Although the demonstration contained many elements which are not present in the normal setting, by
the nature of its membership there are provided characteristics to be
found in both initial and mature groups.

As all beginning groups this group starts out by trying to answer
several basic questions. What are the limits within which we are
allowed to function? What do we have in common that can serve as
a basis for providing group cohesion? What needs do we have which
are pressing and must be dealt with immediately?

The group resembles a mature group in that they are less concerned over the role of the initial group leader, they are ready and

willing to express their feelings to each other, and they are ready and able to accept their responsibility to the group.

As all groups, this one actually moved on three planes simultaneously. One level represents the actual manifest content of the topics they explored. The second level comes from the feelings being expressed through a diversity of content. The last level is represented by the learnings which occur through the actual relationships they establish with each other.

In some ways a group may be likened to a symphony. There are several basic themes that keep winding their way in and out of the fabric of the total piece. Separate instruments try out the theme for themselves. The theme is changed and modified and sounds different as either instruments are combined or two themes are joined together. When we listen to a symphony we enjoy the repetition and embellishments. Unfortunately, in most groups, progress is judged by the newness of the content and the lack of repetition. If the group worker could accept group process in terms of an ever-tightening spiral, he can then begin to perceive how during the repetition of the content new individuals join the chorus, and how associated ideas are integrated with one another.

Topics will not become the focus of the group's attention if they are not meeting the needs of several members of the group at the same time. The topics themselves tend to be less important than the way they are used. To some degree the extent to which a topic is continually prolonged may provide a clue as to the degree to which the conversation is being used as a way of delaying facing something else.[11]

When topics appear loosely related to the objective of the group it is more helpful for the leader to help the group explore what it is doing, rather than switch topics or inhibit discussion.[12]

Just as the content repeats, so too do the underlying feelings crop up again and again. The idea that a person's ability to perceive is a function of his security is the basis for this phenomena. Members of the group move at different rates. They require different relationships to provide security for them. As each person reaches the threshold of security he needs, he suddenly perceives what others may have already understood. Not only is this new insight something he wishes to share with others, but he needs the chance to concretize his insight by testing out if he can use words to communicate his idea to others. The acceptance of individual differences in growth and insights is vital to the atmosphere in a group.

Typical themes in groups include feelings of hostility or warmth toward authority figures or peers, fear of personal inadequacy and the threat of admitting the need for help, confusion over responsibility for self or others, ambivalent feelings of dependency vs. autonomy, and confusion over what constitutes reality.

An illustration of the relationship of content to movement on a feeling level may be useful. In the group session there is reference to a class session where the group explored the sex life of the Eskimo. One could wonder, and appropriately, what relationship this has to a course in group guidance. The actual discussion evolved in the following way. A member of the group commented that she felt the group was getting very close to home because they had begun to discuss their feelings about the difficulty in expressing their anxieties over death, birth, and other phenomena that could not be easily explained. At this point several members of the group related incidents in their lives that were important to them. One told of her concern with a practice near her home in North Dakota. It seems there were times during the winter when the ground was too hard to be able to dig a grave. Bodies were, therefore, stored until the first warm day and a mass burial was held. Another person expressed his attitude toward the loud wailing of his relatives at a funeral. The overt expression of emotion by the Italians led the group to think about the part culture plays in determining how feelings are expressed. Basically, several things were happening. Not only was the group broadening its acceptance of cultural differences, but as each person revealed his own cultural heritage, and found the group able to accept him and his heritage, a more basic security within the group developed. It was after this session, which included the discussion of peoples as culturally distant as the Eskimo, that a silent member of the group participated for the first time. She was a Negro who had migrated from the South. She had learned not to express her feelings and to avoid Negro labels as they led to rejection. In this group she, for the first time, began to feel that maybe she could be accepted as a person. When she began to talk the group became very quiet. They recognized how difficult this was for her. After she finished speaking, person after person told her how much they appreciated her confidence in *them*, by being willing to share her feelings with them. This floored her. She had never believed she had anything of worth to others.[13,14]

One way in which the group succeeded in relating content to feelings was through the use of its daily written logs. Since the log was essentially a personal document it provided each person a chance to record feelings he was secure enough to see in black and white but feelings he may not yet have been ready to share with others. In a sense the writing of these logs formed a kind of rehearsal that enabled group members to discover a way of expressing feelings in a manner they could accept yet in a form others could perceive. Frequently the ideas written in a log one day were expressed verbally in the group the next session.

Because the logs were available over a period of time, it was possible for each person to see how his feelings in relation to specific content shifted. He could also see different types of content discussions that evoked similar feelings in him.

The third level, represented by the relationships in the group, is illustrated by the members' references to each other as sister, mother, or daddy. It also can be seen during the group's exploration of the leader's role and how identification with the leader was only a first step in developing their own leadership pattern.

In many philosophies the use of time is an essential part of the therapeutic process. The protocol provides several examples of concepts related to time: time as giving, time as a limit on doing, time as representative of something you cannot change (a minute is 60 seconds, no more no less), and the use of time as a way of accepting responsibility for oneself.

There is an interesting concept demonstrated by members' reaction to others' use of time. The counting of frequency with which members participate occurs commonly in groups where I am involved. Typically the person who decides to do this is an individual who feels he has been too verbal and resents the fact that others do not talk more, since that would free him from feeling he is being unfair to the group. As the group deals with this situation several insights usually develop. The group tends to agree that to use the group a person must share his thoughts with others. Identifying with verbal members is seen as only one part of a total process. The group then becomes aware of a peculiar phenomena. Although measuring a person's increasing use of group time may provide a measure of behavior, since the total amount of time available in any one session is limited, the theoretically optimal share for each person is obtainable by dividing the total time by the number of group members. It is at this point that the group discovers that the instrument not only has theoretical weaknesses but also it postulates that in a democracy everyone *must* have an equal share of everything. Desiring to preserve the right of the individual to talk or to be silent, the group reaches the understanding that although the person has a theoretical right to equal time *he also has the responsibility of asking for this time if he wants it.*

In other words, where freedom of choice is present, silence can be interpreted as assent. This brings home an associated important lesson. *If you do not exercise your rights you cannot be resentful of others who meet their own needs.* Responsibility to others is predicated on knowing the needs of others. Since we have no right to assume their needs, it remains the responsibility of each individual to make his needs known to the group.

An examination of the way group members were interrupted or supported will provide an example of how a group tends to limit a person they may feel is monopolizing the discussion, while encouraging the less verbal person.

Basic to the use of any group is the feeling on the part of the group members that what they say in the group will not be used against them in outside settings.[15] To insure this security every group rapidly develops ground rules covering the confidential nature of the sessions. This is not as simple a problem as it would appear. Group members are very anxious to use their new found insights in other settings. Typically, groups decide that concepts or feelings can be shared with outsiders, *if* the specific content is not divulged nor the people involved identified. An associated issue is the right of group members to meet together in subgroups outside the group sessions. Although no breach of confidence is involved here, the group discovers that any insights they develop outside the group are not useful in the group, if the group does not understand these ideas. Many groups therefore suggest that, where appropriate, outside discussions of group members be reported in the group so all can share in the thinking process. It is this attitude, among others, which makes it difficult for group members to act out their needs outside the group, rather than in the group session. It is also this attitude which inhibits the development of cliques.[16]

One of the most important aspects of group therapy is the tendency of the group to strive together to solve a problem. They seek to become more self-reliant and less lonesome.[17,18]

Foulkes[19] has presented an interesting rationale as to why group therapy works. He points out that although group members reinforce each other's normal and neurotic reactions, collectively they represent the very norm from which individually they deviate. Redl[20] has pointed out that group therapy, unlike individual therapy, includes elements of societal reality, not the least of which is societal retaliation for perceived misdeeds. Probably one of the most comprehensive descriptions of group life can be found in a series of articles by W. R. Bion.[21] His analysis and presentation has stood the test of time. It is well worth exploration by the reader.

Of all the issues raised by this demonstration, the question of the role played by the leader has major significance. It is within the leader's role that one can find evidence of the psychological theory that a group is using as a basis for operation and evaluation, and within an examination of the leader's behavior lie basic clues as to the skills and personality characteristics found most useful by a group.

I have taken the position that for a variety of reasons it is helpful for the initial leader to lose his position of authority as soon as possible. As he seeks membership status by changing roles in the group, he is then in a position where he must contend with others on the basis of equality. Such a role serves well, after the group has learned to cope with its leadership needs, in preventing the initial leader from using the group to meet his own personal needs in a fashion detrimental to the group.[22]

Acceptance of the group of a leader on a membership basis carries with it loss of any right to maintain special privileges. Readers will note that members of the group refer to the author by his first name. Early in the relationship the question of how to address the author provided the basis around which the group could express its feelings toward authority figures. The way group members fluctuated in using Professor, Doctor, Mister, or Walt provided a sensitive barometer as to how that person perceived the author at that moment.

The protocol should certainly demonstrate the vicarious thrill members seemed to get in controlling an authority figure, at the same time they express concern for the individual in the role.

Basic to the security of any group leader must be the recognition that much of the hostility the group directs toward him is not meant for him personally but rather what he represents. Knowing that all groups go through common stages helps the group leader recognize when the group process he observes is a normal development or is a function of something he is doing.

The chapter that follows is designed to help the reader learn about some of the typical problems faced in groups.

BIBLIOGRAPHY

1. Corsini, Raymond. *Methods of Group Psychotherapy*. New York: McGraw-Hill, 1957.
2. Bach, G. R. *Intensive Group Psychotherapy*. New York: Ronald, 1954.
3. Hinkley, Robert G., and Lydia Hermann. *Group Treatment in Psychotherapy*. Minneapolis: University of Minnesota Press, 1951.

4. Gordon, Thomas. *Group Centered Leadership*. Boston: Houghton Mifflin, 1955.

5. Moreno, J. L. (Ed.). *Group Psychotherapy*. Beacon, New York: Beacon Press, 1945.

6. Hobbs, Nicholas. "Group Centered Psychotherapy," Chapter 7 in *Client-Centered Therapy* by Carl Rogers, Boston: Houghton Mifflin, 1951.

7. Film: "Role Playing in Human Relations." Washington, D. C.: National Education Association.

8. Film: "Activity Group Therapy." New York: Columbia University Press.

9. Film: "Meeting in Session." New York: Bureau of Publications, Teachers College, Columbia University.

10. Film: "Belonging to the Group." Collaborator R. Havighurst, Encyclopaedia Britannica Films.

11. Talland, G. A., and D. H. Clark. "Evaluation of Topics in Therapy Group Discussion." *J. clin. Psychol.*, **10**, 131–137, 1954.

12. Thelen, Herbert. *Dynamics of Groups at Work*. Chicago: University of Chicago Press, p. 57, 1954.

13. Slavson, S. R. "Racial and Cultural Factors in Group Therapy." *Intern. J. Group Psychother.*, Vol. VI, No. 2, 152–165, April 1956.

14. Wittenberg, R. M., and Janice Berg. "The Stranger in the Group." *Amer. J. Orthopsychiat.*, 1952, **22**:89–97.

15. Lindt, Hendrik, and Max A. Sherman. "Social Incognito in Analytically Oriented Group Psychotherapy." *Intern. J. Group Psychother.*, Vol. II, 209–220, July 1952.

16. Slavson, S. R. "The Nature and Treatment of Acting Out in Group Psychotherapy." *Intern. J. Group Psychother.*, Vol. VI, No. 1, 3–27, January 1956.

17. Powdermaker, Florence. "Psychoanalytic Concepts in Group Psychotherapy." *Intern. J. Group Psychother.*, Vol. I, No. 1–4, 16–21, 1951.

18. Frank, J. "Some Determinants, Manifestations and Effects of Cohesiveness in Therapy Groups." *Intern. J. Group Psychother.*, 53–63, 1957.

19. Foulkes, S. H. *Introduction to Group Analytic Psychotherapy*. London: W. Heinemann, p. 29, 1948.

20. Redl, Fritz. "Group Emotion and Leadership." *Psychiatry*, **5**, 573–596, 1942.

21. Bion, W. R. "Experiences in Groups." *Human Relations*, **1**, 314–320, 1948; **1**, 487–496, 1948; **2**, 13–22, 1949; **2**, 295–303, 1949; **3**, 3–14, 1950; **3**, 395–402, 1950; **4**, 221–227, 1951.

22. Wittenberg, Rudolph M. *The Art of Group Discipline—A Mental Hygiene Approach to Leadership*. New York: Association Press, 1951.

5

Typical Problems in Group Process

For the beginning group worker there is real value in being able to recognize typical recurrent experiences in group behavior. To the degree that the leader can anticipate group movement, he is better able to know when the group is responding to his needs rather than reacting to their perception of what he represents. Although groups differ both in the speed of their movement and the ways they develop in expressing their needs, there are definable phases through which almost all groups go. This chapter is designed to provide the reader with the chance to think through typical problems of group process. Unlike preceding chapters references showing other points of view will be included in the body of the chapter.

The Initial Leader

All groups depend on a catalyst to merge the individuals into a cohesive group. The steps involved in achieving cohesion are very much a function of how the initial leadership in the group develops. Studies in leadership[1,2,3] have demonstrated that no one can become a leader if he represents ideas or behaviors that are beyond the group's present knowledge or acceptance. The best leader is the one who helps the group achieve their desired goal. To do this he needs to help the group examine each of the following ideas:

1. What common goal exists among group members? [4]
2. What can they expect from him as a leader?
3. What group roles does the group need? In many groups these

roles are defined and acted out on an unconscious basis. Generally all groups seem to need people seeking help, those willing to provide help, and those who represent societal reality. In the previous chapter the group labeled these roles as those of client, therapist, and "wall" respectively. Other groups have had their moralists, seducers, advisors, etc.

4. What can the group members expect from each other?

5. What limits does the group wish to set on their own behavior?

6. What limits exist which set boundaries on group actions or goals?

It would be relatively simple if all the leader had to do was to raise each of the questions above for discussion, have members vote, and record the group's decisions. Unfortunately, for those seeking simple solutions, groups get the answers to the above questions through observing each other's actual behavior rather than the words being spoken. This means that what the leader does from the very first moment describes to the group the leader's actual desired role in the group.

One way of demonstrating concern for the group is by providing them with an immediate opportunity to express their feelings and concerns. Typically, groups start by expressing their insecurity over unclear boundaries. (Are we supposed to . . . ?) From the very beginning, groups will need to test out the leader's reaction to their needs. The earliest needs to appear in the group will be those of dependency-independency, love-hostility, and the need for acceptance by both the leader and the group.

Each person will try to cope with the group situation with his existing repertoire of defenses. If he can get others to respond to him in the expected customary fashion, he has no need to consider change or to examine himself. Since change is threatening, part of the leader's initial job will be to develop sources of security in the group to meet these threats.

The major role of the initial leader is to be able to recognize the needs expressed by group members as being a function of both the person and the group setting, rather than merely a reaction to the leader personally. The leader not only tries to reflect the feelings being discussed, but also probably of greater importance, helps point out the similarity and differences in feelings among group members. By showing how different members, using different content, are expressing similar feelings he helps the members see their common concerns and facilitates identification between members.

In similar fashion, by accepting feelings of hostility directed toward him and by not responding with hostility, he helps the group learn how to help others look at their feelings without the need to be defensive.

Basically, the leader's initial job is to help the group learn to direct its attention on each other rather than on a leader. He achieves this by continually focusing on:

1. The meaning of an idea to the group.

2. The issues the group seems to be in disagreement over and which they feel a need to resolve.

3. The feelings they are expressing through their behavior rather than their spoken words.

4. The ways they are forcing others into roles or behaviors.

5. The actions or problems which the group raises and needs to solve.

6. And by helping the group see the continuity between group sessions and themes raised.

The following protocol may demonstrate these ideas.

(A few minutes chatter and discussion about the tape recorder.)

W: Where would you like to go today?
   Laughter
D₁: What did we do yesterday? Somebody take a quick five minutes to summarize.
L: I nominate you.
M: _____ didn't take part too much yesterday so he should do it.
D₁: The person who didn't take part yesterday summarize.
Do: Who's going to volunteer for that?
D₁: Who's going to volunteer?
   Short silence
Do: Sort of putting someone on the spot.
   Laughter
Do: I felt like I didn't take much part yesterday.
Ro: Don't forget the difference between oral and mental participation.
W: This is a point—can we be part of a group and yet not have the group feel that we are sharing? (*Short silence*) Putting it another way—can you have a group on a purely mental participation basis?
R₁: The Quakers seem to be able to feel that. And I feel it when I'm among the Quakers.
M.L.: Sure, deaf people have groups.
W: We are raising the question, really now, as to what is a group.
E: I think even more basic than that is the idea of whether you can participate in anything without actively participating. You can listen to a record and participate, some can participate and listen, and some can just shut up for a minute.
W: You have a full house of people at the Virginia Theater all participating in watching the movie—do you have a group?

L: Yeah—the environment is the same and the goal is the same—it's an awfully loosely knit group though.

E: And yet all their emotions will be tied up in the same thing.

Rı: More so than if they were all sitting listening to a lecture.

Ro: Depends on the movie.

M: Is that spectator kind of thing a group?

Ro: Of course, we are all spectators at some time in the group.

Dı: Are they interacting now, or are they only reacting to a common stimulus?

Ro: Well do you have to have interaction for a group?

M: I think so. You could have people writing letters to each other in different parts of the world—they have some commonality but there is no actual change—I think you should have a face-to-face relationship, don't you?—a give and take, if not orally at least gesturewise.

Ro: You think then a group has to have a face-to-face relationship to be a group, M?

M: I think so.

Ro: That would be limiting the group to an awfully small (*interrupted*) . . .

E: Wouldn't you say in regard to religion that everybody in a religion no matter where he is, is more or less a group?

M: Yeah, but sort of secondary—just because people think alike does that make them a group?

E: Well, some people it does—it depends on how strongly they feel about what they are thinking about.

B: Would you say the spectators at a basketball game were a group?

B: They were all actively participating in a certain way not in the actual game; they were all having the same goal.

L: During a period of the game they would be a group.

W: Seems to me we have two or three ideas that have been presented. One is that a group is defined as any, I'm trying to pull out some of the common elements as I think I heard them, ah, any collection of people who have something in common. We have also said that a group is any collection of people who are reacting to a common stimulus. We have also said that a group, and this is somewhat different from the others, is a group only when the people are interacting with each other, and then we further defined that this interaction is predicated on a face-to-face relationship and that they cannot interact unless they can perceive one another. We have had several different ideas expressed here.

E: I would like to carry this religion thing a little farther too. You take the Jewish religion. Some people who feel strongly about their religion will do some things for other people that they have never seen before, so long as they are the same religion, or orphan groups, or clothing for Israel, or whatever else. And there is something there. I don't know if they are really a group; there is something there that a mixture of other people without the same kind of goal wouldn't have.

W: I'm wondering if you are saying this, I'm reading into your remarks now, this isn't exactly what you said—I'm adding something to this— are you saying people feel a group if they identify with the others?

E: Yeah (*hesitatingly*).

W: I wonder whether it is necessary to identify with people in order to have a group?

E: No, it isn't necessary (*interrupted*) . . .

W: But this is one possible way of getting it.

L: I was going to ask, on this interaction with a face-to-face relationship, when the people disband such as when we meet here—then the group no longer exists?

M: No—I say it still does—ideally.

L: Yes, now in a case where it still exists ideally, you would incorporate her idea, ah, whether it be religion or a common goal in a schooling situation.

M: I'm beginning to . . .

L: If it disbands every time—if every time it disbands, it dissolves, then the next time they met face-to-face, would they have to start from rock bottom again to become a group? And how can you ever form a solid group, if when one disbands, the group dissolves?

(*Short silence*)

L: Now like the group at the game last night—they dissolved and will never be a group again until there is another athletic situation where there will be stimulation of the formation of another group, which is not the kind of group which we are really interested in. But you take the group like the religious group or, ah, within a school. If you develop school spirit you are trying to develop a group actually, and you are trying to develop a group that will maintain this group feeling outside of the school building. If that can't be done, I think you are sort of lost before you start in a school situation.

M: I think that my differentiation is that the people in the group not only have to identify with the people in the group and with the group as a whole, but they have to work together to do something.

L: Still that could be incorporated under any collection of people with a common stimulus or something in common—a common goal.

W: Let me ask this question. I don't know whether it will help in the thing we are talking about, but when people form in a group in the sense in which you are talking about it now, does this entity represent something different from the people involved? Is the total more than the sum of the parts?

R: Definitely. I think so.

L: I think it's the melting of the parts rather than the sum of the parts.

W: Is this something we are all in agreement on?

In the preceding protocol, group members were using an attempt to define what constitutes a group to achieve several goals at once. They were forcing other members to define their ideas so they could see if their own ideas would be acceptable. At the same time they were testing the limits *this* group would impose on group membership. (Do I have to talk to be considered a participating member?) Less visible, but also present, is the group's concern over the possibility that group membership in some unclear way may have effects on them in other situations. At one point, the leader appears to have the need to point out the importance of members identifying with each other.

Since it is his need and not the group's, they ignore him and continue on.

The leader can check his own behavior by asking himself the following questions.[5,6,7,8,9]

1. Have I defined societal limits to meet my needs, or is greater flexibility possible?

2. Have I used words or behavior which forces others to look up to me and accept my knowledge and control?

3. Was I aware of the feelings people were trying to express, or did I become more interested in the content or ultimate goal?

4. How did I respond to hostile, affectionate, or other disturbing needs members expressed toward me?

5. How did I relate to a group member who represented my ideal?

6. Was I more accepting of group members who were helping the group more than I was of those whose needs prevented them from relating to the group as a whole?

7. Have I been hostile or sarcastic or critical toward any group member?

8. Did I have a personal goal I would have liked to see the group accept?

9. Was I reacting to sexual charms of the opposite sex?

10. How did I react to emotional demands of members of my own sex?

11. Did I foster total group decision, or did I support a subgroup?

Since answering these questions demands a level of self-understanding all of us may not have, other cues may be easier to locate. The leader can ask himself

1. Was there any time when I found myself perspiring? What was the group talking about at that time?

2. Did I ever raise my voice? Why?

3. Were there points at which I was uncomfortable and wished the group would move on?

4. Did my mind ever wander to things outside the group discussion?

5. Are there members of the group I'd like to spend more time with?

6. Are there members of the group whom I wish would drop out of the group?

If any of a leader's answers to the above questions were in the affirmative, he needs to re-examine the needs he has which could best be met in other settings. In the event the initial leader can comfortably handle the problems raised, he will find the group increasingly taking over responsibility for individuals and group process.

Although all groups do not develop in the same way, typically after the first period spent in orientation and testing limits, there will be a sharp rise in tension and hostility. It is almost as if the group must discover if members will accept each other at their most obnoxious level. The following two excerpts demonstrate rising tension and hostility, while the group is attempting to discover ways to relate to each other.

M: I wonder—are we picking at each other intellectually or not?
Do: What?
M: Are we picking at each other intellectually?
Do: Well . . .
E: Yeah, I kinda get the feeling that we are not doing anything. We are just talking to pass time.
M: Using big words—that's about it—or not—I don't know.
W: Talk accomplishes nothing?
E: Well it all depends—I just don't feel that we have a goal. I think that everybody is just saying something to get the tension out, and doing a very good job of it.
Ro: I think it's increasing rather than decreasing.
Ri: I was just putting down (in her notes) that every time somebody says something, someone interrupts and that this isn't going to get us anywhere.
Do: I didn't feel that we were picking at each other, I feel that we are getting tense and anxious because we can't solve our problem.
E: Well, what is the problem? I don't even know what the problem is!
Do: The problem is what are we going to do . . . what . . . we found that . . . I hate to use the word define—we're trying to define what this group is going to be—trying to come to some kind of a conclusion. A. has given his conception of what he thinks it should be. I gave mine, ah, . . . we are throwing out things actually to try to get some kind of problem solving here, and we seem to be complicating it more than anything else.
W: At this point we are pretty clear on what everybody else doesn't see *our* way, but we are not quite sure what we see together.
L: And I think, even in this group, when somebody takes the role where they become a professional analyzing the core group feeling in the group, even we resent this.
A: Because we realize that they're just as involved as the other members.
L: It's just that we don't like someone putting themselves in a position to say "Well Daddy will look at you and decide what he thinks is wrong with you."

In groups meeting two hours weekly, the author usually finds this happening after 10–16 hours. If, at this point, the leader remains calm and helps the group face its anxiety, the group rather rapidly breaks loose, and it begins to define problems to be solved. They then continue on to seeking causes and possible solutions.

Frequently after helping a member work out a rough problem the group will appear immobilized. If the leader explores this apparent plateau with the group, it frequently is defined by the group as a sort of breather. During this calm spell the group recoups its strength to face the next issue.

As the group grows with maturity, leadership functions are so consistently carried by group members, that an outsider observing the group would be unable to determine who was the initial leader.[10,11,12,13] Each person serving as leader needs to discover ways of communicating to the group his desire to help but not direct. No one behavior is the answer, but the following illustration may serve as a clue to help the reader decide what his typical behavior might be.

As was indicated in Chapter 4, the author discovered that people in his group tended to look visually to the leader for guidance. He, therefore, began to systematically shift the place where he sat each session. This not only made it difficult for the group to develop a set place to look for help, but by changing his seat, he also forced group members to shift their seats as well. This brought many members into contact with each other who had not really perceived each other before. Symbolically it also demonstrated the initial leader's desire to be free to become part of the group and his desire to have mobility of thought and action.

It has been pointed out that a group seeks security by discovering the societal limits within which they must function. This question of society versus the group, with the group seen as a subculture has been described very ably by Beck.[14] For readers interested in the sociological implications of group psychotherapy, her article will be of particular interest.

Initially, the leader is treated as an authority figure despite his own desires.[15,16] It is the author's belief that a verbal structuring by the leader is helpful. As illustrated in the protocol in the preceding chapter, the group hears the words used in structuring but does not accept them until they experience the behavior that goes along with the idea. One might ask then, why bother talking? Why not just start right in and let actions speak for themselves? This might work if group members are familiar with the helping process. If, however, a person's behavior does not coincide with the group's past experiences, being able to recognize what is happening in the group makes it less threatening. Now, having both words and action, the concepts can more easily be integrated into the group's own storehouse of ways to relate to others. Explaining this within the context of learning theory and connecting words with behavior, develops cue responses which in the future can cause the words to carry new meanings and stimulus value.

The role being suggested for the leader is an active one. To the degree that the leader feels a need to structure every eventuality, he could so limit members' perception of their freedom to act that nothing he does later could convince them of their freedom to act. It is here that sensing the feelings of the group provides the leader with clues as to information the group wants, rather than what he feels they eventually might need. If he is to be the leader in the true sense, the people who make up the group will define for him their goal and the needs which must be met.

As the group matures it will begin to recognize the need to explore more effective ways of meeting its needs. In the following protocol we see the group struggling with this problem.

E: The thing is, a need doesn't always have to be solved in a certain way— say the need for recognition—a kid might use a loaded pistol . . . A kid might also draw a picture to get his need satisfied. But it is frustrating to him if you sit down and discuss with him that guns aren't so nice to carry around and that he'd better draw a picture. (*Several talking*)

Ro: In the first place, he has this need to carry the gun or the pistol or to draw the picture; that's what we're talking about. Some place he's been blocked if he has this need. Does he not?

E: What you are saying is that in order to have a need you have to have first been blocked, which I don't agree because when you are born you have needs.

Ro: No . . .

Do: Let me ask this question. Whose thinking through which answer is better? Is it yours or the child's?

E: Both.

Do: No. You see you are saying it is better for him to paint a picture because he'll get recognition. You see this, but he may not see it.

E: I'm not saying I'll say "You paint the picture."

Do: Until he does see it, until he does go through it, he's still feeling a frustration of some need until he finds a substitute or sublimation.

E: The point is, say that he's carrying this loaded gun, and so he's satisfying his need he thinks. And you don't take away the gun. Wait a week and then say "Paint a picture." But it's a process that's continual, and you don't take away something and then replace it, but you do both at the same time.

Do: You see *you* are doing the replacing, not the child. The child may not see this connection you are telling him exists.

E: Yeah, that is why I'm saying it is a slow process.

Do: And until he sees this—what I'm saying, in this transition period, until a person learns to satisfy his needs in a socially acceptable manner, he's not gong to feel that he is satisfying his need, and he is going to be frustrated. And he may be hostile and he may have anxieties about it because . . . until he is able himself to realize that this is connected up to him in some way . . .

E: I don't know whether I'm wrong in what I am saying or you just aren't understanding what I am saying.

E: Just that it's not a process where you break and then support, but it's a process where you are breaking and supporting at the same time. You are not pushing, I mean you are not forcing. And as the kid begins to see that he is doing something that is not only socially unacceptable but it is also something that is causing him more difficulty, then you begin replacing it with a more constructive kind of activity. (*Several talking*)

Ro: But what if the kid doesn't recognize the support—therein lies the frustration.

Do: I'll agree with the process and transition, but what I'm trying to say—how do you perceive the child in this process of transition? How does he feel?

Voluntary and Involuntary Groups

One of the first questions one raises in looking at a group is the nature of the group membership. Is this a voluntary or an involuntary group? In other words, although the group members may share a common concern, did they come together of their own volition or were they forced by some societal agency to belong? Although there is little doubt that groups that arise because of the desire of the members for a vehicle to meet a common need have the edge over involuntary groups, since there is no problem of motivating members to cooperate, it is unwise to assume that any other kind of group must of necessity fail.

To better understand the problems associated with the character of a group it might be helpful to examine a group where the initial motivation for membership was not present. During World War II the author was assigned to serve as a Psychiatric Social Worker at Welch Convalescent Hospital.[17,18] Welch was an Army hospital specifically designed to help rehabilitate patients suffering from combat fatigue. The labels change with time, in World War I they would have been called shell shock cases. Despite labels, these were men who were confused, hostile, with a variety of psychosomatic complaints, with guilt feelings about their inadequacy, and with a common desire to be discharged from the Army. Getting well carried with it the possibility of return to harsh Army discipline, and even more frightening, a return to possible combat and death.

The hospital setting represented the stereotype of the place rich men go when they wish to retire. Situated in Daytona Beach, Florida, it included several swimming pools, athletic facilities, well-equipped shops and classrooms, and had access to deep sea fishing and other forms of entertainment. The men were assigned to treatment battalions where a team of psychiatrist, psychologist, and psychiatric social worker tried to provide help. It was the psychiatric social worker's job to help the men plan their day's activities and, in group settings, to examine their problem and possible solutions. Initially, because the men focused all of the hostility caused by their troubles on the Army, they were freed of as many assigned duties as possible. Given the freedom to use or not use the camp facilities, large numbers of men preferred to lie on their beds dreaming and isolating themselves from each other. After a period of time all professional personnel realized some changes were needed. An order was issued outlining a schedule of activities for a day. Men were forced to go *to* the activities but were then *free* to decide on the level of their involvment. Some interesting things happened.

In Army style the men were lined up and marched to the occupational therapy shop. Once inside they were free to spend the hour as they wished. Initially, they wandered around making hostile remarks at the patients who were busily engaged. Several questioned a man working on a bracelet as to why he bothered. He told them he had been successful in selling the bracelets. It suddenly hit some of the men that if they, too, could sell bracelets they would have money to get liquor. The shop suddenly became active.

What were some of the dynamics beneath the behavior described in the foregoing experience? There seem to be several concepts that emerge:

1. For all groups, but especially for involuntary ones, society's demands on them must be clear and pressing.

2. Given the freedom to explore ways of relating their needs to society's demands, people will tend to meet their most consciously perceived needs first.

3. In the process of meeting primary needs, within a societal framework, clients learn that at least at that simple level they have the capacity to help themselves. Proving even this level of competence is

the first step toward tries at more difficult problems. In other words, people can only get confidence in themselves by experiencing success that is meaningful in their own eyes. This last idea is frequently misunderstood. The teacher who wishes to provide success to a youngster by giving him honorary jobs or frequent compliments may find his efforts to no avail. The compliments have to be perceived by the youngster as having been merited by his behavior. The jobs have to be ones perceived as desirable by the youngster, too, not just by the teacher. In other words manipulating the environment fails when the client does not perceive the new setting as the manipulator anticipated. Rather than guess at desirable experiences the helping person is safer when he assists the client to relate content and meaning within the client's frame of reference.

One of the female members of a group guidance class phrased it very well when she said: "I enjoy having a boy take my arm to cross the street, but if I felt he did this because he thought I couldn't make it across myself, I'd resent his action."

Membership in an involuntary group can also be a source of security. Recently while working with a group of men in the stockade at an Air Force base, the group explored its feelings about being in the stockade. Although, to a man, they would have preferred freedom, the group admitted some ambivalence. While in the stockade they could not easily get into more trouble. Most of their primary needs were being met. They could allow themselves to be quite dependent people and not have to feel responsible for their lack of responsibility since they could blame society for their presence in prison. To put it another way, not being secure enough to face their own need for help, it was comforting to initially be able to get help while pretending they accepted it only because of outside limits.

The issues described in involuntary groups raise the following general questions:

1. At what point does society have the right to place its demands before those of the individual?

2. When will society's demands serve as a basis for help rather than interfering with the helping process?

3. How can a group resolve confusion arising from their conception of the demands coming from society and those which represent their own needs?

Unfortunately, there are no neat answers to these questions. They do, however, represent the common starting place for groups regardless of whether they initially are composed of voluntary membership or not.

The nature of membership in groups has been presented as but the first step in a client's acceptance of responsibility for his behavior. The nature of his group affiliation also may involve his acceptance of the limits imposed from society and his acceptance of his own limited individual capabilities.

Group Composition

If the group atmosphere is a function of the composition of its membership, then the question of who shall be included in the group is of importance. Slavson,[19] working from a psychoanalytic point of view, believes a potential group member must be evaluated in terms of (*a*) having had at least minimal satisfaction in his primary relationships during his childhood, (*b*) not being too sexually disturbed, (*c*) needing a quantity of ego strength, and (*d*) having minimal development of his superego. Bach,[20] working from a different orientation excludes people from the groups he leads if (*a*) they have insufficient reality contact, (*b*) have culturally deviant symptomology, (*c*) are chronic monopolists, or (*d*) have psychopathic defenses of an impulsive nature.

Both of these authors, thinking essentially in terms of severely disturbed people, seem to be saying that they are looking for people who can relate to others and do not have mannerisms others find too disturbing or offensive or who by their aggressive nature will present the group with problems of setting and maintaining group limits. Bach,[20] and Powdermaker and Frank[21] seem to agree that at least two of any one kind of personality is helpful, since it will prevent the person from feeling isolated. They, also, seem to agree that when the differences between group members are not too radical it tends to facilitate learning, since it exposes the client to a wide range of experiences.

A quick rereading of the last two paragraphs should demonstrate that the emphasis is not so much on the presence of a characteristic as much as it is one of degree. Unfortunately, the author has not been able to locate any dependable device that both calibrates the quantity of the characteristics discussed nor which can suggest the number of adverse traits any specific group can assimilate. In reviewing the literature in this area one always discovers that the ultimate composition of these groups reflects "clinical judgment" and in some cases more likely reflects what the leader believes *he* can tolerate. Studies like the one by Ash[22] certainly raise questions about the reliability and validity of clinical judgment.

Certainly if one is developing a group for therapeutic purposes the organizer has every right to try to develop a group which he believes will be most effective. Unfortunately, most of us will find ourselves in group situations where membership is not open to our approval even if we were sure about the criteria we ought to use. Does this mean groups with an unselected membership are bound to be untherapeutic? In the author's opinion nothing could be further from the truth. The degree to which any group can represent society as a whole certainly will effect the usefulness of that group as a testing ground of ideas. The issue then is not so much one of how to limit people from membership as it is how to achieve a heterogeneous group that has the tools to control the elements within it that may lead to disintegration.

It is on this basis that it is felt that the primary basis for membership ought to be common concern over a situation or interest. Cartwright[23] has pointed out that for a group to be effective as a medium for change it must first of all be important to its members. Thelen,[24] following up this idea, and summarizing research in the area, indicates that groups composed of friends are likely to have more energy to spend in participating. Being initially secure with each other they are free to use energies in other ways. He also points out that groups composed of friends are more likely to deal with whatever problem they need to, whether it centers around school achievement or another area of concern.

For a group to be therapeutic there must be help given to enable members to discover the need for different roles than those typically played in friendship groups. Generally, we want friends to see things our way. We want their sympathy and support. Friends serve as a source of comfort rather than threat. As was pointed out in Chapter 3, however, the helping role demands empathy not sympathy, information not advice, and both support and reality factors instead of dependency relationships. These understandings are the tools of the initial leader. It is illogical to expect a group to know how to relate most helpfully without prior experience. It is only as the initial leader himself relates to others in the ways to be learned that group members have a chance to know, evaluate, and use these therapeutic tools. As groups try to set limits, like the group below, friendship *vs.* therapy becomes an issue.

A: In other words, I don't have to worry about my interpretations or my response to his actions if it's friendship.

Do: Can you be a therapist part time and a friend part time? Can you switch roles?

A: Inasmuch as, in my opinion, these people tend to pick out friends that satisfy certain types of needs.

Rɪ: Friends can have therapeutic effects. (*Chorus of "Oh, yes!"*)

Dɪ: But are they therapists?

Do: No!

Dɪ: This solves what I was going to say to M., because what I was hearing in M. is that all a counselor does is give support, and I'm sure she didn't mean it. (M: "No!") But this is all your argument . . . your whole argument was . . . all a counselor does is give support.

M: That's right, Di, you know this is something that we talked around . . . a little different angle . . . if you are in love with someone—your wife, or not your wife or sumpin (*laughter*), and, ah, is that love relative to the reciprocal need satisfaction (*laughter*), I mean if you love somebody . . . You know what I mean?

Do: Say it. It's better to say it out loud than just think it. (*Laughter*)

M: Love means getting your needs satisfied and helping another person satisfy his needs.

E: Or is love something ethereal . . . ?

M: Which you *just* feel!

Do: I don't believe in ether.

M: You don't?

Do: I don't believe love is ethereal.

E: No, he said he didn't believe in "ether" [not either].

M: No.

A: Somebody once defined love as a state of mutual dependency.

Do: I think that is part of it. I think it can even be the whole relationship. But I don't think it's necessary. People go through life doing this—I know people that have done it. I wouldn't want it for me though.

A: Well essentially though is this any different than choosing a friend because he satisfies a need? When I'm saying dependency, I don't mean it in dependency types of needs, but any type of need satisfaction.

Dɪ: You're pushing it pretty far . . . (*Laughter*)

Ro: If you choose your husband to satisfy your needs or your friends to satisfy your needs, I disagree with that.

M: Don't you though?

E: How else would you choose a husband?

The protocol above provides a clear illustration of the group member's fear of the price he may have to pay to get his needs met. The play on words and the underlying sexual connotations of the discussion show the importance of the need for affection and concern over the appropriate way to express these feelings. Group laughter is a helpful clue to point out areas of tension and hidden needs.

Out-of-Group Sessions

Confusion over how to preserve the confidential nature of the group, while recognizing that in most societal settings group members will have occasion to meet outside of the group, causes groups to examine early in their life how best to handle the multiplicity of relationships group members may have. This area is one of marked disagreement among writers in the field. Some authors insist that it is necessary that group members do not see each other outside of group sessions. For isolated therapy groups this may be possible, but when groups are formed as part of an existing institution, such a limit is unreal. Although the simpler the relationships are between people, the easier it is to cope with them, it is rare in society for a person to be able to so purify his relationships with others. If, on the other hand, the group can develop clearly defined roles for in-group and out-of-group relationships, group members have a chance to learn the basic idea that different behaviors are appropriate in different settings.

The following protocol illustrates the awareness of the group of their desire to maintain the group atmosphere in other settings, and then awareness that this may not be possible. Being concerned over the effect of these out-of-group meetings, this group set up a rule which obligated group members to feed into group settings ideas or relationships developed outside the group between members, which would effect group security and cohesion.

Rɪ: I always wanted to be the first one to arrive in our dorm at college and the last one to leave, and I didn't want to miss a thing. (*Laughter*) Even if I had an important committee meeting or class, I would feel threatened if I didn't go out for coffee because I've always been that compulsive about it. I sat at one of these big tables, and at another table a lot of people were talking and I didn't know what was going on . . .

E: I just thought when Ro said that—God, I wish I was that normal!

Do: (*To W*) This is what you meant when you said that your wife wasn't going to see you all semester.

Ro: I also missed E. not being there.

M: We go out for coffee a lot, and I think part of it wasn't there.

Rɪ: I don't think we can stop these between class meetings because we can't stop seeing each other, and if I were to see M. and if you were to see E. and have coffee this would be a subgroup of our group, and we can't make a vow that we don't see each other in between time. It may be we can learn how to deal with it. Personally, I don't know how you felt about it, but when we left yesterday, I said something about, if you

want to know what we talked about the other time we had coffee I'd
be glad to tell you, although it wasn't particularly related to class.

B: Well that's why I said it, because I was interested in the type of things
you talked about.

E: This kinda reminds me of a family now we're getting so close it's kinda
like a mother and the mother doesn't want to let go of any of her kids.

Do: Who's the mother? (*Laughter*) The group.

Dɪ: I think one thing we can do to reduce the threat about some of these
meetings is geared to what W. said he would like for us to do. We do
not discuss class at the luncheon. (*Refers to session where confidential
nature of group was explored.*)

L: But, Di, I don't think it's only a matter of discussing class. It's a matter
of people liking you and . . .

Ro: A group feeling.

Do: I think we are going to have to live through it a while.

It has been suggested that specific situations represent a helpful
core around which people can learn to relate to each other. Because
interests and behavior of people change with age it is logical that the
basis for group formations will differ at varied age levels. It is also
to be expected that the manner in which they choose to communicate
will also change. Little children still accustomed to acting out their
needs may find play and activity groups most natural to their typical
behavior.[25,26] Adolescents form a special problem in group counseling. This is a period of very rapid growth in both emotional and
physical drives.[27,28] It is a stage where speech is highly developed.
There is a growing ability to express themselves verbally with less
need for physical activity to release their needs. Being a period of
rapid shift, however, group activities may not remain stable in one
mode or the other.

Thelen[30] has suggested that the major need of students is to find
their places in the group. They are also concerned about their ability
to adjust to authority and to explore and define their assets and limitations. It is these needs that he believes primarily color what they
learn in class and the meaning to them of the material learned.

Certainly parenthood with its concomitant increased sense of responsibility forms a ripe basis for group help.[29] As parents see themselves through other parents' eyes they may be able to better evaluate
their behavior. As their own information increases and as they are
better able to empathize with their children, their total adjustment
improves. To the degree that they discover that other parents share
their feelings and anxieties, they feel less guilty and can feel better
able to relate more positively to their children and mates.

Although society and peers are important at all ages, the role of
group counseling with older people deserves special attention. The

growing sense of isolation experienced by people as families grow up and become self-sufficient, when added to the isolation caused through both the death of friends and loss of physical contacts, increases the sense of loneliness of the older person. Inability to hear, see, and travel all form special problems to be explored when working with "senior citizens."

There are two other important concepts associated with group membership, namely size and the length of the group's life.

Group Size

Size has a direct relationship not only with the defined purpose of the group but also upon the possible relationships between group members. In a two person "group" there is no escape from the need to react to each other. With the increase of each additional group member it becomes increasingly possible for a person to diminish his interactions with others. At the very least he can participate by identifying with active members. Since the security of the group depends upon being able to communicate and to receive a sense of acceptance, a point is reached where it becomes physically impossible to be aware of all people present. Because visual cues are part of communication, too, the increasing size of the circle needed to accommodate more people creates a distance where words need to be shouted, and where too many people lose the chance to express their ideas since the time available for the total group is limited. Authors differ on when this magical point is reached. The popular upper limits are between 8 and 15. When the group gets beyond this size the group may find the need to operate in subgroups at critical points to re-establish the conditions needed for emotional involvement and release. Under good conditions, where group involvement is high, and large numbers of people in the group tend to identify with each other, it has been possible to have groups of as large as twenty-five work and help each other despite the size. Certainly the larger the group the more difficult it is to achieve the level of group security needed to explore threatening ideas or behavior.

Length of Group Life—Fixed and Continuous Groups

The length of a group's life is partially a function of whether the group initially is conceived as a fixed or continuous group. Fixed groups are composed of a defined membership and are organized for a definite purpose. When the purpose has been achieved the group either disintegrates or develops a new goal around which to unite. An example of such a fixed group might be a citizen's committee organized to elect someone to office.

Continuous groups are not dependent upon a specific membership for existence. Their goal tends to include societal needs which are ongoing in nature. Fraternal organizations like the Masons or Elks would fit this definition.

Admitting New Members

In both types of groups the admission of a newcomer to the group, after initial organization, involves considerable group concern and attention. Each group develops its unique atmosphere. The flavor of the group comes from the rituals, limits, permitted behaviors, and interpersonal relationships they develop. When admitting a new person, the group basically is faced with two alternatives. Shall we indoctrinate him into the mores of our group so he doesn't change the status quo or shall we allow him to examine present traditions and make recommendations for modifications which would increase his security in the group? The way any group handles this question provides a rapid clue to the security of the membership. The more rigid groups will tend to find their security in form and content rather than personal relationships. Groups that are secure about themselves and the value of their ideas do not feel threatened by competing ideas.

The basic thesis of this text has been that groups serve as a tool to meet individual needs. The termination, continuation, or modification of the group, therefore, becomes an issue that the group itself needs to face, examine, and resolve.

When, because of the setting, a group's purpose and way of functioning has been predetermined by an outside agency, it is the responsibility of that agency to interpret to any prospective member what group membership will demand of him.

In schools, the teacher has the responsibility of interpreting to the student the defined goals of a class, the way the class operates, and the demands that will be made on the student. Similarly, any referral of a client to a group setting carries with it the responsibility of helping the client face and evaluate what potential group membership could mean to him.

It is not wise to place a person in a group at the time of a specific crisis in his life. He will feel the need for immediate help, which the group will share, but which realistically cannot be offered by the group. Feeling inadequate to help in a crisis will precipitate considerable hostility against the referring agency which put them in this spot.

The Silent Member

In previous protocols the concern of the group over members' participation is made quite clear. Although group members accept nonverbal signs of participation, a time is reached when the highly verbal members feel guilty and exposed by all they have said. At this time they begin to pressure silent members to talk. Their motivation is complex. Not only do they desire a feedback and reaction to their ideas, but they also wish to make all members equally vulnerable since everyone is treated the same. This pressure, coming from the group, is far preferable to leader-based techniques designed to pull silent members into the group. Not only would action by the leader reinforce his authority role, but it would also threaten the group, since each member would wonder when he would be forced into a role he might find uncomfortable.

In the protocol which follows there is demonstrated how a group, while applying pressure, provides support by identifying verbally with *Ir*. This protocol also demonstrates a typical reaction of a silent member. Frequently the silent person says little because she feels inferior to her peers. As the silent person talks, and as others identify with her and accept her feelings, she feels more worthwhile.

Do: I would like to, ah, change the subject a little because I have a little need—I would like to know something about Ir. Ah, we all had our say about our background . . . I don't know anything about her except that she's sitting there. (*Laughter*) I know her name is Ir ——, and I would like a run down of your background (*to Ir* ——). I think we should give her the same treatment all of us had.

E: May I pose one thing now? I don't know if anybody else is doing this, but I was upset because Ir hadn't said anything. And I think maybe, I don't know whether . . . I was trying to think up some way that I could get Ir in. I didn't know this was your need too (*to Do*), but this is what you felt too . . . is it that you want to know about *her*, or is it that you want to bring her into the group?

Do: Well . . . well, I think that's up to her—I just wanted to know about her so I could feel more comfortable, and I think we should give her the same treatment in terms of the group. This is one of the ways I feel we could bring her into the group—I mean pretty much the same thing.

We are all talking about *our* needs while Ir is sitting there. (*Laughter*)

Ir: I am, ah, getting all my needs satisfied . . . I'm more or less trying to find out where I am 'cause I came in late and, ah, the class had already started . . . but, ah, my background is very slim—I got out of school in June last year and I started last summer doing graduate work and when E. said something about being scared about these people, I had an experience in the summer 'cause I was the only person in any of my classes who had done no work at all—I had no experience and everything was done in terms of experience.

Do: What kind of experience have you had? You were an Illinois grad?

Ir: No, I got my undergraduate degree in Mississippi.

Do: Uh huh.

Ir: And I came to Illinois last summer and started my graduate work.

Do: What did you do your undergraduate work in?

Ir: Social Sciences.

Di: Teaching of Social Sciences or . . .

Ir: Yeah, social science education.

E: And now you are going into guidance work.

Ir: Uh huh—so there. (*General laughter*)

Do: Are you married?

Ir: Yeah.

Ro: She was telling, before class, that she has her husband in the hospital ever since the first of January and she is kept rather busy running back and forth between here and Chicago.

Ir: Oh. Right now he has pneumonia. On the first of January he had a punctured gall bladder.

Do: Got any children?

Ir: I just got married. (*Laughter*)

Do: Well, the only way to find out is to stumble into it.

Ir: I've been married about four months.

Do: Oh! I see.

Do: Ir, you and B have a lot in common.

As suggested before, silence usually reflects fear on the part of the silent member. Silence may indicate a desire not to reveal too much or to expose feelings. Sometimes silence represents a fear that no one would listen if they did talk, coupled with anxiety over testing the hypothesis out. It is not unusual for the quiet person to strongly desire to speak but to be genuinely unable to break through his own resistance.[31] Since, basically, these people fear that speaking will cause them to be looked down on by the group, there are two avenues open to help the quiet ones. The first and most preferable approach is to help the person feel wanted and secure in the setting so that his fears lose force. The second and less usual approach is to allow the person the security of knowing that they can enter the group when and in the manner they find most comfortable.

An illustration may help demonstrate this second approach. All patients in the author's battalion at Welch Convalescent Hospital were informed that at a set time all men were expected to attend group therapy sessions. The men would gather around the center of the long barracks and arrange their foot lockers in a circle.

One of the men chose a bed at the far end of the barracks, and to all appearances went to sleep. A few days passed and instead of sleeping he now read comic books. After a few more days he began to move from bed to bed, getting closer to the circle. The day finally came when he arranged a foot locker in a concentric circle to the group. He listened intently to the men discussing their fears in combat and freely admitting their reactions. He would nod his head in agreement. The next day he further identified with speakers by saying "Me, too," or "I'll say!" Finally, the day arrived, when, listening to the men he broke in saying, "You think you guys had it tough, well . . . ," and at last he was a full-fledged participating member.

This man's feelings of inadequacy were such that any pressure from the leader or the group would have forced him to defend himself by building a higher wall so others could not penetrate or reach him. This illustration may sound extreme, but have you ever watched a small timid child in a play area? He may choose a toy which he appears to be using, but which actually permits him to observe others freely. Slowly he moves into the group choosing the children who threaten him least. The shy adolescent at the party who gets busy fixing punch to avoid being forced to cope with the total group is not too different either.

Silence in the Group

Just as with the individual, silence in the group can be a sign of resistance. To interpret it this way all the time would be in error. Silence can also represent the fact that all members need time to digest the ideas that preceded the silence.

In so-called leaderless groups, the start of a session frequently is marked by silence. Group members chat with one another waiting for all to arrive. When everyone is present, the chatter dies down, and the group prepares to shift gears. One sign of the security of a group is their ability to tolerate silence when it represents the need of the members to gather steam or face a block.

Regardless of the cause of the silence, just like in individual counseling, the group learns that the ideas expressed immediately after a silent period tend to be ones loaded with meaning for the speaker.

For many groups, where social convention is strong, lack of talk is felt at first to be rude. Along with this is the feeling that people must constantly interact verbally to be productive. Ultimately the group learns that you can't think and talk at the same time. Neither can you think your own thoughts and listen at the same time. At that stage, silence becomes something precious. It provides a chance to think without pressure from others, but with the security of knowing the group is there if you need them.

The Missing Member

In the preceding section it was stated that cohesive groups feel a strong kinship to each other. In a sense every member is essential to the total group. This feeling is expressed by the group's reluctance to start until every member is accounted for. Members experience this sense of being important to the group. Early in a group's life it is not unusual for members to react with hostility toward people who are late or who are absent without letting the group know ahead of time. The hostility, when explored by the group, quickly is traced to the feeling of loss by people present. There is a real feeling of being incomplete and missing a part the group needs to function well. This attitude becomes so strong a part of group life that members rarely miss sessions unless physically unable to attend. This group practice is particularly helpful for members who have been chronically late in the past or negligent in their responsibilities. The reconditioning process, for them, is immediate and consistently maintained by the group. While receiving the support that comes from realizing how important a person the group feels the missing person to be, the missing person receives the full blast of their hostility. Unlike in polite society, the absent member learns the price he is paying for his behavior.

The Missing Leader

Particularly in groups where the leader has been initially active in trying to help the group learn how to use the group setting, there may be a residual dependence on him. Despite the fact that group members may have served as temporary leaders for topics of concern to them, the group has difficulty in forgetting the status of the initial leader. The group seems to experience security in feeling that if any situation should arise that they cannot handle, the leader is present and will bail them out.

If, for unavoidable reasons, the leader cannot attend a session, the group is faced with proceeding on their own. As was demonstrated in Chapter 4, typically the more active aggressive member tries to step into the status leader role. If, by this time, the group has learned to use its own resources, any attempt by the new leader to direct action as he thinks it ought to go will precipitate rapid censure of him by the group. With the second leader deposed, another member may try his hand. In this fashion member after member seeking status recognition learns that in this group status comes from helping others not controlling them.

The Monopolist

Many authors have stated that the monopolist represents a category of behavior that inhibits group growth. Although no one can take exception to this idea, the question certainly is raised as to how groups can learn to cope with people like the monopolist, if they are not given a chance to learn to do so. In many ways the monopolist resembles the member who seized group leadership described in the preceding session. He tends to be a person with strong status needs and frequently is a rather basically insecure person despite his overt behavior. The monopolist has learned that as long as he controls topics and direction, people cannot raise issues that will threaten him. It is this last dynamic that spells out how a group can both control and help the monopolist.

The monopolist's behavior causes hostility in the group. When the group has learned to express its feelings, these hostile reactions will be verbalized and directed toward the monopolist. When this happens, the monopolist is confused. Why, he wonders, are people acting this way? "I'm trying to help them and they don't appreciate me." As his anxiety grows he reaches a point where, since he is dependent on group approval, he asks the group to help him understand their reactions. In a way he has learned that the group's attack on him demonstrates that they really care about him (supportive) but that he isn't getting the relationship with them he desires. Since the monopolist tends to have used his aggressive tactics for a long period of time before the group started, these crises in the group may have to occur repeatedly until the monopolist has learned a new mode of relating equally effectively to his unwanted controlling tactics.

At all points of hostility between group members, it is the role of the person serving as leader to remain objective and help the participants examine their behavior.

Resistance

Looking at one's behavior or feelings creates anxiety. Every member present has established some way of coping with his environment. His present method is working sufficiently well for him to get some rewards. Although each person dimly suspects that life could be more rewarding, he is not sure he has the ability to change nor that changed behavior will be an improvement. Feeling this way, there is a strong effort on the part of group members to maintain the status quo.[32]

Resistance takes many forms. As with the monopolist it could represent an attempt to control the environment. With the silent person it can be achieved by remaining beyond the reach of the group. These are both direct and clearly observable methods. Group members employ more devious techniques that are not always easily recognized. One person in a group the author worked with kept his mouth full of chewing gum until the group observed the repetitious nature of this act. For another person, taking voluminous notes provided a "legitimate" excuse for lack of verbal participation.

Catharsis

At the opposite extreme from the nonparticipating member is the person who, while under pressure, bubbles out ideas and feelings to the point that he feels empty and exposed.[33] As all of us know, being able to blow off steam from time to time makes us feel better. The problem is that a certain amount of steam (anxiety) is needed to motivate a person to solve a problem. Just like the steam engine with a hot fire underneath, letting out steam may relieve the pressure, but as long as the fire is lit, pressure will build up again. Letting out the steam, then, is symptom treatment but doesn't get to the heart of the trouble.

Because losing symptoms gives a feeling of relief, and since the experience of catharsis is part of group members' societal tools, a group needs help to learn how to deal with this device to achieve more therapeutic results. The person who is permitted to cathart without group intervention may discover that, while reacting to the pressure, he has verbalized feelings or ideas he is not ready to face. Feeling threatened by what he has exposed, the person grows hostile toward the group. His hostility reflects a feeling that they have no right to know things about him even *he* doesn't wish to face. He is also hostile, defensively, because he anticipates rejection because of what he has said or done.

Some authors would feel it was more important that the ideas the member expressed be verbalized, hence available for inspection, than to be concerned over the period of hostility which may result.

This author believes that ultimately the person and the group grow faster if the group setting can maximize rather than minimize security. Accordingly, when a person catharts under pressure, every effort is made to continually reflect to the catharter, the feelings he is expressing. By helping the member hear what he is saying, as he says it, the group enables the person under pressure to decide if he wants to continue to reveal himself. At the same time, by continuously reflecting feelings, the group provides the person with evidence of their support. They also demonstrate that the ideas being expressed are not effecting the person's acceptability to the group.

The Role of Stereotypes

The word stereotype has developed an unpleasant meaning in our society. It tends to indicate a tendency to think of others in terms of characteristics that are assumed to be universal for a certain type of person. We resent a person's tendency to stereotype because by so doing he robs the person of his individuality and overlooks worthwhile characteristics and personal feelings.[34,35]

In any interpersonal situation, and certainly in a group setting, people try to relate to each other in terms of things they share in common. Initially knowing nothing about the other person, we tend to predict, based upon our past experiences, what a person like the one we are talking to might be interested in. Failing that, we tend to assume that the other person is not too different from ourselves, and, assuming similarity, we use our interests as a model.

Neither of these two bases for stereotyping is inherently bad. As a matter of fact, we couldn't function without using bases like these. The problem of stereotyping others becomes "bad" when, after having put forth ideas we think others might like, we fail to hear in the person's response anything that would prove our initial diagnosis incorrect. In other words, being able to perceive the uniqueness of another person's response is an essential second step needed after the initial stereotype.

People do not correct their misperceptions when to do so might prove threatening. For some, just the fact that they misperceived initially would cause them to feel others would reject them. It is easier to defend their stand than to admit error. For many, perceiving the uniqueness of another is threatening when they feel they have no existing way of dealing with this new and strange kind of person. In either case, willingness to admit failure and being able to get support to meet new situations certainly are characteristics of group members who have found security and acceptance within their group.

Although, in this description, stereotyping has been presented as an initial response, this attempt to find security in the familiar can occur at any time in a group's life. The protocol, which follows, is an example of this.

R₁: That's why I'm so mad at you all saying, "Let's do that damn sociogram."

D₁: I was going to say, was anybody mad at me yesterday, Do? I was doing this to a certain extent.

Do: It was because I could look at what you were doing and I seemed to feel that you purposively put it down in your notes—I happened to read a note he wrote—"I do not feel like I am a group member"—period. And, ah, this was early in the meeting I felt that he didn't want to be a group member—for a good reason, ah, I didn't know what it was exactly, but I sort of felt on the pan, because I was opening myself up and he was sort of sitting back and saying that he was not going to be a group member. Although some of the other people who do not speak I don't mind, because I feel that they are a group member, but I . . . there are certain groups that you find people that just sit but you can see that they actively are participating in a sense and this is tolerable in terms of the group.

W: You are saying that as a person you are secure in a group where the individual is consistent with your perception of what his behavior in the group ought to be.

Do: Uh huh. That's right—in a way.

W: Suppose that your perceptions of Ro and A's perception are different.

Do: I hope so. . . .

Helping the group perceive the accuracy of their perceptions and cues that they are using to interpret what they are perceiving is a basic part of the group's work.

Decision Making—To Vote or Not to Vote

From the very beginning each group faces the problem of the method to use to achieve group decision. Partially because it is the most familiar technique and partially because it seems most expedient, groups use voting to make decisions.

Similar to the experiences reported by Gordon,[36] the author found that voting brought with it problems the group was not sure how to solve. Desiring to provide all the needed time for discussion, the group could not decide when to vote. When several members of the group are ready to vote, but the others are not, they find themselves voting about whether to vote. The group perceives how ridiculous this is, but initially knows no other way of solving the dilemma. Robert's *Rules of Order* provides a method, but does not recognize individual needs.

When, because of individual pressure a group votes prematurely, they frequently ignore the decision and act out their unmet needs. In one group, based upon discussion by group members, it was decided to end each session earlier than originally planned, to enable a group member time to get to her next activity. The following several sessions the group found itself in animated discussion at the new closing time. Despite the fact that the young lady got up and left, the group continued to their initial time limit. When the young lady pointed out how the group was failing to respect its own limits, the group was forced to examine its own behavior. In so doing they discovered that although they desired to help the young lady, they resented losing time they originally had. Seeking ways to solve the problem they explored with the girl ways she could solve *her* time problem. Several members provided solutions that would involve their help. This they did willingly, in order that the total group could meet as originally planned.

This sensitivity to the needs and rights of the individual makes it difficult for a group to accept the concept of a minority subgroup within the total group.

In one group with which the author worked this concept of the rights of the individual met the supreme test. A young man, whom we will call Mr. X joined a group knowing its purpose and typical method of operating. He reasoned to himself that if this group was truly democratic he had the right, as an individual, to participate or not as he chose, and to vote or not, when he chose. Participating or voting when he didn't want to, represented coercion of a minority member by the majority.

The total group, desiring to respect his needs, found themselves immobilized because they:

1. Did not want to set up limits he would not respect (confidentiality, time, etc.)

2. Were threatened by his perception of them when the absence of feedback made them unable to know his true thoughts.

3. Felt cheated by not getting a contribution from him that would enrich the group.

In trying to solve this problem the group developed the following concepts:

1. Groups have a responsibility to be aware of minority group needs and the effect of a majority group decision upon the minority.

2. Minority group members have the right, following a group decision, to continue to work toward changing the beliefs of others so that their values might someday represent majority opinion.

3. Minority group members need to be helped to evaluate the price they are paying for their decision *and* to discover other needs the group *is* meeting that makes giving up a specific need worthwhile.

4. The majority group recognized that if it has met the previous criteria by providing opportunity and support to minority members, then when a group decision is being made silence must be construed as consent.

* 5. In a democracy people not only have a right to vote but beyond that have a responsibility to do so. Failure to vote involves more than individual rights. Failing to vote is taking from others something they need to be successful. Being interdependent no man has the right to receive group benefits without accepting his share of responsibility.

It is this last concept that our schools and citizenry have failed to comprehend. Unless youngsters are helped, early in group life, to learn the lesson of their voting responsibilities, no government using votes as a method of group decision can succeed.

As a sidelight to the illustration above, the reactions of the author to this situation might be of interest. Like the group, he was threatened by this behavior. Feeling responsibility as the initial leader, it became important to try to understand the needs behind Mr. X's behavior. Feeling that it might be difficult for the author himself to be objective about the situation, he asked an outside person to provide answers to questions the author needed answers to. The questions and answers received were:

1. Is Mr. X a psychopath? No.
2. Is Mr. X a monopolist? No.
3. Is Mr. X a cultural deviant? No.
4. Is Mr. X deeply neurotic? No.

* Major rule in group's eyes.

5. Does the group appear to be accepting and supporting Mr. X? Partially accepted by three people. Acceptance of his ideas but not his emotions.

6. At what point do you feel this group's demands on the individual are going beyond the rights of the group? Felt group had no right to insist on verbal participation.

7. Is Mr. X a person who cannot be helped in a group? Why? Mr. X has a real need for help, but at present seems unable to face receiving help from this group.

As the reader can see, the answers suggested a lack of real support for Mr. X and an impatience by the group at the rate of his ability to participate.

Within these examples, it is felt, lies the whole crux of the democratic philosophy. At some point a truly democratic group needs to accept that one of the limitations of this way of life is that it can move only as fast as the slowest member. With this concept comes the corollary that the speed of movement of the individual is a function of his security in the group which the group has the responsibility of facilitating. Last, but not least, the contribution of each individual makes for total group strength and, therefore, no person is truly expendable.

In the last analysis then, voting is meaningful and helpful only when the needs of all the members have been evaluated and where the group is able to accept loss of some freedoms as a price for having others.

Responsibility in a Group

One of the fundamental assumptions behind the philosophy presented in this book is that individuals, given the freedom to grow *and* the help to perceive what they are doing, will accept responsibility for themselves and others. They also will choose solutions to problems that are healthy and societally acceptable.[37]

This philosophy is one many people find difficult to accept. Not infrequently people respond to this idea with the feeling that the idea is all right in the abstract but would not work in their concrete situation. At times, the author himself has wondered if he was in an ivory tower. When such moments have happened typically he has tried to put himself in these "impossible" settings and see what happens. The following illustrations represent some such experiences.

When the author worked with a teacher group concerned about discipline, he found that several of the teachers felt that greater controls were necessary because children were not old enough to handle responsibility for their behavior. The author suggested that people learn to be responsible only by handling responsibility (along with support to face the anxiety it raises) and that children not only could handle responsibility but that they might have good solutions to the discipline problems we were worried about.[38,39,40] To test this hypothesis it was decided to help the author secure a group of youngsters and see what happened. One fifth-grade youngster from each of six different schools was chosen. Purposely the children differed as to race, socio-economic status, intelligence, school adjustment, and verbal ability. None of these youngsters knew each other.

As planned, the author met these youngsters for one hour before going with them to a teacher's meeting where they were to conduct a panel discussion. It was explained to the children that the teachers were concerned about discipline and that they felt that maybe the students had some good ideas which would help.

The youngsters' initial reaction was one of concern. They raised questions like:

"I would like to tell about the troubles in our class, but I wouldn't want to hurt my teacher."

"If I tell about something they will think it's my problem I'm talking about. What will they think of me?"

"How can we say things so they will not laugh at us?"

To summarize, the group was concerned about defining limits and protecting their security and the rights of others, while trying to find ways to be helpful and communicate clearly. The group was helped to see the problems it was raising. It developed several ways of coping with these problems. The author was instructed to tell the audience that the things the children said were to represent the thoughts of others who were not present—that they had swapped problems so that the source could not be identified and that they were interested in solutions rather than criticisms of the status quo. The youngsters did a particularly fine job of proving how able and ready they were to handle responsibility. One example of a problem faced in the panel session might demonstrate this:

One youngster complained about the slow learner in his class who was monopolizing the teacher's attention. Although the youngster did not say so, this was a good example of possible sibling rivalry in a class where a teacher gives different or favored treatment to those she feels may require it. Faced with this problem, the group decided that the brighter youngsters who finished earlier should help the slower ones. They felt students could explain in a way another student could understand, and that by this help the total group would be speeded up. In other words, they solved the problem by accepting more responsibility themselves.

In a completely different setting, the author was asked to help a high school age church group plan a regional conference.[41,42] The group came to the planning session loaded with suggestions from adults as to what they thought it would be good for these youngsters to discuss. Idea after idea was rejected. Finally, one boy said "everyone tells us what to do and think, why can't we be free to do as we please?" This feeling seemed to be highly popular in the group. The author, picking up this feeling, asked the group if maybe this feeling itself might not serve as a theme for their sessions. Rather quickly then things fell into place. The group decided that their theme would be "If I could do anything I wanted as long as the people with me agreed to it, what would I do?" Since they did not want to be told answers to their question, they organized the conference around work groups. Each group had the same problem of answering the idea raised in the theme. Being curious about other group's decisions, they planned on a general session where ideas from each group could be reported and where they could see what they had in common.

Given the freedom to organize society to meet their needs, the groups happily tackled what they considered failures of our society. The role of the family, sex, money, government, politics, freedom to think, and problems of minority groups all were areas for decision making. Some groups, with tongue in cheek (and partially to test adult reaction), suggested organized prostitution, no family life, etc. It was particularly interesting to see the total group reaction to such proposals. They questioned which of the girls were willing themselves to serve in degraded roles. They also asked if anyone really did not feel he wanted someone special to share life with. In other words, when faced with living out the ideas that initially seemed to represent freedom, time after time the total group decided on a way of life which was closer to existing society than ideas that meant overthrowing the past. The major result of the sessions was that the youngsters now had reasons that made sense to them for the rules and limits of society. These limits were now seen as desirable rather than as something being imposed on them by others.

As a last example there is the case of the group of residence hall workers who were up in arms over the behavior of their superior.

They came to the author seeking help in finding ways of coping with the situation.

Each of the women recited grievances and problems she experienced. The author clarified feelings, pointed up areas of similarity and disagreement in the perceptions of group members, and helped them feel free to express their negative and hostile feelings. Following release of these feelings the group began to examine how they might more effectively deal with their superior. Feeling accepted themselves, they began to try to perceive the feelings or needs the superior was having. In the process they found many needs she was expressing to be ones they could meet. They also began to realize that just as they were threatened by her, so too, the group was a source of threat to the superior. Ultimately the group began to accept responsibility for their own behavior, for their obligation to provide support to the superior so she could be better able to perceive their needs, and to help her see how she could relate to them in other ways that would be mutually more satisfying.

These cases are but a few demonstrations of the fact that groups given the security needed to face themselves, react with increased responsibility for themselves and others.

Other Tools and Techniques

Beyond the ways discussed thus far in this chapter, groups employ a vast array of devices to help group members express, practice, and facilitate interpersonal skills.

Probably most common is the use of role playing.[43,44,45,46] Some groups employ available scripts depicting scenes representing areas of common concern to the group. Others have the individuals in the group describe situations they desire to work out. The client selects the other roles needed to develop the setting, and he instructs group members in the kind of person they are to play. The way people are introduced into this acting situation very readily reflects the concept the leader has of the group's role and purpose. Some groups[47,48] have developed groups within larger groups, with the outer group serving primarily in a spectator role. Groups or leaders needing[49] a more structured setting have worked from textbooks, where the text serves as the common denominator toward which all members relate feelings and experiences.

At the other extreme there is a wide range of projective methods[50,51] using art, puppetry, adult play therapy, music, etc., to help provide members with a means of expressing feelings they cannot or are not ready to put into words.

Common to many groups is the use of food as a basis for making the setting more comfortable and informal. Psychoanalytically oriented leaders see food as meeting the succorance needs in the group as they are met in family life. In the author's groups the ritual of deciding on coffee, making it, and cleaning up becomes a vital part of group growth. Through this area the less verbal members typically make an active effort to take their share of responsibility. In this way they demonstrate their concern without having to expose their needs to the group. The group also discovers that coffee served in the middle of the session has a disrupting influence, and eventually groups make and serve food at the beginning both to facilitate communication and to avoid later confusion.

All of the techniques mentioned in this section have as their ultimate purpose improving communication and the relationship skills of group members. They basically are but a means toward an end, and their continued use may reflect the lack of maturity ultimately needed in groups. Truly secure and mature groups require no subterfuges to permit them to express their real problems and feelings.

Summary

This chapter has included a description of a number of problems and practices typically found in groups. At best it can represent just a few of the more critical situations in group life. In the chapter that follows, the reader will find descriptions of the application of group techniques in working with several groups. The problems raised in this chapter will fall into perspective when viewed from the significance of their effect on group growth and maturation. The mature reader will find the appendix specifically helpful in obtaining a longitudinal view of a group. As indicated at the beginning of this chapter, other points of view on each situation have been cited at the appropriate points within the body of the text.

BIBLIOGRAPHY

1. Jennings, Helen. *Leadership and Isolation.* New York: Longmans, Green, 1950.
2. Haiman, Franklyn S. *Group Leadership and Democratic Action.* Boston: Houghton Mifflin, 1951.

3. Hare, P., E. Borgatta, and R. Bales. *Small Groups*. New York: Knopf, 1955.
4. Bettelheim, Bruno, and Emmy Sylvester. "Therapeutic Influence in the Group on the Individual." *Amer. J. Orthopsychiat.* **17**, 684–692, 1947.
5. Winder, Alvin, and Donald Stieper. "A Prepracticum Seminar in Group Psychotherapy." *Intern. J. Group Psychother.*, Vol. VI, 410–417, October 1956.
6. Hadden, Samuel. "Countertransference in the Group Psychotherapist." *Int. J. Group Psychother.*, Vol. III, 417–430, October 1953.
7. Kotkov, Benjamin. "Vicissitudes of Student Group Psychotherapists." *Int. J. Group Psychother.*, Vol. VI, 48–52, January 1956.
8. Knopka, Gisela. "Knowledge and Skill of the Group Therapist." *Amer. J. Orthopsychiat.*, **19**, 56–60, 1949.
9. Slavson, S. R. "Qualifications and Training of Group Therapists." *Mental Hygiene*, **31**, 386–396, 1947.
10. Blocksma, Douglas D. "Leader Flexibility in Group Guidance Situations." *Educ. psychol. Measmt.*, **9**, 531–535, 1949.
11. Gorlow, Leon. *Nondirective Group Psychotherapy: An Analysis of the Behavior of Members as Therapist;* 1950, Columbia University, Microfilm Abstract #2109. Also in *The Nature of Nondirective Group Psychotherapy*, Leon Gorlow, Erasmus L. Hoch, and Earl Telschow. New York: Teachers College Press, 1952.
12. Gordon, Thomas. *Group Centered Leadership.* Boston: Houghton Mifflin, 1955, pp. 197–200.
13. Gibbs, J. R., Grace Platts, and Lorraine Miller. *Dynamics of Participation Groups.* St. Louis: J. Swift Company, 1951.
14. Beck, Dorothy Fahs. "The Dynamics of Group Psychotherapy as Seen by a Sociologist." *Sociometry*, Vol. 21, 98–128, June 1958.
15. Bach, George R. "Observations on Transference and Object Relations in the Light of Group Dynamics." *Intern. J. Group Psychother.*, **7**, 64–76, January 1957.
16. Glatzner, H. T. "Transference in Group Therapy." *Amer. J. Orthopsychiat.*, **22**, 499–509, July 1952.
17. Tropp, Emanuel. "The Military Social Worker as a Discussion Leader." *J. soc. Case Work*, Vol. XXVI, 377–383, February 1946.
18. Cotton, John M. "The Psychiatric Treatment Program at Welch Convalescent Hospital." *Research Publ. Assoc. Nervous Mental Disease*, **25**, 316–321, 1946.
19. Slavson, S. R. "Criteria for Selection and Rejection of Patients for Various Types of Group Psychotherapy." *Intern. J. Group Psychother.*, Vol. VI, 13–30, January 1955.
20. Bach, George. *Intensive Group Psychotherapy.* New York: Ronald, 1954, pp. 18–27.
21. Powdermaker, Florence, Frank J. Powdermaker et al. *Group Psychotherapy —Studies in Methodology of Research and Therapy.* Cambridge: Harvard University Press, 1953.
22. Ash, P. "The Reliability of Psychiatric Diagnoses." *J. abnorm. soc. Psych.*, **44**, 272–276, 1949.
23. Cartwright, D. "Achieving Change in People: Some Applications of Group Dynamics Theory." *Human Relations*, **4**, 381–392, 1951.
24. Thelen, Herbert. *Dynamics of Groups at Work,* Chicago: University of Chicago Press, 1954, p. 62.
25. Little, Harry M., and Gisela Konopka. "Group Therapy in a Child Guidance Center." *Amer. J. Orthopsychiat.*, **17**, 303–311, 1947.

26. Konopka, Gisela. *Therapeutic Group Work with Children.* Minneapolis: University of Minnesota Press, 1949.

27. Axelrod, P. L., M. S. Cameron, and J. C. Solomon. "An Experiment in Group Therapy with Shy Adolescent Girls." *Amer. J. Orthopsychiat.,* 14, 616–627, October 1944.

28. Spotnitz, Hyman. "Observations on Emotional Currents in Interview Group Therapy with Adolescent Girls." *J. Nervous Mental Disease,* 106, 565–582, 1947.

29. Barnes, M. J. "The Educational and Therapeutic Implications of Working with Parent Study Groups Around Problems of the Normal School Child." *Amer. J. Orthopsychiat.,* 22, 268, April 1952.

30. Thelen, Herbert. *Dynamics of Groups at Work.* Chicago: University of Chicago Press, 1954, p. 44.

31. Slavson, S. R. "A Contribution to a Systematic Theory of Group Psychotherapy." *Int. J. Group Psychother.,* Vol. IV, 3–29, January 1954.

32. Redl, Fritz. "Resistance in Therapy Groups." *Human Relations,* 1, 307–313, 1948.

33. Slavson, S. R. "Catharsis in Group Psychotherapy." *Psychoanal. Rev.,* 38, 39–52, January 1951.

34. Thelen, Herbert, and Watson Dickerman. "Stereotypes and the Growth of Groups." *Educational Leadership,* 6, 309–316, February 1949.

35. Gage, N. L. "Understanding and Helping Your Group." *Adult Leadership,* Vol. V, No. 2, 57–59, June 1956.

36. Gordon, Thomas. *Group Centered Leadership.* Boston: Houghton Mifflin, 1955, p. 269.

37. Turner, Marion E. *The Child Within the Group: An Experiment in Self-Government.* Palo Alto, California: Stanford University Press, 1957.

38. Hymes, James L. *Discipline.* New York: Teachers College Press, 1949.

39. Stendler, Celia. "Climates for Self-Discipline." *Childhood Education,* 27, 209–211, January 1951.

40. Sheviakov, George V., and Fritz Redl. *Discipline for Today's Children and Youth.* Washington, D. C.: Department of Super. and Curr. Development, National Education Association, 1944.

41. Cope, J. Raymond. "The Church Studies its Emerging Function." *J. soc. Issues,* 6(1), 5–13, 1950.

42. Coffey, H. S., M. Freedman, T. Leary, and A. Ossorio. "Community Service and Social Research—Group Psychotherapy in a Church Program." *J. soc. Issues,* 6(2), 1950.

43. Schwebel, Milton. "Role Playing in Counselor Training." *Per. & Guid. J.,* Vol. XXXII, No. 4, 196–201, December 1953.

44. Boring, R. O., and H. L. Deabler. "Simplified Psychodramatic Approach in Group Therapy." *J. clin. Psychol.,* 7, 371–375, October 1951.

45. Horwitz, Selma. "The Spontaneous Drama as a Technique in Group Therapy." *Nervous Child,* 4, 136–205, April 1945.

46. Haas, Robert Bartlett (Ed.). *Psychodrama and Sociodrama in American Education.* Beacon, New York: Beacon Press, 1949.

47. McCann, Willis H., and Albert A. Almada. "Round Table Psychotherapy: A Technique in Group Psychotherapy." *J. consult. Psych.,* 14, 421–435, 1950.

48. Moreno, J. L. "Psychodramatic Production Techniques; The Technique of

Role Reversal, the Mirror Technique, the Double Technique, and the Dream Technique Transcript of a Didactic Session." *Group Psychotherapy,* **4,** 243–273, March 1952.

49. Samler, Joseph. *Vocational Guidance Through Groups.* Washington, D. C.: The B'nai B'rith Voc. Service Bureau, 1943.

50. Bach, George. "Dramatic Play Therapy with Adult Groups." *J. Psychol.,* **29,** 225–246, 1950.

51. Moreno, J. L. *Psychodrama.* Beacon, New York: Beacon Press, 1946.

6

Group Techniques Applied

There are at least two points at which group procedures can assist in the learning process. Groups can be highly effective in creating an atmosphere of security where it is possible to consider new ideas, and as has been pointed out, group decisions are powerful forces providing the motivation for change. In this chapter devoted toward exploring the application of group techniques in concrete applied situations, both the needs for security and a desire for change play critical roles in the way these needs become a function of the fashion in which a group is organized and run. In previous chapters the concept of structuring was explored. This technique in large measure represents the primary purpose of the first group to be discussed— the group set up to provide an orientation of new people to an unfamiliar situation.

Orientation

The problem of helping new people adjust to the mores and practices of an organization is one shared by groups with widely disparate goals. Although social work agencies have long used in-take interviewers to partially serve this function, few have tried group methods for orienting new clients. One of the primary sources of confusion in this area comes from the difficulty in separating informational needs of clients from their anxieties over facing unfamiliar demands and threats. The use of lectures, handbooks, and movies all have served to provide background information about an agency; but as counselors and teachers subsequently discover, they appear to fail in helping the clients accept their role as it relates to the agency. They also fail in providing the client the support he needs in facing his feelings of inadequacy in a new situation.

In a Community Agency. When the Hunter College Veterans Guidance Center was initially organized, the staff explored all the steps a veteran had to complete prior to his working with a counselor. Beyond an initial screening by a Veterans Administration representative, to insure his rights to the service, a new client was asked to fill out a series of forms that provided background information about himself, his family, and his goals. Over a period of time it became apparent that the clients' attitudes toward the agency were being structured by their reactions to the forms they were being asked to fill out. As indicated by their questions, clients seemed to be asking themselves: why does anyone else need to know these personal things about me? What will they do with this information? How is this helping me achieve my goals? Where is all this leading?

To meet these kinds of concerns, the Center tried another procedure. All new clients were asked to come to the Center at a time set for a group meeting. After being seated informally, a member of staff started the session by indicating that people had many different reasons for seeking counseling and many questions about how a counseling center functioned. This meeting then was called to provide a chance for people to ask questions about anything that they wanted to know. The more courageous people started the ball rolling by expressing their concern over the seriousness of the vocational choice that they felt a need to make. Others in the group felt reassured when they discovered they were not alone in their confusion and feelings of guilt over their prior inability to make a decision. As their anxiety about seeking help began to diminish, the group slowly moved toward a more positive orientation. They became interested in how they and the counselors could solve their problems. As a response to their questions, it was possible to tell them everything about forms, procedures, etc., but *this time* it reflected information for which they had already perceived a need and which could now be seen as something in which they were sharing rather than as operations being used on them.

This illustration was chosen deliberately because it demonstrates how group procedures can be used in community settings and also points up a major concept.[1,2,3,4]

Although a major role of orientation is to provide information, it falls on deaf ears if the hearers have not been helped first to perceive the need for the information and then to face the anxieties the new situations may provoke.

For readers desiring more information about similar programs, Chapter 5 and Appendix B in Shostrom and Brammer[5] will be of interest.

For some time, schools have been concerned about improving the articulation between the different levels of schooling. Increasingly, representatives from the next higher level of schooling visit youngsters prior to their admission to junior high school, high school, or college, as the case may be. Studies like that of White,[6] which discusses the value of orientation handbooks, have pointed out that for a handbook to be successful its immediate objective must be to make students feel welcome, important, and secure in their environment. White found many handbooks presenting a tone that was authoritarian, prescriptive, and dictatorial in nature. One handbook that comes to the author's mind had more than 50 per cent of the book devoted to rules of the school and the penalties for infractions. It always brought to his mind the reactions of soldiers in the service who were forced to listen to the articles of war, and who responded either by tuning out the speaker or by open hostility.

Failures of handbooks or other inanimate devices in completing the orientation process represent a lack of awareness on the part of the users of the fact that receptivity and acceptance of any information given through impersonal devices is based upon several prior assumptions:

1. That all people want to know the facts available through the booklet, film, etc.

2. That the words used in these devices are understood by the recipient in the same fashion as the author intended.

3. That the recipient is able to transfer the meaning of an answer from one situation to another.

4. That the material not only reflects the needs of the agency but also meets needs of the recipients.

The discussion about handbooks is to point out that using group guidance orientation lectures, like handbooks or devices, can result in the economical transmission of a body of information, but unless these group settings allow for a two-way exchange of ideas and feelings, they are likely to be no more effective than the written word.

The problems involved in the *process* of orienting students to a new level of schooling are not different for the various levels of schooling, although topics explored may differ. Basically the purpose in all cases is to help the new person relate his goals and needs to the structure of a new setting. An exploration of college orientation problems can therefore provide clues for other levels as well.

Surveys like those of Bookman,[7] Copeland,[8] Fitts and Swift,[9] and Kamm and Wrenn[10] have documented the wide range of procedures used in the orientation process. Bookman's study, although somewhat dated, suggests that orientation is given more lip service than real, thoughtful planning. During the recent Twelfth Annual Conference of Orientation Directors held at Southern Illinois University it appeared evident that although schools were increasingly concerned about their orientation role, there was still evidence of marked disparity over the goals and techniques to be employed in orientation programs. The cleavage still exists between the group that holds "Students are too immature; you've got to tell them what to do and think" and the group that states "We want to help students get answers to their questions because giving information too early is a waste of time."

Increasingly handbooks are becoming the products of upper classmen rather than faculty members. These students try to recall their earlier concerns as freshmen and bring to these texts a more accurate survey of real student concerns. They also tend to phrase their thoughts in a way that reflects current student jargon and thus facilitates communication.

More and more schools are selecting a group of freshmen to come to school before the school year and receive training as leaders so that they can help orient their peers. Although this has typically been true on the college level, some high schools have tried this technique successfully. More frequently schools use upperclassmen as freshmen advisors, on a big brother or sister basis. Although these devices overcome many of the problems that arise when an adult tries to offer information and advice, these programs often fall short of their goal because schools have not provided adequate training of their students to help them be competent in these group leadership roles. Hopefully, this book has demonstrated to this point, that the skills involved include more than a knowledge of *Robert's Rules of Order* and the material the administration wants all new people to know and accept. If schools wish to increase their effective use of peer group leaders, prior systematic training of these people must be planned.

Studies by Goodrich[11] and by Lowenstein and Hoppock[12] suggest that moving orientation to college down into the high school or into precollege clinics is effective in improving student grades and adjustment to school. Equally effective results could be expected at the elementary and junior high school level where comparable programs are instituted. But like the studies reported, these orientation programs cannot be appendages to other programs with differing climates and goals. A homeroom program where much of the time is spent in announcements or school-controlled activities does not lend itself to use for free-flowing discussions.

The emphasis on orientation to this point has been on helping people get information needed immediately, and in helping them understand and accept the procedures and demands of the institution. Rogers[13] has pointed out, however, that orientation needs are an ongoing thing.

> Suppose that instead (of the usual college orientation program) students met once a week during the first semester in groups of not over 20, to talk out their confusions, their fears, their resentments, their feelings of inadequacy, and their sense of growth. The group could be conducted in such a way as to make it their group, and an opportunity to develop a clear and realistic orientation to their own situation.

Some colleges are achieving this goal through residence hall programs. The topics such groups discuss are interesting because they provide one clue as to the kinds of concerns people have with which typical orientation programs do not deal. One group of girls discussed "How do you handle yourself on a blind date?," "Now that we made college, what's the value of getting good grades?," "Is college the place to get a man or prepare for a career?"

Although high schools frequently do not have groups that are unstructured enough to allow equal concerns to be voiced, some high schools have used club activities as one way of developing comparable group settings.[14]

In one high school, a group of senior boys met in a series of bull sessions. Their concerns are of interest since they demonstrate the unusual and unexpected anxieties typical structured programs fail to deal with. These boys wondered "Is it true that on the first day you enter the Army they inject you with a four-inch square needle?" "Why should I listen to all that jazz about college, I can make more than my old man right now?" and "Why bother to take scholarship exams? Even if you pass, if you aren't top dog it doesn't matter anyway—also, if I make the grade, my folks will really ride me."

Successful orientation programs need to allow enough time for real concerns to be explored and faced. They need to offer information at the point where the group has discovered its need for the information. The structure of the group should permit feelings to be expressed and the freedom of group members to introduce topics that represent their concerns. The leadership needs to be skilled, and if effective, will help the group reduce its anxiety as the individuals discover they are not alone in their feelings of inadequacy. Also, as groups explore the mores and rules of the institution they have a chance to discover personal reasons that enable them to either accept the status quo, or failing that, to uncover socially approved ways of obtaining change. No orientation program can ever really end, since adjustment is a continual process. Planning, therefore, on continued sources of support and release in a group setting may facilitate the continued integration of people into the framework of the institution.

Group Guidance Programs

Typically the term group guidance has referred to programs designed to help youngsters solve problems of an educational, vocational, social, or personal nature. Although the term group guidance is typically used in relation to school settings, the concepts being explored are equally applicable to youth groups like those run by the Y.W.C.A., Y.M.C.A., Y.M.H.A., Y.W.H.A., B'nai B'rith, or similar groups organized by community agencies. The defense for group guidance all too frequently has been that this approach enables one counselor to disseminate information to many people at once and thereby conserves time.

Certainly, as time goes by, the tendency to divide a youngster's problems into areas is becoming less popular. Increasingly group leaders have realized that it is impossible to discuss vocational choice without considering a person's values or socio-economic pressures. Parental attitudes, desires for peer group acceptance, capacity to accept one's abilities all become an integral part in considering future vocational goals. Although public pressures make group guidance programs focused on educational or vocational planning more acceptable, groups that are free to explore all aspects of the problem cannot fail to explore areas considered more personal in nature. Acceptance of the role of any agency is dependent upon the public's understanding and acceptance of the program. These should be explored with the public prior to the inauguration of any new program. Parental resistance to programs dealing with personal problems frequently reflects anxiety over the fact that if children need help in these areas it implies failure on the part of parents. Freeing parents of these guilt feelings enables them to permit children to get help where and when they can use it.

Although there can be no question of the value and time saved in using groups to cover common informational needs, as previously discussed in the section on orientation, it is based upon the assumption that the primary need of the group is information. This argument also fails to educate the public to other gains available in group sessions.

The studies by Sinick and Hoppock[15,16] demonstrate that courses on occupations are successful in increasing earnings and job satisfaction of students, following graduation. They also improve academic achievement at college. In their study of the effectiveness of various devices they found that plant tours were more effective than film strips, whereas tape recordings showed no advantage over the reading of occupational literature in terms of the criteria of improving adjustment to training and work. There was also evidence of real inadequacy in the teachers' backgrounds in occupations. Similar findings are reported in the study by Lowenstein and Hoppock.[17]

The bulk of the studies[18,19,20,21,22] that compared the effectiveness of group counseling against individual counseling suggests no material benefit in using one method over the other. All, however, found that group counseling was more effective than no counseling at all. Although the studies differed in the criteria they employed, basically they used as their measures student satisfaction with his vocational choice, his certainty of his vocational choice, and the realism of the choice.

Each of the studies reported differed materially in the way the group was conducted. It should be obvious therefore, that any book which sets forth *the* way to organize a group guidance class can do so only to promote a pet belief rather than on existing evidence proving the most appropriate techniques to employ.

On a pragmatic basis, however, based upon teacher reports and discussions at professional conferences, there does seem to be consensus about approaches that secure better student and staff acceptance. Agreement seems to be high that:

1. *Any group program, to be successful, must consider the interests of potential group members.* An established curriculum of topics routinely covered in grades 7, 8, 9, or in a boy's club, etc., fails to recognize that groups that may be comparable on a chronological age basis may differ markedly in their social sophistication and concerns. There is as much individual difference between groups as there is between group members.

2. *To insure that all members of a group share common concerns, it is helpful to involve members in locating areas of concern and in*

establishing the limits of the group. An institution's concern that members receive the information they need at critical choice points frequently overlooks the fact that if these really are points of common concern, group after group on their own volition will choose to cover the same ground. The major difference will be their attitude and motivation to participate, not necessarily the areas discussed. Some agencies to achieve this goal have found that helping group members take instruments like the Mooney Problem Check List or SRA Youth Inventory[23] provides youngsters with two kinds of help. Since both of these inventories list common problems all youngsters face, it helps structure potential common sources of anxiety. For the youngster, learning that these inventories are *common* concerns frees him of feelings of anxiety and enables him to consider these topics for group discussion. Comparable instruments are available for adult groups.

It is this need to secure common understandings that should underlie the development of courses in "Ethics for Living," "Problems of Everyday Living," "Careers and Occupations," and schoolwide activities like career days and college days. In the development of any of these programs an initiating agency should ask itself the following questions:

(*a*) Has the group had a chance to clearly define the information they desire? Within the defined purpose of the group, have they explored the concerns most group members wish to face first?

(*b*) Has the group developed a setting in which its members will feel secure in using the group? For example, what is the effect of college day programs on noncollege-going youth?

(*c*) Has the group developed skills in evaluating the accuracy of the information they receive from resource people? For example, do the guests at a Career Day Conference provide an objective picture of their areas of interest?

(*d*) Has the group secured sufficient prior information so that it has a basis for evaluating the current program? For example, prior to a Career Day have the members considered what they need to know about their interests and abilities so that they see the way in which occupations being presented match up with their pattern of similar skills and interests?

(*e*) Has the group had a chance to develop skills they see a need for in achieving their goals? Have devices like role-playing and sociodramas been used to help the group see how they are coping with present situations—and at the same time have they provided the group with a chance to learn and practice new skills?

Each of the questions above should point up one major factor. No group guidance activity can be successful unless it is considered in terms of the total context of the agency within which it takes place. The meaningfulness of any group experience is definitely related to the things that both precede and follow the group activity. Local research into the effectiveness of any program highlights areas needing additional study.

Consider the following table. It reflects data gathered by Harley Neal (Rockford, Illinois) in a study of the vocational preferences of

DISTRIBUTION OF CHOICES FOR TEN MAJOR OCCUPATIONAL FIELDS COMPARED
WITH WORKERS ACTUALLY FOLLOWING THESE OCCUPATIONS IN THE
JEFFERSON JUNIOR HIGH SCHOOL AREA

Major Occupational Fields	Student* Vocational Preferences (1959)	Locally† Employed Parents (1956)
Professional, technical, and kindred workers	66.4%	7.4%
Managers, officials, and proprietors, except farm	0.0%	10.5%
Farmers, farm managers, foremen, and laborers	0.8%	1.4%
Clerical and kindred workers	12.5%	3.2%
Sales workers	1.1%	3.7%
Craftsmen, foremen, and kindred workers	8.7%	42.8%
Operatives and kindred workers	0.0%	9.7%
Service workers, except private household	9.6%	7.6%
Private household workers	0.6%	1.4%
Laborers, except farm and mine	0.3%	12.3%
Total per cent of distribution	100.0%	100.0%

* Information was obtained through Ninth Grade Vocational Questionnaires.
† Information was obtained through the cumulative records of ninth-grade students.

junior high students. These youngsters were going to attend a Chamber of Commerce sponsored career conference. Although the job distribution of their parents approximates the national job picture, clearly the student-expressed job preferences suggest an inadequate understanding on the students' part of the jobs they reasonably might hope to get. Such data certainly not only raises questions about the role the school must play prior to the conference, but also it raises questions about the nature and purpose of a career conference designed to help youngsters make realistic plans.

3. *The atmosphere of the group must stress security and freedom to explore ideas, along with the responsibility of the group to its members.* This is one point where the administrator of an agency frequently becomes unhappy. For example, the use of the homeroom for group guidance activities makes for easy school programming and simplifies the organizing of on-going programs. When the home room includes youngsters with widely different needs or values, or when the relationship of the teacher to the group involves contradictory roles (disciplinarian vs. permissive leader), it is difficult for all the people involved to feel security in the setting. It is important to realize that even if the teacher—or to translate this concept to another setting, if a minister—can effectively live and serve in two roles, it is not always possible for group members to perceive or accept him in both roles.

Since the home room[24] is so well established in schools as one way of meeting guidance needs, it is worth reviewing typical reasons as uncovered in studies by McFarland[25] and McCorkle and O'Dea[26] as to why home rooms fail. The five major causes as found in these studies were:

(*a*) Lack of time available for groups to explore areas of concern adequately.

(*b*) Failure to use home room appropriately. Use of time for announcements, role call, etc., all distort atmosphere and meaning of the hour.

(*c*) Leaders (teachers) are indifferent. Many find themselves in a role in which they are uncomfortable and discussing areas they would rather not face in themselves.

(*d*) Tied in to (*c*), there is an absence of an adequate number of trained personnel.

(*e*) Inadequate program planning. Programs are either not planned at all or reflect overstructuring by leaders to meet their needs.

All of the above comments could be applied with equal accuracy to typical Sunday School programs.

4. *Teachers or leaders of the group need to be comfortable in their role.* As has been explored in earlier chapters, the behavior and needs of the leader have a real effect on the way a group can establish the controls they need to feel secure. Helping teachers or other group leaders feel able to express feelings can be achieved as they are helped to participate in groups themselves, where they can discover what such experiences can mean.[27] In this fashion, too, they can learn how to serve as a leader from within the group. Such experiences also help potential group leaders become sensitive to group interaction.[28]

The concept that the leader needs to feel secure is clearly related to perceiving one's role and knowing how to live out that role. The basis for this security comes from having clearly worked out one's responsibility to the agency in which a leader works. Ethically, the leader's first responsibility is to the agency that employs him. It is only when one knows the limits of freedom available within agency policy that the leader can interpret to a group in formation those decisions a group has the freedom to make for itself, and those that they are not permitted while continuing to derive the benefits of the agency.

An example here might help. One common goal in activity groups is to help youngsters find socially approved ways of expressing hostility. One leader may tolerate curse words but ban destruction of the building, another will allow wrestling and jostling but ban fights where the battlers use weapons other than their bare hands. The limits of the situation really become defined at three levels. First there is the limit set by the agency. Second there are the limits developed through the structuring that occurs through the initial group leader. These limits frequently reflect the biases and needs of the initial leader. The third and operating level develops as a group establishes mores designed to cope with and reconcile their needs with those of the agency and initial leader.

Group Techniques in the Subject Matter Classroom

The defined goal of the public school and many other agencies in our society is to transmit the culture and heritage handed down to us from our forefathers. A typical question teachers hear is "Why do we have to study math—or English—or?" The question implies two major concerns of the students. First of all they are challenging the meaningfulness of the experience to them. Second they are reacting to having the limits of a specific situation predetermined.

When the leader can accept the feelings of hostility that arise from youthful rebellion to society limits, the group is then freed to use its energies toward discovering ways in which the course involved can be made personally meaningful to them. At this point it is most helpful for the group to be given responsibility for getting answers to the question of the value of the material.

One example of this comes to mind. A chemistry teacher who was accustomed, on the first day, to having students groan as he outlined the concepts to be learned, decided to reverse his approach and ask the group to see what ways they could think of that chemistry was effecting their lives. After a few socially approved schoolbook answers, the children went off on a more personal basis. "I'd like to know what makes lipstick kissproof." "I want to know if detergents really make washing easier." "I want to know what makes high octane gas better for cars."

At this point the instructor indicated on the blackboard the kinds of learnings society expected them to know at the end of the semester. (Limit of the course.) He then asked the group to see if they could see any relationship between the questions they wanted answered and the skills they needed to learn. Together they mapped out projects that would answer their questions while involving school skills needed to get answers.

This first illustration represented an area in which the focus is typically subject matter knowledge. Certainly as the group became motivated to learn, and as they discovered ways to make their experience meaningful, their whole attitude toward the classroom situation changed. In areas like social studies, English, and guidance, helping children relate their needs to the course content becomes less tenuous and difficult. Ojemann[29] has completed a series of studies designed to discover why, despite the relevance of courses like English and social studies to the development of human relations skills, people still grow up with a surface approach to behavior. He found that typically texts and teachers treat human behavior in other ways than those that focus on the dynamics which cause typical human reactions. It is his finding, and that of Stiles,[30] that to develop causally oriented children we need teachers who both teach in a causal approach *and* practice causal approaches in their daily relations with pupils.

As Seeley[31] has pointed out, even when classes use class time to discuss human relations at the expense of time spent on subject matter, the classes achieve well in subject matter learnings.

One interesting way of combining subject matter and human relation goals has been developed by the Illinois Curriculum Program.[32] In their *Reading for Living* bulletin they have developed an index of fiction reading materials that have been grouped according to the way they might provide answers to problems students checked on the Mooney Problem Check List. The concept here was that as youngsters could empathize with fictional characters having problems similar to their own, it might provide a cathartic experience along with alternative solutions to problems. Coincidently, it provided students with the motivation to read, since the content of the books had very personal importance to the reader.

As cited earlier, Stiles found it important to have teachers who practiced causal approaches in their teaching. One report, written by the author,* of a course taught in this fashion, may clarify the relationship of the group processes discussed as they can be applied in the classroom.

The classroom situation, if carefully controlled, can approximate a group therapeutic situation where the teacher serves a dual role of leader and counselor and the students are seen as the equivalent of clients. In the development of any class having this kind of orientation, the therapeutic quality of the group would appear to require the inclusion of the following factors:

The group must have a common purpose which represents real and recognized student needs.

The teacher-counselor must be proficient in the use of group therapy techniques.

All of the participants, including the teacher-counselor, must feel secure in the classroom situation, and

The nature of the group's responsibility and method of operation must be clearly defined and agreed upon at the earliest possible moment.

The initial leadership responsibility of the teacher-counselor is to help a mass of students become a group. He can best do this when everyone involved has security in the situation. People tend to feel secure where they know what is expected of them and know what they can expect from others. This need was given priority by the author in the group being reported on, when he provided the group with an early opportunity to meet informally with their classmates and to report to the rest of the group the kinds of things they had learned about each other. The author at this time tried to indicate his position in the group by also being interviewed by members of the class and by reserving no rights for himself that differed in any way in quality or kind from the responsibilities and demand that the group was making upon each other.

At this time the author, still serving as initial group leader, pointed

* This section is adapted from Walter M. Lifton, "Group Classroom Techniques," *Progressive Education*, Vol. 30, No. 7, May 1953. Describes a course in "Counseling Techniques."

up similarities of interests, problems, and needs verbalized by the members of the group, in an attempt to cement these early bonds and enable the group to feel closer to one another.

Identifying Group Goals

Although it was the purpose of the author to present to the group, both verbally and by manifest action, his own desire to enable the group members to secure within the course gratification of their own needs and their own interests, it was recognized by all concerned that the reality situation set up limits within which these needs could be fulfilled. Since a clear definition of limits enhances security, the author then clearly defined the purpose of the course as indicated in the college catalogue and also presented the unwritten goals that the author felt the group might need to achieve in a course of this type. These unwritten goals were:

To realize the effect of the counselor's personality and behavior on the counselor-client relationship.

To become aware of the discrepancy that may exist between verbalized goals in a counseling situation and actual behavior.

To recognize the difference between manifest and latent content of words.

To compare their typical counseling behavior with existing philosophies.

Once the point was reached at which the author felt that the group had developed sufficient familiarity with the job to be done and his role as he perceived it, it was then possible to throw open for group discussion the areas that the group wished to study, and to evaluate together the techniques by which the skills and insights expected by all could best be achieved. Both by physically altering his position from the front of the class to one close to the students, and by restricting his activity, the instructor removed himself from his position of group leadership and tried to help the group members develop leaders from among themselves.

As a result of group decision, fifteen major areas of interest with which the group desired to concern itself were defined. These areas were listed as: Directive Counseling Theory, Nondirective Counseling Theory, Interview, Follow-Up, Community Resources, Testing, Case-Study, Observation, Questionnaire Techniques, Information Giving,

Records, Bibliotherapy, Hypnosis, Psychodrama-Sociodrama, and Self-Analysis.

Chronologically, then, the group had accomplished the following things:

1. They had gotten to know each other and had discovered areas of interest where they could exchange ideas and help.

2. The instructor's role as a resource person was defined and tested by the group. Following acceptance of the instructor's status as a group member, it was possible to shift the leadership role to other members of the group.

3. The major areas in which the group wished to operate were defined by them, and the problem of developing skills consistent with the limits and the purposes of the course were then left to be faced by the group, as their major remaining problem.

Following group discussion, in which some of the works of Dr. Shartle, the Group Dynamics Researches conducted at Bethel, Maine, and other similar groups were explored, the value of using role-playing as a means of developing proficiencies in counseling techniques and also for an evaluation of each individual's characteristic behavior was explored. At this point the instructor as a group member took an active role in suggesting the need for structuring the evaluations of each role-played situation so that the integrity and security of the participants could be preserved. This was important in order that the group members would not need to feel defensive about their behavior in the group but rather might see the group as devoted to helping them to improve themselves. To accomplish the goal of helping this group think through how it was possible to constructively evaluate each other, the instructor borrowed two questions frequently used by Dr. Robert Hoppock of New York University. The questions suggested were:

1. What did you like about what you have observed the counselor do?
2. If you had been the counselor, what would you have done differently?

These questions were purposely selected to help students present in a positive fashion those areas where their perception of the correct approach differed from the one employed by their classmates.

In the selection of situations to be role-played, and in the people who would serve as counselor and client for each mock situation, the class subdivided into subgroups developed from the diversity of interests among the class members. The group, therefore, had a subgroup of people whose primary interest was in the area of clinical psychology, another focused toward working as counselors in a high school situation, and still others training for administrative responsibilities, and so on. Within the subgroups, the major problems of interest to each subgroup were defined and situations selected that could be role-played to enable the participants and their observers to evaluate how this situation could be handled, and also how the actual participants could be helped in improving their skill.

Using Records for Self-Evaluative Purposes

It became necessary to have the group members maintain some record for themselves of their progress as individuals. Accordingly, several of the members began to keep logs of what they observed within the class and the questions raised in their own minds. When it became important for the author to resume his responsibility as a teacher, the mid-term and final examinations were developed to represent extensions of this self-evaluative approach. On the mid-term, the students were asked to answer the following questions:

1. In light of the goal that you have set for yourself in this course, indicate any ideas that you have received which you believe you will actually be able to use. Give illustrations.
2. Based upon the things discussed in class, indicate those areas which were interesting, but which you feel, as an individual, deserve additional emphasis to clarify themselves for you.
3. Indicate those areas not yet covered in the course which you would like to see included within the remainder of the term.

The author reserved for himself the responsibility of tabulating these data and reporting back the group results, so that it was possible at that time for the group to reformulate its procedures and goals for the remainder of the term in light of any changes in values that might have developed from the beginning of the term. To indicate the kinds of answers obtained from this examination, illustrative quotes from two students' mid-term exams are presented:

> The first thing I did was to think again about what happened at the first meeting of the class. A feeling of friendliness was established, which has remained and grown throughout the course. I like the members of the class, and know more of them well than in any other class of its size that I have. The fact that the structuring of the method of procedure in the class, given at the first meeting, has been adhered to throughout this period has given me confidence in the class. At the time I didn't trust

completely that this "permissive" method of handling such a class would work, and for a while my attitude was one of watchful waiting—but for exactly what, I don't know.

I came into the course with a pre-determined attitude of "eclecticism" in counseling. I didn't have a philosophy of counseling, though I knew what the major philosophies stood for. I was going to use this course as a tool for the choosing of the "best from each of the methods of counseling" and for learning how to put them together when the situation called for it, or to use one method or the other according to what would work best in each case—even "switch in midstream" if it seemed best in a particular case. Not only that, I was a pretty "hot-shot" counselor anyway. People had been running to cry on my shoulder quite a few years now, and I always knew all the answers, and if I didn't I certainly could make up some for them to try. My opinion of myself now is just about as humble as that was exalted.

Later in the exam he stated:

In view of this change of opinion on my part, I found it necessary to re-evaluate my qualifications. I have felt compelled to test myself in various ways, to decide what kind of person I am, if by nature I am the kind of person who could be successful as a non-directive counselor.

There are a number of things about the class that I appreciate in particular. One of them is the complete freedom to read what I think I need the most, and to incorporate into my own thinking the ideas that I myself consider important to me. I'm not expected to assimilate a comprehensive array of facts for the purpose of later proving that I have done some work in the course. As a result I read a lot more than I would otherwise. I also appreciate the fact that I do not have to take lengthy notes in class, because I remember everything I need to know.

Lest these excerpts present too rosy a picture, the following excerpt may illustrate the kind of confusions arising in the students' minds during this process and some of the questions that had developed. Another student stated:

Another difficulty arises out of the permissive role of the counselor. If I am interviewing a student, he must have full freedom to express his opinions. Is this freedom likely to cause a deterioration of student-teacher relationship in the classroom? How might this relationship be expected to change? How might any undesirable change be prevented? During one of the class periods there was some discussion of the Ethics of counseling. It was stated, if I remember aright, that the solution arrived at by the client must be one which was satisfactory to him. I believe a rather extreme case was cited as an example. But, at what point must the counselor's respect for the client's right to reach his own solutions give way to the counselor's obligation to society?

In private discussions this student stated that his feelings toward the course, particularly in terms of his previous concepts of the role of an instructor, were forcing him to rethink the implications of status relationships in the classroom.

The final examination contained two questions. One involved an evaluation by the students of the technical, philosophical, and ethical implications of a quote that was presented. The second question, which had as its purpose trying to present to the students the concept that their responsibilities for their own growth did not cease with the end of the course, was versed in the following way:

> Based upon the repeated evaluations you have been asked to make of yourself and this course, what one area in your development as a person and as a counselor do you now believe needs priority in your list of tasks that remain to be done?

As in the mid-term examination, the author reported back to the group the kinds of general problems faced by the group and some of the issues where further investigation on their part appeared indicated by evidence of confusion or errors in their papers. Prior to the final examination, the issue of evaluating progress in therapy was discussed in class. A sub-group of the class who were particularly interested in this problem agreed to take on for themselves the responsibility of trying to prepare a rough draft of a device which might evaluate what had happened to them in the course. Since it was recognized that this process of evaluating an instructor might contain elements of threat to the individuals within the group, they worked out a procedure whereby their own identities were protected but where the grouped data would be available for a report back to the class, so that a further evaluation of both the course and this evaluating experience could be obtained by the group.

Up to this point, the author has been trying to present a description of what happened in a course that he taught, and what techniques he believed caused the students to increase their understanding of themselves. It might not be inappropriate at this time to state briefly how this experience affected him.

Effect of Course Upon the Author

Basically, it freed the author from setting up a rigid schedule that might match a school calendar, but that would not necessarily be representative of the needs of the students. To the degree that the course really represented a gratification of the expressed needs of the students, no problem of motivation or group interest occurred. Rather, the author was challenged to keep up with the group so that he could supply the members with materials, information, and the support that would enable them to continue in the direction and at the speed they had set for themselves. Not having to pose as an authority who was infallible and all-knowing enabled the author to be freer in participating with the group. To the degree that the group actually accepted the author as a group member, he was able to improve and revise his approaches in terms of the ever-changing and developing needs of the group.

As Applied to a Workshop

One other example of the use of group process skills in an educational setting will be presented. The example chosen involves a workshop setting where the goal of the group involved learning skills members feared, and where some of the membership was of an involuntary nature. This example was chosen because it involves mature teachers, not young children. But, as is indicated, the problems of group development are very similar.

For some time the Illinois Curriculum Program under the direction of Dr. Fred Barnes has been concerned about ways to interest classroom teachers in doing research.[33] In evaluating the problem, Dr. Barnes and his associates felt that they needed to achieve several objectives.

1. Doing research had to be seen as desirable by teachers. In other words, they had to see value in it for them.

2. Teachers had to feel secure in doing research, since people do not voluntarily choose activities which are unpleasant or threatening to them.

3. In line with number 2, teachers had to have a chance to develop skills in this area in a setting where failure would not cause them to lose either peer or self-respect.

4. During the learning period, information needed had to be available. Consultants and textbooks were on hand to supply data on techniques or design.

5. A group atmosphere rewarding research-focused activities needed to be developed to provide support to the individual and to reinforce the desire to learn a skill that meets group approval.

To achieve these objectives several experimental workshops were held where ways of developing subgroups interested in common problems were devised, and techniques for giving these groups responsibility for their achievement and to the total group were perfected.

Dr. Barnes and his associates recognized that one of the major problems associated with securing total group participation was the underlying fear of failure felt by workshop members. Accordingly, it was decided that in a subsequent workshop the sessions would start with a period devoted to helping people feel free to express negative feelings and to exploring their motivation to participate in this type of activity.

A socio-drama was planned that was to represent a faculty meeting where the school superintendent was to describe a forthcoming workshop and a member of the faculty was to be selected (drafted?) to attend. The workshop members were encouraged to represent their own teaching levels and specialties at this mock session. Rather quickly the group expressed resentments, fears, and needs that were common to workshop participants. At this point the role-playing was stopped and the group was asked to evaluate what they thought was happening in the group and why the needs which had been expressed were present. As the group evaluated the role-playing the focus shifted from the "characters" to the ways in which the workshop participants identified or perceived the situations.

One effect of this session was that the workshop members soon discovered that they were not alone in their anxieties and fears. At the same time they were discovering that it was permissible in this setting to express feelings that were blocking their ability to examine content and relate it to themselves.

In typical counseling fashion, after the group members had catharted their negative feelings, they were free to discover and accept the positive possibilities in the setting that they were in. Achieving this positive attitude, the group then became aware of its desire to develop skills to meet its own needs and not because the skills were required to meet external demands. Later, in the subgroup work sessions, the groups periodically had to take stock of their feelings and the way the group was proceeding. At stated time intervals the groups were given a chance to rate the preceding session. In this fashion the groups had objective evidence of their feelings about different activities, and could, through this form, express both positive and negative feelings. These illustrations indicate that in improving group atmosphere in the classroom we need to think about many factors and values.

Although most teachers have had training in relating to students and in recognizing the needs of individuals, the classroom atmosphere typically revolves around the teacher and the curriculum. There are authors who when talking about the group dynamics of the classroom really are describing teacher centered groups where movement, direction, and rewards are all determined by the teacher.[34]

Harris,[35] Maas,[36] Perkins,[37] Laycock,[38] the A.S.C.D.,[39] Cantor,[40] Prescot,[41] and Trow[42] are but a few authors who have tried to focus on the group centered climate needed for optimal assimilation of social and content learnings in the classroom. The article by DeBoer[43] relating group dynamics to instruction in English may serve as a basis for seeing group process in a subject matter setting.

Gillies,[44] Metcalf,[45] Cole,[46] Elkins,[47] and Jenkins[48] have described how, within the school framework, it is possible to develop groups having a therapeutic goal as their major objective.

Studies on Work with Failing and Underachieving Students

Three illustrations of the use of groups that are therapeutically oriented to achieve better academic adjustment may help demonstrate these concepts.

At Sullivan, Illinois, all youngsters who were failing in school were seen by the school counselor. In the counseling sessions with each youngster, each child was given the chance to join a group that would meet after school and would be composed of students who were doing poorly at school. Over a period of several sessions there was developed an in-group feeling which provided members with feelings of worth to replace their former feelings of social rejection. Guilt over their not having measured up to parental standards was alleviated and replaced by group support in learning new ways of adjusting to school and themselves. Grades improved and antisocial acts decreased.

A major study involving several groups of gifted underachievers was conducted at Evanston Township High School (Evanston, Illinois). Youngsters who were getting acceptable grades but were not achieving up to their potential were given a chance to join counseling groups and see if they could discover why they were not doing as well as they could. During group sessions many dynamics for desiring to fail became clear to the group. As reported by Dr. Broedel.*

* John Broedel, Merle Ohlsen, and Fred Proff, *The Effects of Group Counseling on Gifted Adolescent Underachievers*. (John Broedel, who is now employed at Ohio State University, read this paper at the American Psychological Association meetings in Washington, D. C., on August 29, 1958.)

Although underachievement was the identifying trait of the sample of gifted adolescents involved in the study, the evaluative instruments and the clinical assessment of the research team showed them also to be characterized as hostile persons. Prior to group counseling they rejected themselves, including their giftedness, and they were rejecting of others. The administration of a projective instrument, the Picture Story Test, before and after an eight week period during which two experimental groups participated in group counseling, demonstrated that the fourteen experimental subjects made significantly greater gains in acceptance of self and others than did a similar number of non-counseled control subjects.

One reason for desiring to fail became graphically clear in a group of college women who were meeting in a dormitory to explore their feelings about the grades they had received that quarter. An attractive young lady asked the group the following question. "I wonder why I don't study. I get B's without cracking a book while other kids work hard for the same grade. If I even tried a little I know I could get A's, but I never do. I wonder why?"

The group continued in its discussion only to be interrupted by the girl a little later on. She said, "I know why I don't study! If I got A's my mother would say, 'Why don't you do better!' " For this young lady this insight then was followed by questions she needed to think through. Why was pleasing her parents her goal in college? What did she need to do to feel she had really achieved something? Were her goals and standards realistic?

Clubs and extracurricular activities offer a vehicle for group counseling and serve in that way frequently without prior planning. The writings of Coyle,[49] Driver,[50] Haas,[51] Fedder,[52] and Hoppock[53] will be helpful in exploring ways in which agencies have used these group settings to meet counseling goals. The following illustration shows the way group process skills have been applied in working with student councils.

Student Councils*

In 1952 the Illinois Association of Student Councils was faced with the problem of planning its convention for the following year. Desiring to use the initials of the organization as the basis for their theme

---

* This section appeared in Walter M. Lifton, "Counseling the Student Council," *Educational Administration and Supervision*, Vol. 41, No. 2, February 1955, pp. 103–108.

they decided to focus the convention on the idea that "Intelligent Action Stimulates Cooperation." It was a motto that rang true, offended no one, and was not limited in meaning. Having surmounted this problem, they then went on to select a guest speaker and a student panel to discuss the implications of the slogan for student councils. It was at this point that the author, as guest speaker, became involved in the plans.

As a person in the area of guidance, it seemed appropriate to employ the concepts of the field on the job to be done. A check list was developed containing the following questions:

1. How can the slogan be made meaningful?
2. What are the needs of the group and how can we meet them?
3. How can the setting of the panel at the convention be arranged to provide maximum security for all, so that all could be free to think and participate?
4. How could the planning and action of the panel be used to illustrate dynamically the ideas being expressed?

Having been given a free hand in organizing the panel, the author corresponded with the panel members to get their ideas as to how we could best work as a group. Every letter written had copies made so that each of us received all of the letters we were writing to each other. This facilitated communication and made all feel a constant sharing in the group's planning. We all agreed that for the panel to be interesting we should be talking about the issues the membership was most concerned about.

To meet objectives 1 and 2 (making the slogan meaningful by tying it to the needs of the group) we went to the grass roots (student body) to discover what needs they had. The following letter was sent out to secure the information we needed.

ILLINOIS ASSOCIATION OF STUDENT COUNCILS

Peoria, Illinois
April 9, 1953

Dear Member of I.A.S.C.:

In order to have the planned panel discussion on "Intelligent Action Stimulates Cooperation" at the I.A.S.C. convention be one that really makes sense, and is worth while, we need your help.

We would like the representatives of each school to determine those problems in their school which the students see as ones where cooperation from the student body or from the faculty has been slow in coming. We plan to summarize these difficulties and use them as a basis for our panel discussion.

The more specifically you feed to us the issues and stumbling blocks you are facing, the better the pay-off will be when the panel tries to help you with your concerns.

The panel discussion will become real and interesting to you if you will participate by sending us your problems. This must be done immediately, for the convention is close at hand.

Please send the information to:

Dr. Walter M. Lifton
College of Education
University of Illinois
Urbana, Illinois

We need your cooperation! Don't let this be a stumbling block to the panel. Respond as quickly as possible.

Yours for Stronger Student Councils,
Michael Lipkin
1st Vice Pres. I.A.S.C.

It was the returns from this letter that not only helped us plan our convention program, but also clarified for us why many of the student councils were not succeeding. The returns were grouped, and the final tabulation was reproduced so that we could distribute this material at the convention. This duplication of material was done to accomplish objective 2—to help contributors feel that their contribution was recognized and to facilitate the cohesion of the group as they discovered the many problems they shared in common.

Summary of Problems Submitted

(After the general problem area appears the number of problems in that area which were submitted.)

I. Definition of council's role and duties: (24)
   1. Should there be student government in high school? (3)
   2. How much power do councils have and how much should they have? (6)
   3. How much say should the students have in making their own constitution? (3)
   4. Need better leaders: elections not a popularity contest. (7)
   5. Better communication needed between council, faculty, admin. and student body. (9)
II. Administration and faculty: (18)
   1. Lack of respect and confidence from either of those groups; neither group very interested or cooperative in many schools. (11)
   2. Lack of clear definition of power the above groups will allow council. (2)
   3. Detention, assignments, class and library situation. (5)
III. Student body: (66)
   1. Development of school spirit and interest in council, all school activities, etc., for better care of building and grounds and better participation in all phases of school life. (43)

2. Traffic: in the building and out. (8)
3. Cliques and other selfish individuals and groups. (2)
4. Detention, assignments, and class atmosphere. (5)
5. Manners: courtesy and respect for one another and faculty. (8)
   One school wrote that they have no problems to submit.

The forum panel was composed of six students representing high schools from different parts of the state. Although as a group we had been successful in gathering data for our use, we felt we needed to get together and discuss how best we could present the material so that our audience would be interested and become involved in the subsequent discussion. The group spent several hours together informally getting to know each other and swapping ideas on how to best do our job. As alternatives were being considered one of the group said he felt if the convention could be in the room with us then, relaxed as we were, they surely would get as interested as our own group. Another member of the group volunteered the idea that the thing he hated about meetings and conventions was the boring lectures, and he surely didn't want to have to be one of the speakers people listened to.

Rather suddenly we hit on our solution. Instead of lecturing panel fashion about the data we had available, why not recreate on the convention floor just what we were doing then? Each member of the panel scanned the letters we had received and picked out those ideas and attitudes he felt most strongly about. In order to find a theoretical setting where we could express these ideas, we planned our role-playing scene in a family living room where friends from different high schools were rehashing the doings at the convention and the problems of student councils. In this fashion we achieved our third Objective—a setting where participants and observers could be relaxed and feel more secure. Through our mouths the audience could hear and react to the ideas of their peers. By identifying with or reacting to one of the members of the panel group the larger group could share and become involved in the ideas being explored.

During the presentation of the program, panel members were seated in a semicircle so we could see and talk to each other. Microphones were placed so our audience could hear us, but at no time (after the panel program had been explained) did the panel talk directly to the audience. Each of us in our own way expressed ideas obtained from the original letters of the members. We tried to express ideas like the following:

> The most tremendous problem we have is putting over the idea to the student body and faculty that the student council is a government body

instead of just another school club or organization. Since our council is relatively young, this problem confronts us the most.

We have trouble in rousing interest in the student body toward various campaigns and activities that we sponsor throughout the year, such as, clean-up campaigns, dances, fire drills, etc. Another outstanding problem that hinders us is lack of respect from the faculty. Some of our elderly teachers refuse to accept the up-to-date thinking of the student council. They do not respect our meeting time and fail to give their cooperation in council sponsored activities.

How can we overcome too much rivalry and not enough cooperation between the classes?

How can we promote better understanding between teachers and students?

Everyone wants more and better parties but won't help to get them, what can be done?

How can we get the parents and students together to form a Teen-Age Recreation Club?

What methods are used most widely in choosing class advisors?

I would appreciate a discussion by the panel on the area of student council authority. My students have a mistaken idea that the council is all powerful. Needless to say I have discouraged the idea by explanations but the idea doesn't get across. (This idea came from a faculty sponsor.)

In our school my council members feel that too much is expected of the council. We are very active. Any good idea presented by the students is acted upon. If the council meets defeat, then the students feel that the council has failed. This is our big problem.

The members (elected) not always being the best of the school. (Students sometimes elect those they like instead of those who can serve best.)

Some older teachers resent certain student rulings such as checking the rooms for cleanness and so forth.

After about fifteen minutes of role-playing we opened the discussion so that the audience could participate. Questions and ideas came rapidly and were directed not only to the panel members but also to other members of the audience who expressed ideas.

In closing the session we achieved our 4th objective: using the actual content of our planning and panel session to point up the ideas being explored.

Basically we decided that each of the following points was necessary for a successful student council.

1. The rights, responsibilities, and authority of the group should be clearly defined from the start. Once defined they must be con-

sistently maintained. (We had checked with the officers of the IASC as to our freedom in planning the session.)

2. The purpose and focus of the student council must reflect the interests and needs of the students rather than to have it serve just as an extension of the administration. (We sent a letter to the grass roots to tap their interests.)

3. For the student council to survive it must serve as a means of feeding responsibility back to the grass roots rather than to relieve them of responsibility by acting for them. (We didn't lecture on what ought to be done by members but considered the problems and solutions available.)

4. Communication about all activities must be designed to reach and involve the entire student body. (Both our mimeographed material and use of microphones were designed to involve the total group.)

5. Faculty and administration can best develop the student council by vesting in the council rights, responsibilities and authority which are indicative of faith in students as mature and interested citizens of the school. (This arose from the discussion period where the security of the council representatives appeared to reflect their awareness of their rights and responsibilities to their school.)

Moral and Spiritual Values

It would be difficult indeed to describe any group in which questions of values or ethics are completely absent. There are, however, many problems in our society where the major issue is predominantly moral in character. The question of which agency in our society— the school, church, or community—should most appropriately handle these problems is obviously one on which consensus in our society is absent. Begging that issue for the moment, society has certainly failed to utilize group settings adequately to solve some of its concerns. The following illustrations may demonstrate ways in which groups have been used effectively.

One school was greatly troubled by the high incidence of illegitimate pregnancies among the girls in the student body. Lectures in school and at church seemed to have no effect. Courses in sex education also seemed not to be getting the desired result. Finally, somewhat in desperation, the school got the students together and said to them that they believed the students were also concerned about the situation. They asked the students to see what remedies they could suggest. After helping the students set up permissive discussion groups, the problem was given over to the students. After setting up limits and testing peer acceptance of ideas, the boys and girls began to open up. Rather quickly it became apparent that most of the group members had assumed that their acceptance by their peers demanded promiscuous behavior. On an individual basis though, as each member described his picture of the mate he desired to marry, it tended to follow the societal value of the moral person. The group discovered, as person after person talked, that there was an unverbalized but common acceptance of values that were opposite the ones popularly voiced before this. Rather rapidly a new standard became a basis for group acceptance. "Will this behavior get me the mate I desire?" This value did not ignore sex drives but rather helped put them into perspective with other needs.

Another school had a major problem with youngsters recklessly driving hot rods. Following a precedure like the group described previously, the boys and girls again found that instead of only one value system being in operation, a second unverbalized one was equally present. Up to the time the group met it had been assumed that peer group acceptance was based upon proving one's courage by the speed with which one drove. Demonstrating one's physical control by fast driving also seemed a way of proving adulthood. After several group sessions, members began to express some of their hidden feelings. Many had a real fear of being hurt in a car accident. They felt real guilt over the potential injury to others. As person after person demonstrated his feeling that fast driving also implied a lack of concern for others, a new group value began to form.

One school, in developing its guidance program, called in students to become part of the planning group. As the students felt free to express their concerns they raised question after question about the cheating that was going on in the school. Although the teachers had been aware of the problem, they had failed to realize the depth of student concern about it. With the help of the students on the committee a plan was developed to permit students in the school to explore the problem. Beyond providing students a chance to face the situation, the discussion provided new insights for the faculty as to the reasons behind the cheating. Both the faculty and parents were putting extremely high pressure on students to achieve scholastically. Rewards for A students were large and rejection of others equal. Using a curve system in grading, only the very top people could get recognition. As one student after another took to cheating to achieve the desired grades, the person who didn't cheat could not survive. Although they were hostile toward their classmates, they knew no acceptable way of correcting the situation. In this case not only the students but also the faculty and the parents needed group sessions to look at the needs they had which had precipitated the situation.

In an elementary school, a classroom teacher became aware of the snobbery present in the attitudes of the students. Using a phantasy situation she suggested to the class that it might be fun to build an imaginary city. Each student could have any job he wanted. Keeping track of the students' choices, the group discovered they had several doctors, lawyers, and engineers. One individualist wanted to be a bum. The group was then asked to see if the proposed city could survive. The need for farmers, toolmakers, garbage collectors, etc., became clear. In the ensuing discussion the children became aware, for the first time, not only of the inherent importance of every job in our society but also the yardsticks they were using in determining the value of any job or person. The different values in our society that placed premium on monetary rewards, status, social service, etc., moved from the unconscious to the conscious concern of all group members.

For one last example, consider the experiences of a Baptist minister concerned with preparing a group of youth for their confirmation. He was disturbed by their apathy in group discussions and the rote manner in which they were learning their creed. Restructuring the group he tried to help them raise their concerns, fears, and anxieties as they related to their religious beliefs. As they saw him as not sitting in judgment, they were able to voice their doubts and confusion. Having expressed these feelings they were interested in using him as a resource person to see what the denomination had to offer as ways of facing or solving their concerns.

Group Techniques in Developing a Program

Throughout this chapter there has been a repeated emphasis on the need for the leader to be comfortable with his leadership role. Many agencies thrust responsibilities on people without giving them adequate help in learning the skills that go with the role. Whether it be a teacher forced to handle a group guidance program or a parent recruited to teach Sunday School, we have an obligation to prepare the person so he can be effective.

If it were possible to plan most intelligently we would help these potential group leaders learn skills in a nonthreatening environment until they themselves felt ready to handle their group assignment.

The reality situation being what it is, how then can we help people learn skills. One helpful technique involves the case conference method. Providing a group with a problem outside themselves to focus their attention on, sets the stage where the desire to be helpful to others becomes the group more. As person after person presents his perception of the problem and how he would deal with it, the group members inevitably are helped to see ways of coping with the problem they hadn't considered before. This approach is particularly helpful in settings where many old timers are present who may be threatened by new approaches. Being free to listen to others' ideas, they do not need to publicly profess their own ignorance. At the same time, they can learn about new ideas without having to admit that new ways may be superior to their existing approach. If the threat to the group is really great, the leader can help them by preparing a case that embodies problems they will face later, but being fictitious, frees participants from the fear of doing something wrong because of their own ineptness.

One of the commonly accepted concepts in education is that one works from the known to the unknown. In helping groups develop programs or new skills, the speed with which it develops needs to be paced with the security of the group. When a group is truly group centered they speed up or slow down to account for the needs of all the members in the group. As their insights grow, directions will shift.

Consider for example the case of a junior high that was seeking to initiate a guidance program. During planning meetings for which they called in a consultant they became painfully aware of the many activities that needed to be started. They also became sharply aware of their own reluctance to take on these responsibilities. As they explored the problem they discovered that the one place where all the faculty felt there was an immediate need for action which was coupled with a willingness to be involved, was a desire to start an extracurricular program after school. The teachers were concerned about keeping children off the streets after school. They also saw a way in which they could indulge in their favorite hobbies. A science teacher wanted to sponsor a knitting club. A math teacher was interested in teaching children chess, etc. As plans began to form, the suggestion was made that it would be helpful to have students on the planning committee. The addition of students introduced a new and interesting element. The children raised questions as to the students' interests in the clubs that were being proposed. Alternate clubs representing current student interests were suggested by the children. One of the most critical learnings arising out of this experience for the school was an awareness of the concept that any guidance program beyond considering the needs of the school has to incorporate the needs of the children as the children perceived them. This learning was truly major, despite the fact that the total guidance program for that junior high school was limited at this stage to adding clubs to the school.

Discussion

Each of the examples presented differed both in the amount of freedom available to the groups and the degree of task orientation initially present.

Cartwright,[54] in summing up research on techniques of achieving change in people, has developed eight principles that provide a good summary of the goals to be considered in working with groups. The principles are:

1. If the group is to be used effectively as a medium of change, those people who are to be changed and those who are to exert influence for change must have a strong sense of belonging to the same group.
2. The more attractive the group is to its members the greater is the influence that the group can exert on its members.
3. In attempts to change attitudes, values, or behavior, the more relevant they are to the basis of attraction to the group, the greater will be the influence that the group can exert upon them.
4. The greater the prestige of a group member in the eyes of the other members, the greater the influence he can exert.
5. Efforts to change individuals or subparts of a group which, if successful, would have the result of making them deviate from the norms of the group, will encounter strong resistance.
6. Strong pressure for changes in the group can be established by creating a shared perception by members of the need for change, thus making the source of pressure for change lie within the group.
7. Information relating to the need for change, plans for change, and consequences of change must be shared by all relevant people in the group.
8. Changes in one part of a group produce strain in other related parts which can be reduced only be eliminating the change or by bringing about readjustments in the related parts.

To the degree that a group accepts responsibility, they will become increasingly concerned over problems of evaluation. The chapter which follows presents a discussion of the problem of evaluation and how some groups have solved this issue.

BIBLIOGRAPHY

1. Grunwald, Hanna. "Group Counseling in a Case Work Agency." *Intern. J. Group Psychother.*, **4**, 183–192, 1954.
2. Harlow, George. "A Group Guidance Inter-Faith Project." *Pers. & Guid. J.*, **35**, 34–36, 1956.
3. Rosenberg, Bernard. "Group Vocational Counseling in a Rehabilitation Center." *J. Rehab.*, Jan.-Feb. 1956, pp. 4–6.
4. Harlow, George. "A Group Guidance Summer Project." *Pers. & Guid. J.*, **34**, 441–442, 1956.
5. Shostram, Everett L. and Lawrence M. Brammer. *The Dynamic of the Counseling Process.* New York: McGraw-Hill. Chapter 5 and Appendix B, 1952.
6. White, Robert M. "Student Handbooks: Observations and Recommendations." *Pers. & Guid. J.*, **37**, 43–46, 1958.
7. Bookman, G. "Freshman Orientation Techniques in Colleges and Universities." *Occupations*, **27**, 163–166, 1948.
8. Copeland, Theodore. *Freshman Orientation Programs.* Doctor's Thesis. Temple University, 1954.
9. Fihs, Charles T., and Fletcher H. Swift. *The Construction of Orientation Courses for College Freshmen.* Public. Educ. Monograph #3, University of California, 1930.
10. Kamm, Robert, and C. Gilbert Wrenn. "Current Developments in Student Personnel Programs and the Needs of the Veteran." *School Soc.*, **65**, 89–92, 1947.
11. Goodrich, Thomas A. "Gains in Self Understanding Through Pre-College Clinics." *Pers. & Guid. J.*, **31**, 433–438, 1953.
12. Lowenstein, Norman, and Robert Hoppock. "High School Occupations Course Helps Students Adjust to College." *Pers. & Guid. J.*, **34**, 21–23, 1955.
13. Rogers, Carl R. "Some Implications of Client-Centered Therapy for College Personnel Work." *Educ. psychol. Measmt.*, **8**, 545, 1948.
14. Driver, Helen. *Multiple Counseling.* Madison, Wisconsin: Monona Press, 1954.
15. Sinick, Daniel, and Robert Hoppock. "Research on the Teaching of Occupations 1952–1953." *Pers. & Guid. J.*, **33**, 86–89, 1954.
16. ———. "Research on the Teaching of Occupations 1954–1955." *Pers. & Guid. J.*, **35**, 155–160, 1956.
17. Lowenstein, Norman, and Robert Hoppock. "High School Occupations Course Helps Students Adjust to College." *Pers. & Guid. J.;* **34**, 21–23, 1955.
18. Caplan, Stanley Wm. "The Effect of Group Counseling on Junior High School Boys' Concepts of Themselves in School." *J. counsel. Psychol.*, **4**, 124–128, 1957.
19. Hewer, Vivian H. "Group Counseling, Individual Counseling, and a College Class in Vocations." *Pers. & Guid. J.*, **37**, 660–665, 1959.
20. Hoyt, Don P. "An Evaluation of Group and Individual Programs in Vocational Guidance." *J. appl. Psychol.*, **39**, 26–30, 1955.
21. Wright, Wayne E. *A Comparison of Individual and Multiple Counseling in*

the Dissemination and Interpretation of Test Data. Unpublished doctoral dissertation, University of California, 1957.

22. Richardson, Harold, and Henry Borow. "Evaluation of a Technique of Group Orientation for Vocational Counseling." *Educ. psychol. Measmt.,* 12, 587–597, 1952.

23. Singer, Stanley L., and B. Stefflre. "Concurrent Validity of the Mooney Problem Check List." *Pers. & Guid. J.,* 35, 298–301, 1957.

24. McKown, Harry C. *Home Room Guidance,* Second edition. New York: McGraw-Hill, 1946, 522.

25. McFarland, John W. "Developing Effective Home Rooms." *School Rev.,* 61, 400–405, 1953.

26. McCorkle, David B., and David J. O'Dea. "Some Problems of Homeroom Teachers." *Pers. & Guid. J.,* 32, 206–208, 1953.

27. Moustakis, Clark. "A Human Relations Seminar at the Merrill-Palmer School." *Pers. & Guid. J.,* 37, 342–349, 1959.

28. Wright, Wayne E. "Multiple Counseling: Why? When? How?" *Pers. & Guid. J.,* 37, 551–557, 1959.

29. Ojemann, Ralph H. "The Human Relations Program at the State University of Iowa." *Pers. & Guid. J.,* 37, 198–206, 1958.

30. Stiles, Frances A. *A Study of Materials and Programs for Developing an Understanding of Behavior at the Elementary School Level.* Doctoral Dissertation, University of Iowa, 1947.

31. Seeley, John R. "The Forest Hill Village Human Relations Classes." *Pers. & Guid. J.,* 37, 424–434, 1959.

32. DeBoer, John, Paul Hale, and Esther Landin. *Reading for Living.* Springfield, Illinois: Superintendent of Public Instruction, Circular Series A No. 51, *I.C.P. Bull.* No. 18, 1953.

33. Barnes, Fred. *Practical Research Processes.* Springfield, Illinois: Superintendent of Public Instruction, 1958.

34. Strang, Ruth. *Group Work in Education.* New York: Harper, 1958.

35. Harris, F. E. "Techniques for Guiding Group Experiences in the Classroom." *Elementary School J.,* 49, 32–36, 5, 1958.

36. Maas, H. "Applying Group Therapy to Classroom Practice." *Mental Hygiene,* Vol. 35, 250–259, April 1951.

37. Perkins, Hugh V. "Effect of Climate and Curriculum on Group Learning." *J. educ. Res.,* 44, 269–286, 1951.

38. Laycock, S. R. "The Mental Hygiene of Classroom Teaching." *Understanding the Child,* Vol. XVI, 39–43, April 1947.

39. A.S.C.D. *Group Planning in Education.* Washington, D. C.: ASCD, 1945.

40. Cantor, Nathaniel. *The Dynamics of Learning,* Third Edition. Buffalo, New York: Henry Stewart, 1957.

41. Prescot, Daniel. *The Child in the Educative Process.* Chapter 9. New York: McGraw-Hill, 1957.

42. Trow, William Clark, et al. "Psychology of Group Behavior: The Class as a Group." *J. educ. Psychol.,* XLI, 322–338, October 1950.

43. DeBoer, John J. "Implications of Group Dynamics for English." *English J.,* XVI, 239–244, May 1952.

44. Gillies, Emily P. "Therapy Dramatics for the Public School Room." *New Child,* 7, 328–336, 1948.

45. Metcalf, H. H. "Group Counseling at the Eleventh Grade Level." *School Rev.*, **54**, 401–405, 1946.
46. Cole, Natalie R. "Exploring Psychodrama at the Fifth Grade Level." *Sociatry*, **2**, 243–245, 1948.
47. Elkins, Deborah. "How the Classroom Teacher Can Help the Emotionally Disturbed Child." *Understanding the Child*, **20**, 66–73, 1951.
48. Jenkins, David. "Counseling Through Group Activities." *The Clearing House*, **23**, 8, 488–493, 9149.
49. Coyle, Grace L. *Group Experience and Democratic Values*. New York: The Woman's Press, 1947.
50. Driver, H. "Small Group Discussion as an Aid in Counseling." *School Rev.*, **59**, 525–530, December 1951.
51. Haas, Robert (Ed). *Psychodrama and Socio-drama in American Education*. Beacon, New York: Beacon Press, 1949.
52. Fedder, Ruth. *Guiding Homeroom and Club Activities*. New York: McGraw-Hill, 1949.
53. Hoppock, Robert. *Occupational Information*. New York: McGraw-Hill, 1957.
54. Cartwright, Dorwin. "Achieving Change in People: Some Applications of Group Dynamics Theory." *Human Relations*, Vol. IV, 381–392, 1951.

7

Evaluation and Research*

EVALUATION

In the preceding chapters it has been pointed out that an effective group climate[1] produces an atmosphere where group members are continually trying to clarify their ideas and behavior. The protocols in the preceding chapters demonstrated how, as a group matures, they become increasingly concerned about the yardstick to use in measuring their growth and present status. As the question is explored by the group it becomes apparent that there are at least three aspects of the problem of evaluation worth looking at. These aspects include the growth of the group as a group, the growth of an individual from the beginning session to the present, and a comparison of an individual's present functioning compared with "norms" described from society's expectations of people living different roles.

Group Growth

Although authors differ in the areas they emphasize, almost all authors would agree that the following characteristics are typical of mature groups.

1. An ever increasing ability to be self-directed (not dependent on leader).

2. An increased tolerance in accepting that progress takes time.

* Parts of this chapter originally appeared in Walter Lifton, "Group Therapy in Educational Institutions," *Review of Educational Research*, Vol. XXIV, No. 2, April 1954, pp. 156–158.

3. An increasing sensitivity to their own feelings and the feelings of others.

4. Marked improvement in the ability to withstand tension, frustration, and disagreement.

5. Perceptive of the common denominators which binds the group as well as areas of individual difference.

6. A better ability to anticipate realistic results of behavior and to channel emotions into more socially acceptable ways of expressing these emotions.

7. An increased ability to change plans and methods as new situations develop.

8. Less time needed to recover from threatening group situations. Peaks and valleys of emotional group crises become less pronounced.

9. Increased efficiency in locating problems, engaging in problem solving, and providing help to individuals as needed.

10. Prestige in group now comes from willingness to face own responsibilities and to assist others when help is needed.

11. Acceptance of the right of the other person to be different.

12. Acceptance of the idea that people are different.

It seems odd that there are still people who insist that there can be no such thing as group counseling or therapy. The point that is made is that what is being observed is actually counseling of individuals in a group. This point of view conveniently overlooks some of the characteristics of the group setting which cannot be equated with a one-to-one relationship. The growth that comes about by identifying with another person who is working out a similar problem, the attempt to define reality by testing how many peers need to see something the same way for it to be real, and the learning involved in assuming a leadership role are all samples of phenomena that are based on group life. No equivalent experience can be presented in the individual therapy session.

Despite the many problems in research design discussed in this chapter, the frequency with which studies demonstrate significant findings must make the objective individual wonder if all this smoke cannot help suggest a fire underneath.

Individual Growth

In previous chapters there have been included check lists a leader can use to determine if his behavior reflects a helping relationship or is a function of his own personal needs.

The personal logs of each group member provide data that can be objectified and quantified.[2] Plotting these data over time indicates the direction the person is moving. This helps a person have a basis he can use in looking at himself. Log data can be analyzed in some of the following ways. The logs provide:

1. A comparison of the frequency with which the log deals with content *vs.* feeling areas.

2. A comparison of the locus of attention on self *vs.* others.

3. A record of the changing attitudes toward specific group members and the reason felt as cause for this change.

4. A record associating specific content areas with the type of emotional reaction it precipitates.

5. A record of goals set and those finally achieved.

In many ways logs can serve a unique function. Just as a parent is shocked into realizing how much her child has grown, when she tries on last year's dress, so too, the logs help demonstrate changes that have occurred so slowly that they fail to evoke notice. Probably the greatest virtue of this device is that it provides the reader with a tool for self-evaluation, when supervision or the group itself cannot share in the process. As teachers and other group workers learn to keep a record of their daily activities and impressions, they develop the habit of introspection which is the basis for growth.

A Comparison of Self with Others

One of the most threatening moments in a group's life occurs when the group members realize that the true measure of their capacity will be realized only insofar as others perceive and accept them at that level. This concept occurs most clearly when students have a chance to explore their feelings about course grades and the manner in which the grade reflects their level of achievement.

Because grades have been labels that most students have had no share in deciding, the initial reaction to the grading problem is that grades represent the views of others and therefore the individual need feel no responsibility for the yardstick employed. When, however, as in some of the courses described in this book, they need to share in the grading process, it is no longer possible to avoid looking at grades and what they mean to the person.

Typically groups go through the following stages. The ideas are expressed in the following ways:

1. "Let's dichotomize between individual growth and course grade." "People entered the group at different levels. It is not fair to not reward the person who has grown most." The idea here is that grades are rewards for efforts and not level of achievement.

2. "Let's give everyone an 'A' so no one need be hurt." Since it is painful to accept that some people are better than others, the group tries to make all members equal. When this idea is explored with the group, hostile feelings are expressed rather quickly. Although people wish to help each other, they do not wish to do so at the expense of loss of their own identity. It is soon realized that a common label for all makes the label meaningless and another means of differentiating between people will arise.

3. "Since the true measure of our value to society and to ourselves is in terms of what we offer in the way of skills, how can we determine the skills society anticipates from us? How can we develop ways of recognizing the differences between people while using the same basis for comparison?"

Although the concept of evaluation has been demonstrated in a course setting, where there is need for precise labels, a similar path is followed by groups who are seeking to assess whether they have achieved goals they have set for themselves.

It is in this last stage of maturation that a group begins to examine the bases by which they can determine if they have reached their goal. As they put into words the criteria involved, the associated discussion provides a synthesizing of all that has gone before. Criteria labels become associated with specific group experiences and as such are remembered long after the group dissolves. This association also causes the criteria, and subsequent label, to have personal meaning for each group member.

Because the group has learned that it is easier to face threat when others help, and that the perceptions of others are meaningful, it is not surprising that final evaluations typically take the form of sociometric ratings. Sociometric ratings are tools that have been developed to measure the relative standing or distance between people on a given dimension. The data is gathered in the following way. Members of a group are asked to indicate the name of other people in the group with whom they would prefer to be closely associated in a defined activity. By tallying the number of times each person is chosen, and by an examination of the way a person both chooses and is chosen by others, a clear picture of the intended relationships between group members emerges. Group sociometric ratings differ from the typical classroom use of sociometric ratings in several important ways. Typically, sociometrics are used as a basis for objectifying group structure so that the teacher or leader can see individuals needing help or can locate the people who are in positions of leadership.[3] It often provides the basis for a diagnosis which is then followed by a manipulation of the environment to promote change in the direction the manipulator thinks is best. One rather forceful reaction to this type of activity is the concern now being expressed, in our gregarious society, whether the individual diagnosed by this device as an "isolate" needs to be socialized. Increasingly we are concerned over the need for "isolates" in our society, when this represents the well adjusted person who feels better able to create by himself rather than with others. To put it differently, we are becoming concerned over the meaning of the behavior to the person himself, and we are recognizing that society requires many different kinds of people. Of equal concern with this diagnostic use of sociometric data is the effect on the people completing the instrument. Since typically people are asked to rank others in terms of a specified characteristic, the effect of this action is to focus the perception of people on each other in terms of status derived by their acceptability (or rejection) by their peers on a particular dimension. Since studies tend to focus on one dimension, it tends to create a status hierarchy in the group rather than focusing on the differing strengths of different people. Smucker[4] has raised an interesting and provocative question when he points out that negative sociometric data is equally diagnostically useful in revealing the tension and disruptive potentials in a group.

In contrast to the foregoing description, groups have frequently used sociometric ratings to give the person being rated an objective picture of how others see him. It not only provides a basis for helping a person compare one of his characteristics with other traits he possesses, but if the group shares the total group data, each person can see how he compares with all others on each characteristic. Since the pooled data can be kept anonymous, no person need feel threatened by others knowing how the total group perceived him. The major threat comes, instead, from helping the person face the differences between his own self-concept and the opinions of others. To provide this help groups typically insist that sessions be held after ratings are made available, so that anyone who desires can ask the group for help. At that time, not only is support given, but where confusion exists in the mind of a group member about the reasons for the disparity between his own perception and those of the group, the group tends to try to help by providing examples of behavior which caused their perception to develop.

Probably the most threatening aspect of this approach is the unexpectedly high (in the group's eyes) agreement between group members in the way they perceive specific characteristics in the person being rated. The total grouped ratings also demonstrate to the group that even when all attributes are considered, some people are more effective than others. At this point, if the group can examine the pattern of total ratings for the entire group, it is relatively easy to assign labels or grades. Since this is done without awareness of the scores of specific individuals it carries no implication of group rejection of an individual.

Presented here are two instruments developed by different groups. In both cases the groups were concerned with developing skills in group process. Although derived independently, it is interesting to see the characteristics that both deemed important.

GROUP A

		(Less)					(More)	
		1	2	3	4	5	6	7

How much did ___Joe___

(a) solve his problems through identification with others problems — 1 2 3 4 5 6 7

(b) solve problem by accepting responsibility for his actions — 1 2 3 4 5 6 7

(c) understand (empathy) others' feelings — 1 2 3 4 5 6 7

(d) understand (diagnosis) others' actions — 1 2 3 4 5 6 7

(e) help others feel accepted — 1 2 3 4 5 6 7

(f) show concern with others' problems — 1 2 3 4 5 6 7

(g) show preoccupation with own problems — 1 2 3 4 5 6 7

(h) use others to gain information — 1 2 3 4 5 6 7

(i) offer help to others on request — 1 2 3 4 5 6 7

(j) show consistency between what he says and does (judge from classroom situation) — 1 2 3 4 5 6 7

(k) effectively make himself understood — 1 2 3 4 5 6 7

(l) efficiently make himself understood — 1 2 3 4 5 6 7

(m) change within this group — 1 2 3 4 5 6 7

(n) How competent would this person be as a group leader? — 1 2 3 4 5 6 7

GROUP B

(Rating scales available with each factor)

1. Awareness of group process (See Dynamics of Group Interaction. Helps structure limits, helps group solve problems)

(a) Observer (doing nothing)   (b) Participant (cohesiveness)

2. Does he use others to get answers for himself (parasite)?
3. Does he let others know when he feels the same way?
4. Does he express feelings?

   (a) Positive   (b) Negative

5. When he serves as a therapist can he understand another's feelings without getting emotionally involved himself the same way?   (Does he cry when you do?)
6. Does he try out new ideas (new behavior, new ways)?
7. Listening—does he respond:

   (a) Verbally   (b) Physically

8. Is he a conformist?
9. Is he getting through audibly and clear?
10. Does he dig you?   (Do you feel understood?)
11. Does he focus on others' needs?
12. Does he focus on my needs?
13. Does he contribute when he has something to contribute?
14. Does he assume a client role?
15. Does he assume a therapist role?

Obviously not all of these qualities were rated in the same way. The group had to make value judgments, for example, as to their attitude toward the person who always conformed as compared to the one who never conformed. The result of the rating process in Group B was a sharper perception by the group members of the specific areas needing attention, to improve their over-all effectiveness.

RESEARCH

Research Design. The preceding section was labeled evaluation to distinguish between data used for descriptive purposes and data secured, under controlled conditions, to provide answers to predetermined questions.

It would be nice, in discussing methods of research useful in this area, if it were possible to provide precise clean-cut instructions. Unfortunately, available research designs and tools are not truly adequate for the task to be done.

The person planning research on group process is faced with a choice of possibilities for establishing a control group against which to measure the effects of the experimental variable. One method involves one group only, with data gathered during a period where the variable is not operating, then an equal period involving the experimental variable, and then another equal period where the experimental variable is again absent. This approach avoids the major problem of matching groups on the basis of the group atmosphere that character- izes each group as unique. It has the weakness of not being able to assess the effects of uncontrolled variables, maturation, or the effect of the second phase on the third. Although maturation would appear to be controlled, the assumption is being made that the growth due to maturation during all three phases is constant.

An alternative and traditional method of control is to try to establish a control group that matches the experimental group on the significant variables in the research. Many studies have dodged the issue in- volved here by assuming that if characteristics like age, diagnosis, personality type, I.Q., etc., were comparable, the groups could be con- sidered matched. Although this is a convenient escape hatch, it fails to accept the fact that the major variable in most studies of groups is the group climate itself. Admittedly this is a difficult variable to quantify, but the author believes that it is this problem which most needs our present attention.

The literature does suggest some promising approaches that deserve further inspection. Bach[5] has compared the quality, quantity, and verbal interactions of the same members of a psychotherapy group when they faced reality (discussion) *vs.* fantasy (play-drama) condi- tions. Martin, Darley, and Gross[6,7] have developed an "Index of Co- hesiveness" and an "Index of Mutuality," which attempt through sociometric choices to equate groups in terms of group atmosphere. Canter[8] has developed a multiple-control group technique as a means of factoring out unwanted variables. Statistically, it is possible to establish control. To accomplish this purpose one needs a large enough population so that group members can be assigned to groups on a random basis. If the number of people and groups is large enough one can assume comparability between groups. Unfortunately, few studies can capture a large enough sample to use this approach with a real sense of confidence.

Zlatchin[9] used two groups of subjects, his experimental group and another composed of all boys in the same grade level. The initial and final test results of the untreated group were intercorrelated and treated by correlational-profile analysis and multiple correlation to obtain two independent, weighted, composite measures. On the basis of *each* measure, control groups were matched with the experimental population to form two control groups, one for each major measure. In other words using a large pool of subjects, matched experimental and control groups were developed independently for each variable studied.

One of the other sources of difficulty in research on groups comes from the role of the leader or therapist. The literature has amply illustrated the effect of the leader's personality and value system on his behavior and relationships with the group. Control groups using different leaders certainly have introduced a major variable that will effect the results. Unfortunately, using the same leader in both experimental and control groups does not solve the problem either. Since group composition, in and of itself, will effect the reaction of the leader, it is impossible for any one person to relate equally to two groups. Differences here are compounded when the leader employs different methods in each group, since few people are equally adept at alternate methods of working with others.

The measures the investigator employs will very readily reflect his concept of group process as being individual learning in a group or a group which represents something different than the sum of individual reactions.

The range of techniques developed to quantify group process is both varied and long. It includes sociometric techniques,[4,10,11,12,13] interaction-process analysis,[11] group dimension scales,[14] genatypical dimensions (reactions of warmth, hostility or flight recorded in terms of direction and intensity),[15,16] client reports,[17,18,19,20,21] and observer reports.[17,18,19,20,21,22]

In a recent study by the author,[23] research reports were tabulated to find the comparative frequencies with which different instruments were employed to measure change in the area of group therapy. There was a slight preference for the Minnesota Multiphasic Personality Inventory, the Thematic Apperception Test,[24] and the Rorschach. Beyond these all other devices seemed equally chosen. This survey also revealed considerable concern over whether the typical absence of significant changes in test scores reflected the lack of sensitivity of the instruments chosen or were in fact evidence of no change in the variable being studied.

There appears to be an increasing emphasis on the use of on the spot observers. The use of tape recordings has ruled out vital visual cues of the members' identification with each other and also the intended meaning of the words expressed. Recent use of television monitors and kinescopes suggests new ways of recording and analyzing data.[22]

The papers by Burchard, Michaels, and Kotkov,[25] as well as those by Frank,[26] and Heyns and Zander,[27] provide excellent summaries of problems of research in the area.

It is not realistically possible within a brief chapter to review the results achieved by all the research conducted to date. Several recent texts[28],[29],[30] have been specifically designed to serve that purpose.

In reviewing these texts there appears to be little agreement over the meaning of the results. For example, studies like those conducted by Fiedler[31] that relate interpersonal relationships in a group with the group's effectiveness seem to suggest that good leaders interpose greater psychological distance between themselves and their co-workers than do poor leaders.

How can readers of this text reconcile these conclusions with the thesis presented in this book that group effectiveness is related to strong empathic relationships between group members?

A close examination of these studies reveals several major defects that may make possible a different interpretation of the results obtained.

The primary source of data in many studies comes from the use of a Q technique to derive measures of assumed similarity. Cronbach[32] has clearly demonstrated some of the mathematical and psychological fallacies involved in the concept of assumed similarity. At the very least there is experimental evidence involving sociometric data[33] that demonstrates little correspondence between whom a child in a study said he liked to be with and with whom he was observed to spend time.

Even if there were no question about the validity of the measurement technique, there still remains confusion if truly effective democratic groups are to be equated with friendship relationships based on identification and sympathy, rather than empathy and acceptance of individual difference. There can be no quarrel that most existing groups tend to function on a friendship basis which equates acceptance of the person with accepting and meeting his needs as he wishes. The entire purpose of this book has been to demonstrate that it is possible to structure groups so that they retain the warmth and support available in friendship but are modified to develop relationships that are more conducive to growth. Given that type of group, the author believes that the leader no longer need be distant to help members of the group use each other most effectively.

One of the definitions of leadership is that the person who is chosen as leader supplies or meets the needs of the group. Part of the security group members have comes through identifying with the leader. Group members also seek to be accepted by the leader and their peers. To the degree that the leader epitomizes an ideal, real identification is impossible because members recognize considerable distance between their capabilities and those they have projected onto their leader image. Feeling unworthy, they then tend to desire a leader who can make decisions for them. As presented in the section on evaluation, groups are faced with ambivalent feelings between desire for equal status of all group members and their need to recognize true differences in ability. This ambivalence is resolved as personal security grows. One common result of studies on therapeutic groups is the observed positive relationship between a person's security and his ability to accept individual difference.

In some ways Army tradition epitomizes the concept that effective groups demand social distance between leaders and the group. Recruits are taught that they are saluting the uniform and not the man (overlooking of course that the uniform can give no support or understanding). The story goes that there is at least one illustration in the service that completely refutes this hypothesis. Carlson's raiders functioned as a total group. Before any operation every man was given the chance to contribute his ideas and all men understood and accepted the goal of the group. Feeling worthwhile as people, this rugged group was able to function in isolation from others. They also were able not only to delegate responsibility, but also to assume leadership roles with no previous definition of status or preserved psychological distance.

The studies cited and illustrations presented all seem to suggest a need for renewed attention to our definition of what constitutes a democratic group and a need to redefine the kinds of affect which relate to effectiveness in groups.

Summary

One measure of the sophistication of a discipline comes from the extent and quality of research that has been performed. There is little doubt that many questions in the area of group process need investigation. Equally obvious should be the need for any researcher to have reconciled for himself, prior to starting on his research, the assumptions and hypotheses he cares to make. The traditional starting place for any study is to review what others have done so far. To assist the reader in taking that first step the bibliography for this chapter includes a separate list of doctoral dissertations that describe research designs, instruments, and areas warranting consideration in future studies.

BIBLIOGRAPHY

1. Perkins, Hugh V. "Climate Influences Group Behavior." *J. educ. Res.*, **45**, 115–117, October 1951.
2. Allport, G. W. *The Use of Personal Documents in Psychological Science.* New York: Social Science Research Council, *Bull. 49*, 1947.
3. Jennings, Helen H. "Sociometric Grouping in Relation to Child Development." In Caroline Tryon (Ed.), *Fostering Mental Health in Our Schools.* Washington, D. C.: ASCD, National Education Association, 1950.
4. Smucker, Orden. "Measurement of Group Tension through the Use of Negative Sociometric Data." *Sociometry*, **10**, 376–383, November 1947.
5. Bach, George R. "Dramatic Play Therapy with Adult Groups." *J. Psychol.*, **29**, 225–246, April 1950.
6. Martin, William E., John G. Darley, and Neal Gross. "Studies of Group Behavior: II. Methodological Problems in the Study of Inter-Relationships of Group Members." *Educ. Psychol. Measmt.*, **12**, 533–553, Winter 1952.
7. Gross, Neal, and William E. Martin. "On Group Cohesiveness." *Amer. J. Sociology*, **57**, 546–563, May 1952.
8. Canter, Ralph R., Jr. "The Use of Extended Control-Group Designs in Human Relations Studies." *Psychol. Bull.*, **48**, 340–47, July 1951.
9. Zlatchin, Philip J. *The Effects of Group Therapy Upon Some Aspects of Behavior, Social Relationships, and Personal Attitudes of Adolescent Problem Boys.* New York: New York University, 1950.
10. Davis, Ruth G. "Group Therapy and Social Acceptance in a First-Second Grade." *Elementary School J.*, **49**, 219–223, December 1948.
11. Evans, John T. *Objective Measurement of the Therapeutic Group Process.* Cambridge: Harvard University, 1950.
12. Nelson, Alice D. *The Effect of Group Self Study on Sociometric Ratings.* East Lansing: Michigan State College, 1951. Abstract. *Microfilm Abstracts* **12**, No. 6, 852–853, 1952.
13. Pepinsky, Harold B. "Measuring Outcomes of Classroom Therapy." *Educ. Psychol. Measmt.*, **7**, 713–724, Winter 1947.
14. Hemphill, John K., and Charles M. Westie. "The Measurement of Group Dimensions." *J. Psychol.* **29**, 325–342, April 1950.
15. Joel, Walther, and David Shapiro. "A Genotypical Approach to the Analysis of Personal Interaction." *J. Psychol.*, **28**, 9–17, July 1949.
16. Thelen, Herbert, and Dorothy Stock. *Methods for Studying Work and Emotionality in Group Operation.* Chicago: Human Dynamics Laboratory, 1954.
17. Baruch, Dorothy W. "Description of a Project in Group Therapy." *J. consult. Psychol.*, **9**, 271–280, November 1945.
18. Lawlor, Gerald W. "Psychodrama in Group Therapy." *Sociometry*, **9**, 275–281, November 1946.
19. Lifton, Walter M. *A Study of the Changes in Self Concept and Content Knowledge in Students Taking a Course in Counseling Techniques.* New York: New York University, August 1950. Abstract. *Microfilm Abstracts* **11**, No. 1, 55–56, 1951.

20. Metcalf, Harold H. "Group Counseling at the Eleventh Grade Level." *School Rev.*, **54**, 401–405, September 1946.
21. Peres, Hadassah. "An Investigation of Non-directive Group Therapy." *J. consult. Psychol.*, **11**, 159–172, July 1947.
22. Noble, Frank C. *A Method for the Quantification of Interaction in Psychotherapeutic Groups.* University of Illinois (Ed.d Thesis), 1958.
23. Lifton, Walter. "Group Therapy in Education Institutions." *Rev. Educ. Res.*, Vol. XXIV, No. 2, p. 156–163, April 1954.
24. Horwitz, Murray, and Dorwin Cartwright. "A Project Method for the Diagnosis of Group Properties." *Human Relations*, Vol. VI, No. 4, 397–410, 1953.
25. Burchard, Edward M. L., Joseph J. Michaels, and Benjamin Kotkov. "Criteria for the Evaluation of Group Therapy." *Psychosomat. Med.*, Vol. X, No. 5, 257–275, September-October, 1948.
26. Frank, Jerome D. "Some Problems of Research in Group Psychotherapy." *Int. J. Group Psychother.*, **1**, 78–81, 1951.
27. Heyns, Roger W., and Alvin F. Zander. "Observation of Group Behavior." *Research Methods in the Behavioral Sciences*, New York: Dryden, 1953.
28. Hare, Paul, Edgar F. Borgatta, and Robert F. Bales. *Small Groups—Studies in Social Interaction*, New York: Knopf, 1955.
29. Cartwright, Dorwin, and Alvin Zander. *Group Dynamics: Research and Theory.* Evanston, Illinois: Row Peterson, 1956.
30. Taguiri, Renato, and Luigi Petrillo. *Person Perception and Interpersonal Behavior*, Stanford, California: Stanford University Press, 1958.
31. ————. Chapter 16, "Interpersonal Perception and Group Effectiveness," Fred Fiedler, pp. 243–258.
32. ————. Chapter 23, "Proposals Leading to Analytic Treatment of Social Perception Scores," Lee Cronbach, pp. 353–379.
33. Polansky, Norman, Ronald Lippitt, and Fritz Redl. "The Use of Near-Sociometric Data in Research on Group Treatment Process." *Sociometry*, Vol. XIII, No. 1, 39–62, February 1950.

BIBLIOGRAPHY OF DOCTORAL DISSERTATIONS

1. Abrams, Arnold. *Effects of Group Therapy Upon Certain Personality Characteristics of a Selected Group of Institutionalized Male Sex Offenders*, New York University, 1952.
2. Ballin, Marion Ruth. *An Evaluation of Adult Group Guidance.* Stanford University; 1954.
3. Barr, Lawrence. *Changes in Personality Test Measures Resulting from Participation of College Students in Group-Centered Psychotherapy*, University of Southern California, 1952.
4. Blessing, Harold D. *An Investigation of Fantasy and Overt Behavioral Changes in Patients Who Have Undergone Psychotherapy*, University of Denver, 1951.
5. Bosco, Sr. John. *An Investigation of the Effectiveness of Group Psychotherapy in Improving the Adjustment of Adolescent Girls in an Institutional Setting.* Ohio State University, 1951.

6. Bold, Richard W. *The Use of Group Psychotherapy in the Professional Training of Ministers,* Boston University, 1951.
7. Briskin, Gerald J. *An Exploratory Study of Identification in Group Therapy.* University of Michigan, 1955.
8. Broedel, John. *The Effect of Group Counseling on Gifted Adolescent Underachievers.* University of Illinois, 1958.
9. Canter, Irving. *Study of the Relationship of Education to Social Group Work Through an Analysis of Theory and Practice.* University of Maryland, 1955.
10. Caplan, Stanley W. *The Effect of Multiple Counseling on Junior High School Boys' Concept of Themselves in School,* University of California at Berkeley, 1956.
11. Chang, Thomas. *Predicting Selected Behaviorial Characteristics on the Basis of Observation of a Group Psychotherapy Session With Mental Patients,* Ohio State University, 1957.
12. Chenven, Harold. *Effect of Group Therapy Upon Language Recovery in Predominantly Expressive Aphasic Patients,* New York University, 1952.
13. Clampitt, Richard R. *An Experimentally Controlled Investigation of the Effect of Group Therapy,* State University of Iowa, 1955.
14. Croley, Hugh T. *A Method of Analyzing the Process of Group Psychotherapy,* University of Denver, 1950–1951.
15. Daniels, Marvin. *The Influence of the Sex of the Therapist and of the Co-Therapist Technique in Group Psychotherapy, With Boys.* New York University, 1957.
16. Dysart, James M. *A Study of the Effect of In-Service Training in Sociometry and Sociodrama on Teacher-Pupil Rapport and Social Climate in the Classroom,* New York University, 1952.
17. Evans, John T. *Objective Measurement of the Therapeutic Group Process.* Harvard University, March 1950.
18. Feldman, Leonard. *Multiple Counseling: Factors Related to Self Improvement,* University of California at Berkeley, 1952.
19. Feish, Irving J. *Group Therapy As a Technique to Release Tension and Anxiety Existing Prior to Regents Examinations; An Experimental Venture in Mental Hygiene.* New York University, 1954.
20. Fine, Harold J. *Interaction Process: the Analysis of a Group Therapeutic Experience in a Human Relations Seminar,* Syracuse University, 1952.
21. Fisher, Bernard. *An Investigation of the Effectiveness of Group Therapy for the Remediation of Reading Disabilities,* New York University, 1953.
22. Flemming, Edward L., Jr. *An Investigation of Problem Centered Group Discussion as a Technique for Reorienting the Attitudes of the Aged,* Columbia University, 1950.
23. Geller, Max. *Group Psychotherapy with Girls Institutionalized for Mental Deficiency: A Study of Psychotherapeutic Process and Effects,* New York University, 1952.
24. Gerstenlauer, Charles A. *Group Therapy with Institutionalized Male Juvenile Delinquents,* New York University, 1949.
25. Gordon, Ira J. *The Creation of an Effective Faculty Advisory Training Program Through Group Procedure,* Teachers College, Columbia University, November, 1950.
26. Grier, Daniel J. *Orienting Students Through Group Counseling in a College Setting.* Teachers College, Columbia University, 1950.

27. Grob, Samuel. *A Clinical Investigation of the Role of the Therapist in Group Psychotherapy*, Harvard University, 1950.
28. Holden, Ruby M. *Relationship Between Perceived Leadership, Perceptions of the Ideal, and Group Productivity in Small Classroom Groups*, University of Illinois, 1954.
29. Jones, Francis D. *An Evaluation of Group Psychotherapy*, Washington University, 1950.
30. Kimball, Jack F. *An Application of Two Principles of Client Centered Therapy to Classroom Teaching at Harpur College*, Teachers College, Columbia University, 1951.
31. Knox, Wilma Jones. *Acceptance of Self, Other People, and Social Conformity As Effects of Group Therapeutic Experiences*, Pennsylvania State University, 1958.
32. Langworthy, Stanton B. *Content and Procedures for a Course to Provide Prospective Teachers Guided Leadership Experience with Young People Through Activities in Group Work Agencies Supplemented by Classroom Instruction*, New York University, 1951.
33. Leino, Walter B. *Evaluation of Outcomes of A Personal Adjustment Course*. University of Minnesota, 1956.
34. Lewis, Robert T. *An Analysis of Group Cohesiveness as a Function of Different Types of Group Therapy Focus*, University of Denver, 1952–1953.
35. Martin, John H. *A Study of the Measurable Effects of Group Discussion of Adolescent Problems Upon Certain Personal and Social Attitudes of Ninth Grade Boys*. Fordham University, 1946.
36. Mehlman, Benjamin. *Nondirective Group Play Therapy with Institutionalized Endogenous Mentally Retarded Children*, Abstract. Syracuse University, January 1951.
37. Mitchell, Dorothy. *The Validity of the Thematic Apperception Test and Its Implications for Group Therapy*, University of Oklahoma, 1949.
38. Naboisek, Herbert. *Validation of a Method of Predicting Role-Expectations in Group Therapy*, University of California at Berkeley, 1952.
39. Nelson, Alice D. *The Effect of Group Self Study on Sociometric Ratings*, Michigan State College, 1951.
40. Newburger, Howard M. *The Effect of Group Therapy Upon Certain Aspects of the Behavior and Attitudes of Institutionalized Delinquents*, New York University, 1951.
41. Northern, Helen. *The Effectiveness of Social Group Work in the Development of Qualitative Participation*, Bryn Mawr College, 1953.
42. Page, Curtis W. *A Comparative Study of Three Types of Group Psychotherapy Formulations*, University of Denver, 1952.
43. Parloff, Morris B. *An Analysis of Therapeutic Relationships in a Group Therapy Setting*, Western Reserve, 1952.
44. Pivnick, Harold. *Group Discussion and Its Relationship to Social Acceptability and Personality Adjustment in Normal Adolescent Girls*, New York University, 1952.
45. Roman, Melvin. *Tutorial Group Therapy: A Study of the Integration of Remedial Reading and Group Therapy in the Treatment of Delinquents*, New York University, 1955.
46. Rook, LeRoy. *Evidence of Change in a Group Therapy Situation as Described by the Rorschach*, University of Oklahoma, 1949.

47. Rosenberg, Pearl P. *An Experimental Analysis of Psychodrama*, Radcliffe College, 1952.
48. Saloshin, Henriette E. *Development of An Instrument for the Analysis of the Social Group Work Method in Therapeutic Settings*, University of Minnesota, 1954.
49. Scheidlinger, Saul. *The Concept of Group Relations in Freudian Psychoanalysis*, New York University, 1950.
50. Schick, Sarah J. *An Experimental Comparison of Two Methods of Group Psychotherapy*, New School for Social Research, 1951.
51. Seeman, Alice Zerbola. *Group Guidance: An Exploratory Study in Methods of Analysis*, Ohio State University, 1949.
52. Stock, Dorothy. *The Relation Between the Sociometric Structure of the Group and Certain Personality Characteristics of the Individual*, University of Chicago, 1952.
53. Trapp, Edward P. *Role Construct Applied to Group Analysis*, Ohio State University, 1951.
54. Wieder, Gerald. *Group Procedures Modifying Attitudes of Prejudice in the College Classroom*, New York University, 1951.
55. Zlatchin, Philip J. *The Effects of Group Therapy Upon Some Aspects of Behavior, Social Relationships, and Personal Attitudes of Adolescent Problem Boys*, New York University, 1950.

8

Conclusion

Terminating Groups

As it must be with all things, groups reach a point where they end. For continuous groups, the ending is not clearly perceived, for it may represent merely the moving out of one group of people who are immediately replaced by others. For finite groups, however, closure represents a distinctive part of the group's life. As the terminal date approaches the discussions become more superficial as the anxiety increases.

Think of the last day before graduation and the feelings discussed in this chapter may come back to you. Remember the sense of loss of close friendships, the sudden acceptance of characteristics which symbolized the group that was formerly rejected (labels, etc.), the frantic copying of addresses to insure that the bond really wasn't being broken, and the apprehension over your capacity to face the next step alone. In a very real sense groups go through a weaning process. Almost like an ill child, they may revert to infantile behavior as one way of saying they really aren't ready to go off on their own.

The leader who anticipates the sudden upsurge of anxiety and dependency will not himself become anxious. He will be able, instead, to accept these feelings as natural. Discovering that the leader remains calm helps the group achieve perspective and enables them to go on to their next level of responsibility. If in the end, members of a group can perceive what the group as a group achieved and, if they can see what they personally have gained, the value of the group as a social force will remain in their memory for future reference.

Groups can be used in at least three ways. They can serve as a way of helping a person discover how others might help him in an individual counseling situation. For the person receiving individual counseling, it can often be helpful to concurrently relate to a group. The group serves as a testing ground for ideas developed in the individual sessions. Lastly, the person who terminates individual counseling may wish to use a group as a weaning process. Having been secure in a two person setting, he now moves to a comfortable group situation before tackling the world at large.

The Training of the Effective Group Worker

One of the most serious weaknesses of a book of this type is that it must advocate the value of an experience that many have not shared. As we have seen, an intellectual acceptance of the rights of the individual is not enough. To live out one's beliefs, each person needs to have had, himself, the chance to have experienced the rewards that come from a supportive group where individual difference is truly valued.

New behaviors need to be rewarded and to be equally effective with older modes of behavior. If, then, the approach described in this text makes sense to a reader, further implementation of the approach will require more than additional reading.

For the highly motivated person there are specific kinds of preparation that will be helpful. Included are:

1. Courses covering personality theory and the dynamics of human behavior.

2. Courses covering semantics and effective verbal communication.

3. Courses providing background of an anthropological or sociological nature which will assist the reader in recognizing the meaning or symbolic significance of various roles or acts in our culture.

4. Courses training a person in specific counseling skills.

5. Courses providing supervised practicum experiences where the student is helped to discover the way in which his needs are effecting his behavior.

6. Group leadership or member experiences to sensitize the person to typical experiences in the life of a group.

Many readers would welcome the chance to secure formal training but reality factors make the possibility remote. Although pulling oneself up by one's bootstraps is difficult, there are specific criteria one can apply to oneself as a means of gaging whether growth is taking place. After each group session it would help to ask oneself the following questions:

1. How much of the time was I concerned with the content of the group's discussion rather than on the interaction taking place or needs being covertly expressed?
2. How active was I in this session? Were my contributions a reaction to group needs, or was I meeting personal needs?
3. Did I have any trouble in communicating with the group?
4. How accepting was I of the rights of each person to see things in his own way? Do I in fact accept the idea that no two people are really alike?
5. Can I really accept the fact that a group moves slowly and that it takes time to mature?
6. How able am I to stand tension in the group without getting upset?
7. How effective was I in helping the group develop leadership skills so they wouldn't need me?

Using a personal checklist can help. Having a group where others will offer their perception of your growth is even better. The really motivated lay leader will find many other people in the community eager to work with him in developing groups where human relations skills represent the purpose of the group.

Summary

This book has been focused toward helping people become more cognizant of the benefits and problems associated with the use of groups to promote affective learnings. Based upon comments of readers who reviewed this text in its early stages, it appears as if there is no easy way to label the procedures involved without violating the values of some readers. It is hoped that the major goal of utilizing understandings arising in the fields of psychotherapy, education, and social work have not created the impression that the processes being explored were suitable only for the deviant or maladjusted person. To come full circle, it is worth again repeating that it is my belief that no book can be written that will fit the personality, values, or skills of every reader. By necessity each reader should conclude this book with a long list of points of agreement and disagreement with the author. When viewed *in toto* this list represents the operating philosophy of the reader. Each person who finds himself in a leadership role must inescapably decide how he will use this role to promote values in which he believes.

Hopefully this book will have demonstrated that effective group leadership is a skill that requires training and preparation. As one reviews the many techniques employed by group leaders it is easy to conceive of the role as involving only the mastery of a series of tricks of the trade. Of greater importance is an awareness that each technique's effectiveness is dependent not only on how it was employed but also on why it was used. Inescapably each technique becomes but an extension of the needs, values, and biases of the group leader. Although all of us will find ourselves involved in groups and with leadership functions, our ultimate success as a person and as a nation, depends upon an increased awareness of the needs of all to develop group process skills.

Our current preoccupation with academic achievement and conservation of manpower has had one negative characteristic. As we become increasingly more task oriented, the value and rights of the individual are increasingly losing their force as the essential component of a democracy. Let us dedicate ourselves to the task of demonstrating to society that group techniques need not lead to mediocrity, but rather can serve as the key to unlock the potential for individual happiness and growth.

Appendix

A Diary Report of the Complete Life of a Group

One of the dangers in a chapter like Chapter 5, is that it tends to suggest a level of specificity that is not accurate. No group exactly duplicates another. The cross references in Chapter 5 will have demonstrated clearly to the reader the existence of numerous other interpretations of specific situations or definitions of group process.

This Appendix has as its goal the development in the reader of an awareness of the stages through which a group may pass as it progresses from its start to its termination. Since this Appendix provides a picture of the complete life of a group, it carries with it both the excitement found in group crises and the boredom that develops when the same ideas seem to be repeated over and over. This diary of a group should not be read as one would read a play or drama. Use the material instead as a vicarious training experience for yourself as a group leader or member. As you read, ask yourself what you think you might have done at each point. Consider the issues the group raises and reraises, and decide what themes seem to be dominant in the life of the group. If you find yourself bored or angry, ask yourself what needs of yours would help or hinder your activities in the group.

In order to provide the reader with this documentary report of a group, the author has secured permission from Mr. Joseph Srsnick to reproduce parts of the logs he wrote as a member of a group. To maintain the confidential nature of the group's discussion, the logs have been edited. The reader will find some of the comments repetitious, but they have been included to provide a more realistic picture of the way groups return to concepts or problems until they are worked through. The logs also provide a chronological picture of stages in a group's life and the speed with which this specific group

was able to move. The material also shows the integration of therapeutic techniques within structured university class requirements. It
should be remembered that these logs reflect the perceptions of only
one group member.

Log 1

Today we held our first group meeting and Dr. Lifton began by
turning on the tape and mentioning its necessity. He then briefly
talked about the course's limits. He mentioned the facts that we
would be graded and that class members would be required to take
notes, or rather, to make logs of each session.

Since G. and I were new to the group, the members introduced
themselves. This seemed necessary in order to acquaint each other
and to establish some feeling of solidarity. The introductions were
very brief and seemed to be rattled off in a business-like fashion.

. . . E. wanted the leader's opinions on the course's content and
aims. This may have expressed a need for structuring and seemed
also to demonstrate a need for dependence on the leader. E. then
wished that everyone mention their reasons for taking the course, in
the hope that we would get a better understanding of individual goals
and desires. All of this seemed like a desire to establish group unity
and seemed like an attempt to get things going.

Some members seemed to think the group was heterogeneous while
others seemed to think that each had some things in common. . . .
The group seemed heterogeneous in that the members are of different
ages, are male and female, have different positions at this time, and
have had a variety of experiences and backgrounds. It was homo-
generous in that we are all members of the course, all seemed reasonably verbal, all are relatively inexperienced in group guidance, and all
wanted to further their knowledge and skills in the area. . . .

Some member then wondered where we would go from here and
it was pointed out that we had already made some progress and were
beginning to express our views on different topics. . . .

It was mentioned that we could learn group techniques by our
personal experiences in the present group. We would be living in a
group for four hours a week and would gain a working knowledge of
the things that could happen in such an assembly.

The group came to the realization, with the leader's help, that we
had been searching for limits and for ways of feeling comfortable with
one another. . . .

We also came to the realization that communication in groups is not an easy thing to accomplish and various members felt that each member should contribute something to the group—verbally. They could not accept the fact that a member could remain silent and gain from the experience.

Some members expressed the feeling that they needed some verbal contribution from every other member in order to feel secure.

Quite a few of the members seemed to revolt against G. for his statement that he may not communicate with the other members. They seemed, however, to be unaware of G.'s feelings and did not seem to be accepting him as an individual—and to me this does not show respect for him. In fact, the group as a whole had little awareness of the feelings of others and seemed to state their own views instead. . . .

On the whole the session seemed characterized by a searching for limits, for group commonness and unity, and for defining our roles and goals. . . .

Log 2

. . . He then asked the leader's impression of the article as if in an attempt to gain approval or acceptance. . . .

. . . It was agreed that we should try to be understanding of each other and have respect for each other's judgment and opinions—even though these opinions may be counter to our own.

Several group members have reached the understanding that G. has every right to remain silent since we can learn by listening. In fact, it was realized today that we, as a group, were not listening enough to each other but were more concerned with our own thinking. The group did value the perceptions of G. and one member mentioned the fact that G.'s initial silence had aroused hostility in him. . . .

The group seemed to want an authority figure present, to which they could turn in times of confusion and stress. This may be due to the fact that the group had not become entirely secure with each other and had overlooked themselves as resource people. They did seem to eventually realize that the controls and guides would have to be group created. . . .

. . . Toward the end of the session members were beginning to reveal their true feelings, which this writer feels is essential to progress. It was brought out, however, that different people react on various levels. . . .

C., who did less talking than anyone else in the group, seemed to rationalize her silence by saying that someone had always beaten her to the draw in communicating her feelings. I kept wondering why her silence wasn't questioned as G.'s was. . . .

Log 3

. . . E. brought to the group's attention the fact that we often do not give individual members enough opportunity to disclose their feelings concerning a topic that was initiated. Instead of becoming listeners we often introject [*sic*] questions and opinions that really satisfy our own needs; discounting the needs of the person who first introduces a topic. It was realized, however, that the combined perceptions of several members add to the original perceptions or understanding of the person who initiates a question or topic. We thus give mutual help in satisfying needs and enhance the security of group members. . . .

Dr. Lifton tried to point out the responsibility of group members by directing our attention to the fact that we are free to experiment in the group if we assume the responsibility for the effect our behavior has on others. . . .

. . . When E. left the room he was missed and the group felt that they had better wait until his return for continuing the discussion. . . .

. . . At this point, too, the group realized that we support each other "when the heat is on" and have gained a sharpness of perception that lets us know when someone else is reaching his "tolerance point." The group is thus realizing the value of being your real self. When we reveal ourselves to others we allow them to get closer to us. . . .

One of the last points of discussion was the problem of limits, as these relate to confidentiality and behavior toward one another outside of our sessions. . . .

Log 4

Today's session again seemed to hedge around limits, security, understanding, acceptance, and roles. . . .

Our desire to be understood, which leads to acceptance, was illustrated in W.'s, L.'s, and F.'s efforts to explain their behavior of the previous meeting. They seemed to be saying, "I'm explaining my behavior of last week so that you will understand me. I'm not changing my mind about these issues but I want to be sure you understand me; so that you will accept me." . . .

R. seemed to gain insight into the effect emotion has on objectivity and rationality. . . .

A. seemed to be saying: "If I know what hostility means to others I will know what to expect from them, when they get hostile." This again seemed to be a reaching out for understanding. Perhaps the group was wondering how a hostile person would be evaluated. Would we lose respect for one who did reveal hostility? . . . We are looking for constructive ways in which to express negative feelings. . . .

. . . Perhaps some of his trouble centered around his statement that none of us were competent enough to go around analyzing each other. . . .

. . . Others can tell us if we are being perceived as we would like to be perceived. . . .

We also seemed to realize today that we are becoming a more closely-knit body and are beginning to act as a group and are beginning to make more concrete our group characteristics. The mere fact that we stayed on the topic that G. initiated seemed to prove that we as a group can tackle a specific problem and work for the good of an individual or individuals.

The problem of behavior outside the group was again brought up. . . .

Log 5

My feelings at present are those of rebellion. . . . The group seems to want understanding but when someone tries to explain themselves, they are cut off and diagnosed. Even though my needs weren't met I tried to meet those of others. However, there did seem to be insights gained today.

I will try to list some of the positive gains—as I see them.

1. Therapy and learning take place when we put our feelings into words.

2. W. wanted to be sure that everyone understood what the limits are; especially in regard to confidentiality.

3. We should include the group in our thinking.

4. Hostility was amply displayed. This may indicate greater security to reveal our negative feelings. This will probably lead to antagonism but I have faith it will eventually lead to understanding.

5. W. felt that Dr. Lifton should be a group member. Others couldn't or wouldn't see him as such (E.). I believe he should be perceived as a member, a clarifier, and a catylizer.

6. E. noticed we are on guard—or defensive. He verbalized that we cannot be honest if we are defensive.

7. L. wanted to know what kind of a group we were. I don't think her question was answered. We are still trying to determine this.

8. E. admitted that false interpretation can be harmful but he seemed to be interpreting or judging several group members. He doesn't practice what he preaches—as I see it.

9. E. said we should be humble and not use the group solely to satisfy our own needs. I wonder if he practiced this humility?

10. The group seemed to realize we become hostile to those we like. Hostility means that we care.

11. Someone said we should accept people for what they are—even if they are confused.

12. The group realized that we are now becoming aware of what we are doing.

Now I'll list some of my own views and feelings.

1. If we are to be given a semester grade by the others we will try to find out what *they* think a good group member is and then conform to those criteria. By so doing we may not be our real selves.

2. I don't think, at this point, that the group knows what a good member is and I wonder if we can become objective enough to grade each other fairly.

3. We do not give others a fair chance to explain their views but jump in before they are finished talking and contribute our interpretation. We read *too* far beyond a person's words because we haven't given him a fair chance to clarify his views. If we listened long enough the need for interpretation or diagnosis would disappear.

4. I sense a great deal of suspiciousness among the members. We are suspicious of what the other guy *might* be thinking of us. This can be overcome if the members gain enough security to really tell each other just how they feel.

5. When I nod my head in *understanding* I am showing respect for the individual. I am not judging but am trying to demonstrate an internal frame of reference. I am not analyzing anyone—merely trying to look at the world as they do. Others have seen this as having their minds' read. I must clarify this to them if the issue presents itself or if I see the opportunity for so doing.

6. E. has accused me of offering no suggestions in the first three meetings whereas I think I did state my beliefs, goals, etc.

7. Too often we talk for others, as if we knew exactly what they

feel. We do not know exactly how they feel since we haven't given them enough time to talk.

8. After we listen to a person carefully and see his point of view, then we can add our own perceptions. In this way we will get 10 points of view on a topic—including Dr. Lifton—if he desires to contribute. This will lead to growth—I think.

9. I sensed that the group has not as yet accepted the fact that we are self-governing and must take responsibility for most of the group's behavior, direction, limits and goals. Members too often look to Dr. Lifton for direction.

10. I sense that the group does not realize that others besides Dr. Lifton are leaders. However, members do act in this capacity without realizing it. Anyone who suggests a new topic, asks a question, summarizes, or clarifies is taking the role of the leader.

11. Therapy goes on all the time. If a member leaves with a clearer perception of his self-concept, he has grown. Therapy is learning and we are learning. If a person's thinking and/or behavior changes as a result of our sessions, then therapy has taken place.

12. Members should assume responsibility for their behavior but other members can help by verbally reacting to that behavior.

13. We are not communicating enough and certainly are not effective enough. Doubt and insecurity do not lead to group unity.

14. We must learn to listen, accept, understand, contribute our own perceptions, and work for the group's welfare. If we want our own needs satisfied, we must satisfy the needs of others.

15. If each member was listened to long enough, the group could satisfy his needs. He in turn would work with the group in meeting the needs of every other individual. The group works as a group in helping each other and in working toward goals. The members add individually to this endeavor. The members get their needs satisfied in the process.

Now I have put into symbols my feelings. Now I should be able to use problem solving techniques with them. I am not so rebellious now.

Log 6

. . . group seemed more calm. . . . I find it more helpful to list things I have experienced in myself and in the group.

1. It was a good feeling to know the group is beginning to understand me. I experienced a definite sense of greater security.

2. It was disclosed that the group had suspected some sort of conspiracy between myself and Dr. Lifton during the first three or four sessions. They felt that the leader always agreed with things I had suggested. G. felt that this might be due to envy or suspiciousness.

3. A great part of the session was devoted to understanding Dr. Lifton's role. Some members definitely seem to see him as a teacher. It was noticed that A. consistently backs down when the leader appears to talk to him. This appeared as a surrender or fear reaction on A.'s part. Others have noticed this also.

4. I think Dr. Lifton should be accepted as a group member whose responsibility consists of helping the group to understand each other and become more integrated. He consistently directs the group's attention to noticing how the group is functioning. This seems to have been very helpful.

5. The members seem to be recognizing their individuality.

6. Some members seem to want Dr. Lifton to give support, structure and guidance. They still don't seem to realize that each member becomes a leader in turn. Perhaps they don't have enough faith in their own potentialities, as yet. The trend seems to be toward unity and group thinking—but we are slow in reaching this goal.

7. We definitely seemed to miss G. when he left the room and we seem to feel incomplete without him—or any other member who might be absent. The group feels that a legitimate excuse justifies an absence but we expect the absent member to listen to the tape.

8. The group realized that the leader has information on the members that is not shared with the group. This appeared to help the group see him as a teacher. The possibility of sharing the logs with the group did not seem to win favor.

9. Once we test people we get to know them. This leads to understanding and then to increased security.

10. The group sees the logs as a method of making concrete and symbolic our feelings. The logs are also used in rehearsing our behavior for future meetings. The group seemed to realize that we could test our perceptions, that are developed in the log, in the group. The group thus becomes a source of reality testing.

11. Members also realized that in writing the logs we are forced to analyze ourselves and our motives. The logs are thus a source of self-understanding—which is part of therapy.

12. Someone mentioned the fact that we must first analyze ourselves in order to do justice in understanding others. I don't think we fully realize or accept the fact that the greatest opportunity in self-analysis lies in our inter-group relations.

13. Some members seem to be afraid of self-analysis in the group, or should I say, self-analysis through the group.

14. R. pointed out that we often disregard feelings and merely focus our attention on the content of verbal interplay. I believe that focusing on feelings is much more fruitful and productive.

15. It was mentioned that it is hard to put our feelings into verbal symbols. However, until this is done our meetings will be somewhat unproductive. The logs aid this crystalization of thinking.

16. The members are beginning to realize that the ambiguity dimension of our non-directive atmosphere is sometimes uncomfortable. As a result the members strive for support, clarification, and direction. They rationalize this by pointing out that our educational system has always leaned in the "directive" direction. They are still refusing to take full responsibility for group direction and growth.

17. Our verbal content is the vehicle through which group dynamics operate.

18. We are beginning to realize that we don't have a group until we have established some common ground. We must get something from each other.

19. We benefit from others' perceptions of our problems.

20. The group seems to be the type which still does not completely solve any presented problem because we skip around too rapidly from topic to topic. Perhaps we skip in order to look at the problem from different viewpoints and in order to crystalize our thinking.

21. It was also realized that we create limits in various areas by the total import of our actions. Some limits are unverbalized.

22. It was also pointed out that we can gain nothing from an experience unless feelings are present which are experienced and perhaps verbalized.

23. W. pointed out that we can partly determine a leader's function by observing Dr. Lifton in action. We further learn the leader's role by becoming a leader in the group.

24. Some members were afraid of criticizing the leader in the log. This seemed partly due to a fear of hurting him or in losing his acceptance.

25. The secrecy of the logs seems to inhibit Dr. Lifton. However, no one definitely suggested that this confidentiality be changed.

26. It was pointed out that we force Dr. Lifton into various roles by our needs.

27. E. seemed to think that by voicing hostility in the log toward the leader would harm the teacher-friend relationship.

28. By rereading previous logs we can determine our own growth and our movement direction.

29. Dr. Lifton pointed out that it is harmful for a leader to be considered perfect. His reflection of feeling at this point would tend to prevent a real transference relationship from developing. He shows the members that it is their perceptions of him which make him appear perfect.

30. A leader is perceived as he is, due to our needs, his needs, and the environment.

31. All of the above observations seem to verify what has been written in textbooks on group guidance or therapy.

Log 7

In my impression the group seemed to move backward today. Although we have formed some group unity we seem to have drifted apart and have become nine separate individuals. . . .

Although the group decided to admit the new member it took them two hours to arrive at such a conclusion. As F. said: "Why do we fuss so much?"

. . . different individuals have verbalized some excellent insights and suggestions that would benefit the group. The group as a whole has not picked these insights up.

1. Admitting a new member would provide an interesting experiment on the effects it has on the group's unity.

2. We are concerned about an individual's absence and feel incomplete without him. An absent individual has the responsibility to let the group know the reason for his absence.

3. Group unity is disclosed by our feeling incomplete when a member is absent.

4. Dr. Lifton was right when he said that the matter of note taking would someday be a topic of discussion. Each member wants to feel that others are listening when he is talking.

5. It was mentioned that we must allow each member to help himself. We must not make the individual feel that he is helpless.

6. Movement takes place when we reveal our ugly side as well as our pretty side. However, I do not believe that progress depends solely on revealing our hates, etc.

7. Only two people in a group can relate to each other at one time. The others are involved in the meantime.

8. Verbal participation isn't mandatory as an indication of involvement. A listener has value.

9. The whole is greater than the sum of its parts. Nine cumulative perceptions gives everyone in the group a much clearer picture of a topic or problem.

10. If another member doesn't understand me or would like to know something about me, he must ask me to disclose myself.

11. I think our needs sometime blind us. As a result we hear what we want to hear when someone else is talking. We aren't really listening but are projecting our own needs into his talk and interpret.

12. The group members still seem to be analyzing and diagnosing each other.

13. Several members feel the group discussions have some therapeutic aspects.

14. Extraneous talk isn't appropriate to the group discussions; unless everyone agrees to talk on a topic.

15. When we ask someone a direct question and desire an immediate reply, we often confuse him and put that person on the defensive. Communication should be free, spontaneous and willing.

16. The total import of our actions telegraphs our feelings to others, without the necessity of verbalization—sometimes.

17. We aren't able to speak until we feel secure and have formulated our thinking. If we are too emotional we get confused.

18. Listening to group discussions stimulates our thinking and can lead to the solution of problems.

19. Some members feel that we still aren't our real selves in the group but have become an aggregate of intellectualizers.

20. L. pointed out that it might be profitable if we related in the friendly, informal manner that we use in our gatherings outside of the group. No one seemed to appreciate her efforts.

21. In a group setting it is easier to retreat in the face of threat or anxiety. This is harder to accomplish in a smaller group and so we are forced to be more sincere or revealing.

22. The matter of whether we should satisfy our own or other's needs was brought up and didn't seem to be solved. The group can help, understand, support, or assist each member in turn. That member who is being helped then willingly helps another member, in turn. The group meets the needs of the person talking. He then is stimulated to help the group meet the needs of the person who talks next.

23. We can meet our needs through others and then help them meet theirs.

24. We still seem to have a communication problem, perhaps because we focus too much on content and not enough on feeling and understanding.

25. Several members felt that the group might be temporarily slowed down upon the arrival of the new member, since it would take a while to get to know him and work out a secure, comfortable relationship with him.

Log 8

. . . No one seemed to mind the fact that the proposed new member decided not to join our group. This may be one small indication of unity. . . .

. . . This is another sign of unity. Dr. Lifton summarized and clarified the issue by saying that since we are secure we don't mind being divergent. . . .

The mechanism of displacement seems to have taken place between E. and myself. We were reacting to one another the way we would ordinarily act toward someone else. Our perceptions were thus distorted by our mental set. We saw and heard only what we wanted to hear. . . .

E. picked up the feeling which I have noticed in the last three or four sessions. It seems that the members (some of the members) have been competing with each other for some sort of recognition or status; although the purpose of this competition doesn't seem to be clear. I'm wondering whether this is good for the group or whether it is harmful. It doesn't seem to make for unity but for suspiciousness. . . .

. . . Sometimes I feel that the group is making wonderful progress and at other times I feel discouraged. I expect to be misunderstood sometimes and I guess I must try even harder to make my views much more clear.

The following is a list of some of the things I've noticed happening.

1. The group seems to realize that the majority has responsibility to and should listen to the minority. The minority also has responsibility to the majority. In other words, the group's knowledges, insights, and goal-directed behavior is improved and strengthened when everyone contributes and is concerned about everyone else's welfare.

2. W. seems to have faith in the group's capabilities to handle new problems. Other members do not hold this view. I have a great deal

of faith in the group's abilities. If we as a group develop the attitude that we are helpless—we will become helpless. Our mental set determines our thinking and behavior.

3. The group seems to be recognizing the fact that we are individualistic and are beginning to assert this uniqueness. I believe that this does not have to lead to disunity but could contribute to gains and unity. When we become secure and trusting enough to reveal our individuality, we can attack any problem more effectively because each of us will feel free to add our own perceptions to the solution of a problem.

4. The group seems to realize the importance of every member and is anxious to hear his views and opinions.

5. E. especially felt that values and attitudes could be transmitted during the meetings. I agree.

6. Our behavior reveals implicit agreement upon certain values or modes of behavior.

7. We must accept the person for his own personal worth but may disagree with what he says or thinks.

8. R. felt that first impressions aren't necessarily real. We grow to understand a person by listening to him. This is in disagreement with F.'s statement a week ago when she said that we cannot change our original impression of people.

9. B. wanted to know (sincerely) how we can get to know someone. The group sort of told him that we get to know another by employing a two-way process using the internal frame of reference. We get to know someone to the degree that we allow ourselves to look at the world as he looks at it, and we do this by listening.

10. It was noticed that by directing questions and other very direct measures against someone puts him on the defensive. A member will talk only when he feels secure and is not being pressured.

11. Silence has varied meanings to the people who are reacting to someone else's silence. Some of the members wondered how they could meet their own needs when reacting to a silent person; while at the same time respecting his right to be silent. Even though the group seems to have allowed various members to remain silent, we feel more comfortable and gain more clarity in our thinking when these people do speak.

12. We are trying harder to meet each other's needs—this may slow down decision making temporarily. It is a sign of progress in my mind.

13. The group's value system is composed of portions of the value systems of the members. We seem to surrender a little bit of our

values or needs in order to be accepted by the group—or to conform to the group. This in turn enables the group to support us and believe in us.

14. To the degree that another member seems strange, his behavior may appear hostile to us. We see only what we want to see.

15. The meaning of an action or verbalization is the thing that counts.

16. We must take greater pains to express our views and to understand those of others. Only when our own needs are understood and accepted can we more clearly see other people and their needs. We understand others to the degree that we understand ourselves.

Log 9

Meeting eight seemed to start the ball rolling in a productive direction. . . .

Following are things I have witnessed:

1. Each member seems to favor a certain role in the group. We seem to have realized, however, that each member can and should function in several different roles. We seek the most comfortable role.

2. In the "outside world" we act the roles of student, parents, wife, husband, citizen and other social roles. In the group we are not bound by such hard and fast relationships. We don't have to act in any certain way. We can be our real selves here, gain insight into our self-concept, and realize how others see us.

3. Using F. as a guinea pig we discovered that we sometimes focus only on a member's negative aspects and disregard focusing our attention on his finer qualities. We thus discovered one of the group's patterns of behavior to each other.

4. It's hard to live up to the expectations of others. We can't please all people. We sometimes set up expectations of others which may be unfair and unrealistic.

5. We should not pressure any member to speak but should allow for spontaneous verbalization. The more we pressure, question and probe an individual, the more defensive and anxious he may become. By creating a secure, non-critical atmosphere we encourage all members to participate. Respect for others leads to feelings of security.

6. Actions speak louder than words. Our actions may deliver an impression which may not coincide with our spoken words. We are thus focusing our attention on our actions as well as our verbalizations

and are able to detect any ambivalence here. We are thus learning about ourselves.

7. Our perceptions, even though unrealistic, will determine how we act, how we use the group, and how we are perceived by others as a result.

8. A person can be an active participant by listening. Many of our questions get answered by listening.

9. Even though we respect the right of a member to be silent, we cannot be positive that he is listening and gaining. We want others to tell us whether or not they are profiting from the group experience.

10. We satisfy the silent person's need to remain silent. In all fairness then, he should help others satisfy their needs—when their needs call for him to verbalize now and then. It's a give-and-take proposition between all members.

11. The way the group as a whole treat or react to a particular member will cause him to develop certain self-concepts and ideas concerning interpersonal relationships.

12. When the group expects too much of a particular member it causes that person to feel inadequate and misunderstood. We can become more realistic by allowing each member to reveal himself more fully. This can do away with misperceptions to a large extent.

13. We are all teachers in the group. We teach ourselves and others certain things. This might be a definition of therapy—therapy is a learning process.

14. Our ideas should be tested out in the group—a form of reality testing. This technique will prove whether or not our ideas are logical and sensible. The group represents a unique situation in reality testing.

15. We can crystallize our thinking better by verbalizing. When we put our thoughts into words we attempt to be logical. By verbalizing, we can determine any illogic, unreality, or conflict. We must, therefore, give each member a chance to think out loud—by listening to him.

16. Using F. as an example: she seemed to gain a great deal of security and calmness when her feelings were verbalized. The group definitely seemed to understand her better.

17. E., my former antagonist, shook my hand and told me I was conscientious. This made me very happy for I've been trying to get close to E. as a person of real value.

18. If the group as a whole doesn't know what it wants, it may gain more concrete goals as it proceeds. Our behavior, however, seems to

be goal oriented—if even at an unverbal level. All behavior is motivated.

19. The group seems to get what they want from a member. They seemed to want F. to give a talk and appeared content when she did.

20. Group pressure leads to conformity. Since we want to be accepted by the group we conform to the group's standards—at least partially. We do not necessarily have to lose our individuality by so doing.

21. We must assimilate our knowledges to the group's benefit. Each of us add our perceptions to a topic under discussion.

22. Learning results in change of behavior. We internalize our learnings.

23. R. pointed out that we can learn to accept a person for what he is and still disagree with what he says. This attitude can lead to greater understanding. What we learn in the group we carry to other situations.

24. It is hard sometimes, to put our beliefs into action.

25. I realized why the group initially disliked my reflecting and clarifying behavior. Since they did not know my motives they mistrusted me. Now the group seems to realize that more of us should act as reflectors, summarizors, and clarifiers—provided we make known our intentions.

26. Dr. Lifton noticed that some members speak for others—without really knowing how others feel. This is not showing respect for others.

27. We can be too blunt and frank. Perhaps we should be more gentle when we speak our mind. This was the reaction between E. and L.

28. The way we behave determines to a large extent how we are perceived. If we want to be perceived in a certain way, we must make our behavior conform to that picture. The group—through its reality testing ability—can tell us if we are conforming to the picture we would like others to form of us.

29. We must ask for help. If it is given without being wanted, it may be seen as hostile behavior. We must not make a member feel inferior when we offer help.

30. Dr. Lifton tried to show the group he was human when he said that he would appreciate help from the group—help in satisfying his own needs. I feel this was a wise, and humble, and sincere move on his part.

31. A silent person pays the price of being misunderstood. Verbalization seems necessary—to some degree.

32. If we are blunt in the group we may develop an accurate assessment of our actions. In other words, we should be our real selves and reveal more of our true feelings. Only when the other members realize the depth of our feelings can they understand and help us.

Log 10

This meeting continued to implement the gains that were made in the last two sessions. . . .

1. The matter of being more informal in the group was brought up and discussed. It was believed by some that this approach enables us to get to know each other better and seems to be a more comfortable method of procedure. It was pointed out that often our discussions have been intellectual, without too much regard for feeling. Other members felt that we desire something more from the group than merely informal chatting. Perhaps this informal behavior could be used initially to establish that secure atmosphere which would enable us to become more "group guidance" oriented. This seemed to be a striving for a mode of operation or a method of interpersonal relationship.

2. Although W. brought up the topic of "grading" he did not seem to feel that it was a need of his own but stated it was an attempt to present the group with a possible topic for discussion. It was realized that this issue had not been settled and was not settled today. The group seemed to realize that the responsibility is ours. It was felt that lack of decision may influence group behavior. I personally feel that the group has not yet agreed upon a method of evaluation and will arrive at one as time progresses.

3. I personally feel that the group goes about solving problems in a more objective, realistic, group method at this time which is a definite advancement over earlier sessions. We seem to allow more members to present their views while the others listen and evaluate.

4. The group was again concerned about G.'s silence and seemed to be able to pinpoint the cause of their behavior. Because G. once said that he is usually a talkative person, his silence then became object of suspicion. He has, however, clarified his point of view many times and is determined to retain his basic views. He does, however, seem to be aware of the needs of others but will not change his basic beliefs in order to conform, which seems logical. We retain our basic beliefs but conform a little to the group in order to win their approval and support. They help me solve my problems; therefore, I must help them meet their needs.

5. W. expressed a concern with the effects his behavior has on others. I think the group does let us know how our behavior affects them.

6. F. was concerned over the silence of those people who are ordinarily talkative. When members suddenly change their behavior they make us feel uneasy. Perhaps this is due to the fact that we feel more secure when we can predict, to some degree, the behavior of others. E. remained silent because he felt that his efforts in the past were not effective. Learning leads to change of behavior.

7. E.'s feeling that the group atmosphere is still strained and strange led to group investigation into the causes of this tension.

8. The group then discussed the nature and depth of personal revelation to others.

9. There are different basis for judging others. We can judge others by ourselves or by the way they perceive us.

10. If others tell me how I am seen in their eyes, I will know how I am being perceived and will be able to determine if this is the impression I want communicated. It was pointed out that this can be threatening.

11. Some people felt it may not be comfortable to be understood. I feel that a lot depends upon the person we reveal ourselves to. If the person I talk to is understanding, accepting, and non-critical, then I will have less fear of revealing myself for I will feel that he will accept me at any cost. This is the essence of client-centered therapy. However, all people will not be this accepting and understanding, probably.

12. Our false front is part of us. Our feelings, however, are not as easily covered up and become noticeable. They become a doorway to the real self.

13. I believe others become closer to us to the degree that we reveal our true feelings.

14. At various times the members expressed a desire to learn what others thought of them. The group thus seems to be moving in the direction of unity through intimacy—or revelation.

15. Some members today felt that the group as a whole has given only criticism and rejection. They have not given enough support and understanding.

16. The group also realized that we do come to the aid of a person who is being prodded and pressured. We help those who are experiencing anxiety.

17. Sometimes, when we ask a member for help, he may not be

able to give it at that moment. Therefore, we must accept his lack of assistance.

18. We yield to the needs of others somewhat in order to satisfy our own needs. In some degree we conform to group policies in order to be accepted.

19. Others' perceptions of me will determine how they will act toward me.

20. We can become able to describe our conscious self-image to others. Their perceptions of me can be a form of reality testing in that they will let me know if I am presenting the picture of myself to others that I want to present. What we think we are and what others think we are may be two different stories. Their perceptions will at least stimulate our thinking.

21. The group seemed to realize that individual members play many roles during our group sessions—although some people tend to prefer a certain role over others.

22. The group seemed to realize that we often force G. into his silent role—as a means of warding off our criticisms.

23. Our forcing people to talk often leads to defensive, silent behavior.

24. It is possible to reject a person's behavior or beliefs while still respecting him.

25. We are always being judged by others, so why not have them put their thoughts into words.

26. We give up something of ourselves to the group and are responsible for our actions.

27. E. felt that we must establish common goals. He also felt that we are competing for acceptance.

28. In order to be understood we must state specifically what we want, and not beat around the bush.

29. Some members still did not want to accept the role of the leader although each of us has assumed the leader role at some time.

30. We have faced uncomfortable issues today and have been fighting for unity. We are often impatient sometimes and expect results to occur rapidly.

31. Although we initially said that we didn't want to be analyzed or reveal our true selves, we seem to be moving in that direction gradually and consistently—as our security spreads.

32. The group also seemed to be demanding that W. realize and admit hostile feelings. Perhaps they did not want to believe that he is a perfect person without fault. In other words, if he is human, he must get mad; when he gets mad he should admit it. He should gain

an understanding of his real self. So we are, in a sense, forcing people to realize their true selves. I should say, we are forcing people to realize "more" of their true selves. We seem to be moving in that direction.

Log 11

. . . we have developed a more objective method of looking at ourselves and the things we do, as well as in realizing that we do have techniques for handling problems. . . .

1. Because E. felt that we lack free expression and a friendly atmosphere, he suggested breaking down into small groups to attain such an atmosphere and as a means of finding common topics to bring to the group as a whole. Others in the group reacted and added to his idea but seemed to feel that we should attack this problem as a group since it does concern all of us. He felt that we might be able to establish the proper rapport in the smaller groups during the first hour and then carry over this attitude to the group as a whole. This writer pointed out that we usually do get the ball rolling by the second hour and are well on our way in the solution of a common problem. The rapport, which might be gained during the first hour in the smaller groups, is usually established anyway in the large group by the time of the second hour. There would thus seem to be little gain by such a procedure—unless it would be used merely as an experimental device. There would be no guarantee of common problems at the close of the small group sessions.

2. E. pointed out that there seem to be two types of groups: one which has established definite goals and others that are attempting to determine goals. We still seem to fit into the latter category since we haven't verbally agreed upon a goal. Our behavior and attitudes, however, do seem to indicate that we are moving in a direction but this direction may not be realized or agreed upon. I believe that we will become aware of these goals as time progresses.

3. It would be unfortunate if we had to become smaller (in group size) in order to accomplish those things that should be handled as a group. Problems concerning group relationships and ways of relating should be handled as a group.

4. We still feel a necessity to let our hair down more and become personal.

5. R. felt that we still don't recognize that someone has a problem and wants help. Others feel that we still don't give each other enough opportunity to speak.

6. L. suggested we come to the group meetings with some problem we wish to have discussed. I agree that this procedure would keep the process continuing and would allow each other to know what our concerns are.

7. It was realized that someone must assume the leadership role. Some members felt that there should be more people acting in the leadership capacity. E., B. and Dr. Lifton seem to have played this role—or were allowed to play this role. The group seems to permit only certain individuals to assume the leadership role. We have practically agreed upon the qualities of a leader—at least in our behavior.

8. It was mentioned, that in listening to the tapes, we iron out things and keep the ball rolling. As was mentioned, however, we are able to become more objective concerning ourselves when we are listening to things that have already happened. While we are experiencing group interaction, it is more difficult to become objective.

9. Dr. Lifton's device of having everyone relate what he thought had happened during the first hour was a splendid technique to get the group to take a look at the things that happened. This technique is a means of obtaining objectivity, and should be developed.

10. When each member did relate his perceptions relating to the happenings of the first hour, it was realized that we each see a problem from a different standpoint. I think this is valuable for it allows us to obtain many different views of and solutions for various problems. We do seem to reach a degree of group understanding concerning various problems, which is gained after each member is allowed to wrestle with the problem and state it in his own words.

11. We noticed that certain problems keep recurring from session to session. This may indicate that problems cannot be solved immediately but require more time. I feel that understandings and insights are gained during the period of time between meetings as well as during meetings. In other words, the processes that are initiated during the meeting are carried over into daily life and aid us in the solution of our various problems. This, I firmly believe, is one of the chief values of group work.

12. We still seem to cut a person off before he has had a chance to present his views and reach a comfortable solution to an issue. We still have to learn to listen more and try to understand the other fellow's point of view. Until we understand him, we cannot meet his needs fully.

13. Problems mean different things to different people. This leads to the handling of a topic from our own point of view.

14. Some members feel that we need support when presenting a need to the group. Unless we feel that others understand and want to help us, we will probably refrain from talking.

15. We should find out what a particular topic means to each of us. We do not have to view a problem in the same way but should allow each to solve a problem in his own way. We may disagree with a person's point of view, but we should still respect him as a person.

16. There are many different methods of accomplishing a goal or in solving a problem. We are looking for a comfortable, effective method which is acceptable to the group.

17. E. felt that a learning situation must be logical. To obtain knowledge we can point out discrepancies and illogical thinking in the thinking of others, add our own perceptions, and eventually reach a solution. It is a matter of group attack on a certain problem and is a give-and-take method which necessitates some degree of objectivity.

18. It is possible to make contributions without necessarily surrendering our beliefs or points of view.

19. We seem to be looking for a common process to meet our individual needs while at the same time meeting the needs of others.

20. We are also looking for more gentle or diplomatic ways of disagreeing with someone.

21. E.'s desire for small groups has already been realized and could continue to be developed, for we do meet in small groups when we listen to the tape. While listening to the tape we do talk over common points of view more openly and aggressively. All we need do is to communicate to the group, some of the things we have picked up or agreed upon.

22. By looking back over the things we have previously done in a given session, we can find out where we are and what we are. We can then accept ourselves or take steps to change things.

23. B. and I feel that we do have a process of handling problems.

24. We are seeking a comfortable mode of operation.

25. Some members felt that we as a group should experiment with other techniques and thus develop a larger repertoire of methods.

26. It takes a long time, sometimes, to put over a point.

27. We still don't say everything we feel and we should.

28. We are searching for ways of meeting our own needs as we help others meet theirs.

29. Aggression can be more effectively handled in a large group since we come to the aid of each other.

30. If I have a technique that I want the group to use, I must show them their needs can be met while employing it. We thus have to sell

our ideas by making them clear and by pointing out their usefulness.

31. We can't evaluate a situation that seems limitless—as the small group idea. A situation without limits makes us feel anxious.

32. We are still looking for more effective ways of relating what we feel so that this might lead to unity.

33. Support may not be felt as support by the one receiving it.

34. A focus on the content of our verbalizations often leads to irrelevant talk. We must look more closely at the emotional or feeling aspects of our behavior and that of others.

35. We are still afraid that if people don't accept our ideas, they will not accept us. We are thus afraid that if we speak our mind we will not be understood and might be rejected.

36. Greater security can result if we know more clearly what is to be asked of us.

37. Preconceived expectations (set) influence our perceptions and behavior.

38. Although many varied definitions were given of therapy, we seemed to agree that it is partly the experiencing of new behavior in a secure situation.

39. Our members are anti-intellectual when we try to force our ideas upon others.

40. We must operate as a large group because we would otherwise have to relieve the experiences of the small groups in order to gain understanding.

41. We understand a problem which is before the group when we are able to put it into our own words.

42. We still seem to be competing for certain roles.

43. Means of achieving better communication still need to be worked on.

Log 12

. . . Today we accomplished in 25 minutes what it took us an hour to accomplish previously. . . .

1. Methods of handling hostility was brought up again. It seems that we are still searching for more effective means of controlling this type of reaction. As we gain in security we become more able to deal with this issue objectively.

2. Dr. Lifton gave some of the perceptions he gained from his readings in an effort to aid group progress.

3. C. mentioned reading in families, which seemed to lead the group into a consideration of the values that might be gained by having each of us bring portions of plays or selections from books to the group. This seemed to be a method of relating to the group our personal interests, attitudes and beliefs. It would be an attempt to get to know one another better—a vehicle for greater understanding. Other members seemed to imply that we might, gain this understanding by being more frank and sincere in the group—without having to use printed material to put over these points.

4. The group seemed more "ready" to accept such techniques to implement our needs and to further our growth. We thus seem verbally ready for experimentation. W. also seemed concerned about our apparent rejection of E.'s ideas of last week. Some of us are thus apparently developing more concern about other's feelings.

5. E. suggested that we look at ourselves in an attempt to determine causes of group disunity and strangeness. Although looking at ourselves realistically may be painful we would grow and gain understanding by facing such unpleasant issues. We thus seem to be getting more daring, which is probably the result of our increased feelings of security.

6. We also seem to be realizing that strength lies within the group. The group members have much potential for further growth.

7. Some members seemed to wonder whether or not we could state our philosophies and ideas after using outside writings as a vehicle. I feel that we could profit from such a technique.

8. E. tried to test out the limits of his frankness. He tried to determine how far the group would let him go by using what he called "brutal" methods. He admitted that such techniques do not make for getting ideas accepted. He said further that we cannot and should not try to cram our ideas down another person's throat.

9. It was mentioned that we too often attack another's point of view instead of looking at the possible value in the suggestions of others. To me this seemed like a statement of real gain and insight.

10. A. mentioned the fact that he felt we had built up walls between us that make gaining understanding difficult. He felt that we have been and should try harder to find ways of going around the wall. I feel that we should find out why the wall is there in the first place and tear it down.

11. L. pointed out that people often are prevented from arguing intelligently because aroused emotions interfere with logic and objectivity. She felt, and this writer supported the idea, that we could use

our group in the developing of more calm techniques of arguing. Since our group is somewhat experimental we could work out methods of conducting an intelligent, objective argument or discussion.

12. G. and I felt that a person's ideas are part of his personality. I wonder if we can really reject a person's ideas and still accept him, if we believe that his ideas are really a part of him. The validity of our ideas can be tested in the group and in the process we can learn from others. We built up our concepts concerning a topic from the concerted efforts of all group members.

13. E. felt that our personal felt inadequacies, our fear of rejection and evaluation, our discomfort with authority figures, and our ego-centered participation techniques are roadblocks to group progress. I feel that his efforts at understanding are to be praised and I feel that he has added something of value to the group.

14. We have tools among ourselves, which consist of the learnings, experiences, and ideas of the individual member.

15. Even though we are becoming more integrated we still don't give the individual member a fair chance to explain his views but immediately attack and criticize his efforts at being understood.

16. We seem to suppress the possible value of the other fellow's contribution.

17. Sometimes constructive criticism can be felt as rejection—which is threatening and anxiety provoking.

18. Repeated attacks on a person's attempting at explaining himself will lead to a stifling of verbalizing. A person does, however, owe it to the group to explain his ideas and to point out to others the value of them. If he can convince or "show" the others that their needs can be met by employing his techniques—they will probably be accepted.

19. This writer suggested that we consider the feasibility and usefulness of an idea without necessarily attaching these ideas to a person; although, the person should be rewarded for contributing something positive to the group.

20. Our perceptions of a topic add to the knowledge of the subject.

21. We should not be afraid to relate our perceptions and should be courageous enough to reveal our disagreement or misunderstanding of someone else's point of view. If we do not say that we disagree with an idea our silence may be interpreted as consent.

22. It was noticed that not all members become involved in a topic under discussion. In those instances we allow the other members to work things out for themselves.

23. We react dually to a presented topic by trying to understand its author's point of view and by reacting to the idea as such.

24. Our perceptions change from session to session, which reveals growth.

25. We aren't what we want to be but are moving toward the goals of understanding, acceptance, and sincerity.

26. We are making progress but are still too impatient. Growth takes time.

27. We are still searching for a comfortable level of communication and seem to be finding it.

28. The group members do not seem to be as afraid of Dr. Lifton as they were initially. They are beginning to assume the leadership role that Dr. Lifton tried to give them.

29. We can wrongly assume that ideas are becoming realistic to others when it is only my own perceptions that are becoming clarified.

30. We should expect everyone to see things my way but should respect the individuality of the other person.

31. A person can view a topic from several angles and doesn't have to be fully for or against it.

32. Perhaps we confuse the word "reaction" to an idea with "rejection" of it. Thus part of our problem is a semantic one.

33. At times we may not want the advice of others and openly reject it, even though we may realize it has value. We thus seem reluctant to admit that the other person may be correct in his assumptions, beliefs, or ideas.

34. We are searching for methods of rejecting the advice of others without hurting the feelings of the giver. We seem to have a need to give aid but must be more diplomatic about it.

35. We seem to be changing, are becoming more able to accept earlier ideas.

36. There is still some hesitancy to look at ourselves honestly, partly because this is a threatening experience.

37. We are reluctant to admit weaknesses in ourselves, even though this is a first step in their correction.

38. We must feel the support of others in order to gain that courage needed to try out new modes of behavior.

39. We must explain an idea more fully so that it can be understood and possibly be accepted. We must allow each other to explain things more completely. Only by listening to the other fellow can we gain a knowledge of the way he looks at the world.

40. If a member rejects someone else's idea, he should at least have one to take its place. It is thus futile to tear apart an idea without first considering its possible merits and offer remedies to it.

41. This writer is realizing more fully that Dr. Lifton is a group member with rights and privileges of his own.

42. I am happy with my own insights and with the progress of the group. They are continually verifying the faith I have in them.

Log 13

. . . I related quite a bit of the feelings I experienced while working with my groups. The discussion of group therapy seemed to give F. the courage to lay before us a problem of serious concern to her. . . .

. . . The group was calm and listening most of the time while F. spoke. We pointed out the illogicality in her thinking, showed her that the problem lies within herself, and gave her support and suggestions as to how we looked at various issues. She definitely seemed to benefit from the hour. The group has thus jumped into psychotherapy completely—perhaps without fully realizing it. The experience to me was a success and may lead to similar behavior in the future. On the other hand, some members may feel threatened by it initially.

Log 14

Today's clam chowder meal definitely seems to have brought us closer together on a friendly basis. . . .

The remainder of the session was used in an effort to help C. solve a problem she was faced with. . . . It was noticed that when we are faced with a decision we often include far too many irrelevant details for consideration. . . .

We used C. as a means and an end, for by helping her we were bringing some of our own problems into the picture. . . .

Log 15

Today was the first time that W. and B. came in late. This seemed to lead the remainder of the group to spend their time in "small talk." This small talk did have some value in that topics of concern were talked about. . . .

C. seemed more comfortable with the problem she presented last time. . . .

. . . I think both C. and R. realized, and showed the group, that there are many ways of looking at any situation and our perceptions change and become more realistic when we do more exploring or searching for answers.

The atmosphere of the group today—as a whole—was a calm, friendly one. However, this writer, who was pressed with several vital decisions in his life, felt anxious, confused and hostile. The group gave me support and provided information in an attempt to help me reach a decision. I felt a terrific sense of relief after getting my problem off my chest and presenting it to the group. I realize fully the value of sharing a problem with a group like ours. When I felt that others were on my side my problem didn't seem so large and I was actually able to look at it more logically. . . .

. . . B. told us a few of the things he had heard at a recent conference. Until he had organized the material in his mind, he was not ready to discuss it with us. This may be an expression of our desire to be logical in our thinking and talking. . . .

Log 16

. . . We definitely seemed to miss G.; especially when we discussed the topic of needs. . . .

. . . the topics, statements, and insights were so numerous that I am forced to list them in order to keep them clear.

1. It may be profitable to seek synonyms to words that are unclear.

2. Many of the words we use are ambiguous: such as need *vs.* drive.

3. A drive is the resultant reaction to a felt need. Some needs may be unconscious.

4. When we present a topic to the group, which really represents a need, we should try to state exactly what we mean or want.

5. Drive and needs are interdependent.

6. We can meet some of our own needs by helping others to meet theirs. The act of giving help is therapeutic and may meet our need of feeling important and charitable.

7. Because our needs, which are a part of us, are interdependent, we as a group are interdependent.

8. We may be able to find a mutual way of satisfying our needs.

9. We are able to meet a person's expressed needs in various ways —not necessarily in the specific manner he desires. This seems similar to sublimation or substitution.

10. There is a hierarchy of needs which is different in everyone. Some needs are definitely more important than others.

11. In defining needs we may have a small number that are so general that almost any feeling could be categorized in them. On the other hand, our list could become long if we became very specific in our definitions.

12. We may expect our personal needs to be met in quite specific ways only if this does not deprive others of their needs. This seems to be a reaction against immature, ego-centric behavior.

13. We have primary needs (inborn, biological, universal) and secondary needs (learned, social, develop from primary needs).

14. Perhaps in our search for a precise definition of need we are searching for purification where it isn't possible, because human nature is too complex and our verbal symbols are too inadequate.

15. Some of our needs appear contradictory. Example: we may fluctuate between strivings for dependency and independency—one of which may be largely unconscious.

16. Unexpressed needs may differ widely from expressed ones.

17. Perhaps we should decide which need is the most important to our happiness and survival and concentrate on its satisfaction. This again seems to indicate a way of acting mature and of doing without immediate satisfactions in some areas in order to gain greater satisfaction at some distant time.

18. The group realized at this point that our discussion had broadened considerably from the initial topic. In reality, needs are complicated.

19. We should become more intent on recognizing our own feelings as they occur and the needs of others in order to function effectively as a group.

20. We felt that a communication problem still exists, even though strides have been made.

21. Perhaps we still haven't reached a compromise between satisfying our needs and those of others.

22. We seemed to realize that an issue is not dropped until everyone has reached an understanding of it, or until all are satiated.

23. Some members felt that group silence may be a sign of defense and insecurity and not merely contemplation.

24. We seemed to come to the realization that one of our unspoken laws consists in not speaking of an absent member unless he has the chance to listen to the recording of the session. (Respect for the individual.)

25. We were concerned with methods of helping an absent member.

26. Our limits on the matter of confidentiality still are unsettled.

27. If we feel that growth has taken place in the group, we must

clarify this to others. Unless we pinpoint our areas of advancement, they may be overlooked.

28. We must define to others what we see and feel.

29. A. felt that we have developed more affection for each other and have begun to look at Walt (Note: no longer referred to as Dr. Lifton) not as an authority figure. We have thus developed some measure of security, closeness, interdependence and unity.

30. We still have to form a yardstick to measure ourselves and others.

31. L. felt we have become like a family.

32. Serving coffee seemed to direct our verbalization toward conversation.

33. C. gave a progress report on conditions in her dormitory. She related that the minority group has become more integrated with the rest of the girls and have gained insight into the effects of their behavior.

34. The group's yardstick should include common perceptions.

35. Common perceptions are involved in group relationships.

36. We evaluate others in terms of what we expect from them. Therefore, we should let them know what we expect. They will thus be more able to meet our needs.

37. We must become familiar with the yardsticks of others.

38. These yardsticks are not necessarily related to grading in the course.

39. Before we like anyone else we must first be able to like ourselves.

40. Progress will probably result when we consider the perceptions of others as well as our own.

41. Our varied yardsticks cause communication problems.

42. Although some members felt we have talked in circles, others have felt that we have progressed and that we have commonalities.

43. The suggestion came up again that we must share with others our ideas on how we feel the group has progressed.

44. E. was not sure that we have grown as a group. He admitted being impatient with us and felt that our silences were a forced phenomena. He felt that we haven't been willing to look at things. I feel that E. is a man of action who prefers to get down to business. However, F. and L. told us to get down to business during the second meeting.

45. A. gave E. help by showing him that he might be too impatient.

. . . We are getting to the point where we want to solve our problems and not put them off. . . .

Log 17

Today's meeting got under way more rapidly than ever. . . .

1. Some members feel that we have become more affectionate toward one another while others feel that we are not as close as is believed. Perhaps our definitions of "closeness" differ.

2. We often hurt the ones we love but not with malice or forethought. Because we "love" someone we become interested in them and try to help them. When their behavior indicates unhappiness we become very active in our efforts at being realistic, in wanting them to achieve, and be "the best." We can become more blunt with them and often go to extremes to be kind. We are thus in a conflict state in that we try to be kind but our impatience leads us into behavior which could hurt them. A person can move forward (mature and gain insight) in personality development only at a pace in which he is comfortable.

3. Striving for 100% agreement on each topic presented to the group can hinder group progress because all members do not become equally involved in every issue.

4. We seem to want frankness. We want members to be their real selves and not wear false faces.

5. As this writer lists the events, ideas, and insights as they are presented, one gets a feeling of confusion. Many ideas are put forth but we are still working to achieve an overall integration and understanding. All the ideas seem interrelated in that they are expressions of felt needs or are suggestions toward improvement. I think we will eventually reach a stage where we will realize that this integration and harmony and understanding are realized by all.

6. We should display the standards and expectancies that we have in regard to ourselves and toward others. When others begin to understand how we think, our ability to communicate should be improved. By putting our ideals and expectancies into words they become more crystalized and thus more capable of being understood.

7. Our inability to keep our attention focused on a specific topic may be due to the fact that our needs are interrelated. A clear understanding of one issue can be attained more perfectly only when we understand the branches of this issue and its effect on others. In other words, behavior is multiple determined and can be more fully understood when viewed in totality. This is probably related to the learning principle called generalization.

8. When we put a label (a word) on a feeling or insight our thinking becomes clarified because we can handle a symbol but cannot handle feelings as easily. In our attempts to be logical our thoughts become crystalized and organized—progress then can result.

9. This writer agrees with A. in his opinion that we could almost write a textbook on our experiences. Because we have experienced so many things, their import is considerably strengthened and clarified. Our experience is more valuable than merely reading about groups in action.

10. We should be more willing to state our minds without fearing that others will be hurt in the process. Talking can lead to understanding.

11. E. feels that W. is the only one that uses an internal frame of reference in trying to understand someone. Here he is judging us without actually being aware of our own techniques. It becomes our duty, therefore, to clarify our own principles and methods to avoid being misinterpreted.

12. E. wants others to help him look at those things in himself that are not admissible to consciousness but which may be noticeable in behavior. Others thus become a means through which we can achieve greater self-knowledge. Others help us to develop a more accurate picture of our "self." Sometimes we can criticize or evaluate others but be unable to withstand a reciprocal type of behavior. This may also work the opposite way.

13. We may allow an individual member to manipulate the group by inhibiting in ourselves that behavior which he is opposed to.

14. In a sense we cannot help changing or growing because our own thinking becomes more mature, broadened, and integrated as we evaluate and consider the opinions of others. Others serve as a means through which one may gain many perceptions of a topic or problem. Others may help us fill in the gaps in our thinking and develop a broader understanding of ourselves or of an issue that is before us.

15. Perhaps too many members in our group are intent on winning others over to our way of thinking. We must respect the rights of others and not try to prove that our way of thinking or doing things is better than theirs. From the combined thinking of 10 people, we can develop better and more complete ways of looking at life and its problems.

16. We may get 100% seeming agreement on an issue due to the fact that some members may surrender their own points of view and become submissive to the wills of others. We should retain our own

individuality, develop it even further, and think collectively not competitively.

17. F. thinks that there are two major types of people in our group —those who are therapists and those who are clients. She further feels that those who do most of the talking may have revealed less of their true selves than those who talk less frequently but more honestly, or personally. She has felt unaccepted because others did not allow her to remain silent. She feels that we should be more accepting, understanding, and sincere. We should accept people as they are.

18. Acceptance and support from the majority gives the individual greater security and feelings of worthiness. This leads to more communication.

19. An individual member may have a problem that is personal in nature or may be one concerning the group and its process.

20. One of our problems may be "confusion." We may be asking for the impossible when we demand that others put a label on their felt needs. When we are confused we are unable to pinpoint the cause of the difficulty. The confused person is actually asking for assistance in pinpointing the cause of the problem. We need support in facing painful issues. E.'s shock therapy may prevent the members from exploring their problems freely and logically.

21. If we feel secure enough and know the group is on our side, we will not need to cloak ourselves or our problems but would willingly bring them out for exploration.

22. Some members feel that an individual can put before the majority a problem which he believes the group needs to face. It was argued that such a procedure would reveal that such a presentation would show that the individual must have been concerned, to some degree, with the problem or he would not have presented it in the first place—in fact, he would not even be aware of it.

23. The group seemed to disagree as to the nature of group growth. It seemed to become a matter of individual perception and expectation. Growth thus is a relative thing. L. felt that the majority should allow the minority to stay where they wished—to progress at their own rate and in the directions they desire.

24. Since groups are made of individuals, it may be possible to measure this growth as it is experienced in the individual.

25. We seemed to agree that "leaving behind" meant that everyone should feel the same way about all issues; the old idea of 100% involvement on each issue. However, it was expressed that there is no need to have 100% involvement on each issue.

26. Some members felt that we haven't decided on the limits in

which we will function. Our present limits of functioning (agreed upon by our behavior) don't permit the growth we desire. Conflict.

27. E. again persisted in asking others what they thought of him. This led to the feeling in some that we can't give help until the receiver is ready to accept it.

28. We may be able to give our opinions of other members to them but be unable to accept this type of categorizing or judging ourselves. In that event we must communicate to others (in some way) that we are not ready to accept this type of criticism.

29. We can have unity without 100% agreement. Let some members continue to think in their own way. Growth is relative since individual perceptions and expectancies differ.

30. This led to the all important insight that "we have not told each other what we do have in common." A yardstick can be created (perhaps it already exists with us) that can measure common processes. There is a distinct difference between yardsticks and processes. We do have a common process in the group through which we satisfy our needs and this process leads to security. The common process is the *group*, for our needs could not be satisfied without the group. Each of us uses the group in his own way, to satisfy his own needs.

31. What is expected of other members (their behavior) is a limit which does not have to be verbalized to be felt. We are responsible for our behavior. We are unanimous in "our lack of consensus."

32. Those limits which are not realistic can be changed, which would allow movement to take place.

33. What we say and what we do may be in direct contradiction. This makes it imperative to focus on our behavior and feelings. This would lead to insight, clarification, and understanding.

34. The strangeness and anxiety that we occasionally feel, which stifles communication, may partly result from being threatened by speaking in front of nine other people. It is easier to talk and relate to one or two others—it is harder to relate to nine others—but it can be done. Perhaps we are afraid that the others will reject us or look at us differently if we expose our true selves.

35. Until we accept ourselves, we cannot accept others. Perhaps some members are not yet ready to fully accept others. Behavior is always caused.

36. At least four people said they were ready to expose themselves. In fact, F. and others already have started this trend. Perhaps the others will gain enough courage and security to follow suit.

37. The minority has the right to try and convert others to their way of thinking. They have the right to self-expression.

38. A person will change (grow and mature, etc.) when he feels it would be worthwhile and safe to do so. He will change only when the desire to change is strong enough.

39. We can make known our need for help but others may not want to or be able to give help at that moment. This is one value of groups, in that some*one* may at least be able to provide support, when it is needed. "It is difficult to help others when some of our own needs get in the way."

40. We can accept and develop the idea that we can allow others to have different points of view while we retain our own.

41. Our thinking becomes crystalized when we put our thoughts into words. We thus become more able to tell others just how we feel so that they can understand and accept us.

42. The relationship that develops between two group members has effects on the group as a whole. The group is thus closely interrelated. We have more wholeness and unity than we realize. We have unity while retaining our individuality.

43. Accept the fact that there will never be unanimous agreement. We all cannot have the same views on various topics. Once we realize and live with this idea, growth could continue indefinitely.

44. We learn to compromise. To meet our own needs through the group, we help them meet theirs. By giving, we receive.

45. We realized that giving examples of issues clarifies them. I can meet an individual's expressed need in more than one way. A person is mature who realizes that a felt need does not have to be met in exactly the way he desires.

46. Perhaps not knowing how we will be graded threatens us in that we want to maintain a "nice" picture in the eyes of the person or persons doing the grading. We want to remain "acceptable" to the person or persons who will evaluate us.

47. Perhaps we get too emotionally involved in the group which prevents us from bringing out a problem. Strong emotional involvement may lead to disorganization in thinking.

48. Unless we let others know that some of our perceptions have changed, they will continue to react to us in the manner previously formed. They will continue to react to the "older" picture we have given them. It is again the old problem of "communication."

49. We should share with others in the growth experiences we have between meetings.

50. We seem to desire to resolve an issue before we drop it. However, those issues which are not resolved continue to crop up. We do

not resolve issues at the same speed; therefore, they are brought up again for another member to resolve in his own way.

51. G. was a great help in that he caused us to focus our attention on several pertinent areas. G. is largely very honest and sincere.

52. We haven't shown to others our acceptance by giving them support.

53. We bring to the group's attention those matters which have greatest emotional significance. This is in accord with "hierarchy of needs."

54. If we assume others are honest, we will begin to act as if they were honest and thus reveal what we feel.

55. We must be willing to look at ourselves truthfully. We practice what may be called "group confession."

56. G. pointed out that we too often are forced to defend our views.

57. It is better to air out our presently felt feelings and needs, rather than to suppress them. If we suppress them, they will demand expression at a later date anyway.

58. We must learn to use the group in the solution of our problems instead of going to smaller groups.

59. We discovered we are not the happy family we claim to be but we are on the way to doing something about it.

60. If others accept our hostility (our negative side) then we can be sure they accept us in totality.

61. We should not think for others but ask him if our perceptions of what he has said are correct. Don't put words in the mouths of others.

62. We should use the "internal frame of reference" in trying to understand others.

63. It is uncomfortable to be misperceived. It is partly our job to correct misperceptions.

64. We must place before the group those things that make us uncomfortable.

65. Others must give us credit to grow and change between meetings.

Log 18

. . . I feel that the group would grow even faster if these silent people contributed more. . . .

1. We need to become familiar with everyone's yardstick concerning group growth. When we hear the opinions of others we may

gain added insights and new ways of perceiving group relationships.

2. This writer does not feel that we need or could attain common yardsticks in regard to the things we see and feel. Since we are all unique individuals we cannot look at the world in exactly the same way as another. We could, however, understand another person better if we gained some knowledge of the way he looks at the world.

3. Our evaluation, from others, is a helpful way of discovering whether or not others see us as we think they do. This is a valuable form of reality testing. Our group has used this technique but it could be developed further.

4. Some people may not be able to take criticism or evaluation from others since this may be too threatening.

5. Until we understand ourselves, our understanding of others will be limited. Our self-understanding grows by being a group member.

6. Since a member's behavior and talk influences the group, an individual's growth would be positively correlated to group growth.

7. Although E. feels that we as a group haven't grown, others feel that we have. We allowed E. almost an hour to explain his views on groupness. He is a difficult man to follow.

8. Our common purposes and interrelationships make us a group. Added to this are: affection, communication, and interdependence. We also have the common process of satisfying our needs through the group.

9. Some of the behavior and interrelationship features that have been exhibited sort of label us a therapy group. We haven't really called ourselves as such.

10. A leader is a group member since he falls within the group's limits.

11. Some individuals in a group can grow while others may not. Unless a member tells me that he has grown and describes the nature of his growth, I will be unable to judge that he has. Part of his growth, however, will be reflected in his behavior.

12. E. doesn't trust people's politeness since he feels that politeness is merely acquired behavior and may not be a sincere effort at giving help.

13. Since all behavior is motivated, we should consider more closely the cause and effects of our behavior in the group.

14. A group has a unit regardless of purpose.

15. We should examine the latent as well as the manifest content of our speech.

16. E. wants to deal with truths and not hypotheses. This can't be

done since much of behavioral science is still in the experimental stage and human behavior is so varied.

17. Walt pointed out to E. that he has been trying to direct the group.

18. The question of "group mind" came up, but since it is such a new term to us we were unable to reach anything resembling a conclusion or consensus of opinion.

19. Individual growth is a relative thing and depends upon the individual's attitudes, needs, and expectancies.

20. We are becoming more unique individuals because others help us to determine the boundaries and completeness of our differences.

21. The growth processes that are initiated within the group are continued between meetings in other situations.

22. Our growth appears in various areas of our personalities.

23. We become part of a group by interrelating.

24. The ideas of others, when they are stated in our own words, may sound different to the originator of the ideas. No two people look at the same idea alike.

25. Understanding is best achieved if we use similar language.

26. There is a distinction between a yardstick for the group and our own yardsticks. We are still trying to construct a yardstick to evaluate the group. It must be a group enterprise.

27. We have conformity by abiding by the group's limits, and have individuality in our own ideas.

28. Group limits may be different from individual limits.

29. Our self-knowledge is increased when other members help us straighten out our thinking and logic. This is reality testing.

30. We can describe group growth by measuring the growth of each member. Then we focus our attention on interrelationships, dynamics, feelings, and procedures to evaluate ourselves as a group.

31. When people differ with our ideas, we sometimes feel they are attacking us.

32. We should share our inner security and growth by communicating it to others. They will understand us better if we do so and perhaps profit from the way we look at things.

33. When we see a particular member being pressured, we come to the rescue.

34. Some members may grow, in their own way, without being too talkative.

35. We sometimes intellectualize too much and talk around a problem.

36. One sign of growth is that we talk to the group and not to a specific individual.

37. We should let others know how they affect us and how we feel toward them. An undesirable interpersonal relationship can cause group discomfort.

38. F. sees the members as either giving or receiving help.

39. We see ourselves in another member when he presents to the group a problem that we ourselves feel.

40. We are sometimes afraid of shocking someone or of being disloyal. We do not want to become an outcast by the things we say. We want to remain an accepted member and we try to maintain equilibrium.

41. F. tried to act the therapist today. This could be a sign of increased security and self-knowledge.

42. If I say the behavior of another is unacceptable, I must tell him how to act differently. I must tell him how his behavior affects me.

43. F. says she can feel that someone else is sincere.

44. A. revealed some personal problems in order to show his sincerity to F., but she did not comprehend it as such.

45. We should look at our real selves more.

Log 19

This meeting was the first during which Walt was missing. This made us gradually assume responsibility for governing and directing ourselves. . . .

It was again felt that we should seek the causes of our misperceiving others. . . .

. . . we must not suppress feelings toward another because these ideas still strive for recognition and can cause unpleasant situations to develop. If we verbalize our feelings, we can reach a solution to any misperception we might have. It was also noticed that members cannot express their true feelings until they feel secure enough in the group atmosphere and feel that others understand and accept them. . . .

. . . He seemed to be saying that our behavior might get out of control without the limits and clarification that is set by a leader. When others told him that we are all leaders and therapists, he seemed to become more reassured. . . .

. . . We still haven't formulated the qualities of a good group member and thus are somewhat unable to evaluate each other.

. . . As I see it, one of the chief benefits of being a group member is that we can learn about group processes and functioning and then apply it to other groups of which we are either a member or a leader. . . .

Although it is not an easy or pleasant experience to evaluate ourselves, it would be a good learning experience. . . .

Log 20

Today's meeting began when Walt told us he would be out of town when two of our meetings are scheduled. After discussing possible alternative plans, we decided on either extending the time on two regular sessions or on meeting as a group without the leader. Perhaps the group is realizing its own potential and is ready to assume its own leadership.

The rest of our two-hour meeting was spent in discussing systems of grading and evaluation. . . .

We tried to decide whether or not we needed unanimous agreement before acting and this issue was not settled. . . .

It seemed that part of what we were facing today was a new situation with no apparent limits. The unknown, because it has no limits, seems threatening. We imagine that we might become too critical, hostile, or shocking. . . .

The issue was not settled today; probably because it is an important one that cannot be rushed through. We are dealing with a problem that is common to many facets of life. We have certainly initiated our thinking processes in an attempt to reach an understanding of this situation.

Log 21

. . . B. wanted help on a personal problem. This was the first time he had really asked the group for assistance, since he was usually a giver of help in previous meetings. . . .

1. In our daily lives we play many roles and fit many stereotypes.

2. Teachers and ministers are often accepted in a stereotype manner.

3. Since B. is a resource person, we discussed how such a person could be used in a group such as ours.

4. Some limits in group work are unchangeable. Others are changed as we change the criteria that were used in creating them.

5. The matter concerning majority vote on decision-making was brought up but didn't seem to be settled.

6. Group members must take responsibility for change in group procedures.

7. In a sense B. was asking to be evaluated and this seemed to be a follow-up of A.'s suggestion, last time, concerning oral evaluation of each other.

8. We can evaluate others only if we have something to contribute.

9. The problem concerning the difficulty of getting into a discussion was mentioned again. This seemed to be a rebellion against time monopolizing by a few members.

10. A. asked B. how he looked at non-Christians. This seemed to be a question concerning himself for A. has told us, in so many words, that he is anti-religious in some respects. B. had asked to be evaluated and then so did A.

11. B. felt that he did react to a stereotype of "non-Christian" but felt that people in general react to stereotypes of others. Our initial impression of a stranger is largely determined by his awakening in us, learned reactions to certain stereotypes. He becomes a cue to a past response.

12. Walt pointed out that perhaps we were really talking about interpersonal relationships and not reactions to stereotypes.

13. Our roles are determined by our behavior in interpersonal relationships.

14. When we react to a person as if he represented a stereotype, we do not really know the person. Such a reaction may prevent us from really knowing him.

15. This business is related to "labeling" in psychotherapy—which can interfere with growth and understanding.

16. In life it seems that we initially react to a person by categorizing him: is he single, married, a teacher, a father, old person, young person, and so on. Only later, by talking and relating to him, do we really get to know him.

17. In our own lives we probably hope to create certain impressions on others. We do things that help others to see us in certain ways. We try to display a self-concept in our behavior.

18. In group work we should accept another's need for reacting to us in a stereotyped manner.

19. The question was again raised as to which person's need should be met in group relationships. I think this can be answered on a democratic give-and-take principle. In order to have some of our needs satisfied—through the group—we must help others meet some of their needs. By giving we receive.

20. Our behavior doesn't always correspond to our self-concept. In

a group setting such as ours, the other members can tell us how we are being perceived. This is reality testing because we can judge whether or not our behavior is being perceived as we would like it to be perceived. If we are acting in a way not congruent with our self-concept, we are then able to change.

21. There are both verbal and visual kinds of communication. In order to really understand an individual, we must learn his language.

22. We can accept criticism from those that love us.

23. We must correct misperceptions and be frank and honest.

24. Giving help makes the other fellow feel secure—then he can help me. Our relationship thus deepens.

25. In this group we learn to make our behavior conform to the picture we hold of ourselves and wish to give others.

In summary, our meeting was a successful one in that we felt secure enough to discuss important issues. B. was secure enough to ask for evaluations from others.

Log 22

. . . E. felt that we too often criticize a person or issue without offering suggestions for a remedy in the meantime. This very issue was mentioned in previous meetings and was partly answered since we do try to figure ways out of dilemmas. . . .

L. brought up the problem of evaluation again—as it was concerned with majority *vs.* minority rule. . . . In a sense we initiated today a process of evaluation—evaluation in the group. Any group problem of importance comes up again and again until we solve it. A majority decision takes into consideration the needs of the minority. If the majority did not consider the minority, rebellion might result. We came to the realization that we are all unique individuals who cannot see eye-to-eye on all things. We become even more unique and individual as a result of group interaction. When there is unity in a group, the minority will go along with the majority decision because they will not feel left out. . . .

We came to realize that each of us has basic beliefs that are held firmly—they are part of our basic attitudes—those attitudes that help to shape our personalities. . . .

Log 23

Today A. became a leader. . . . Before we could decide upon the grade issue, we had to establish a voting procedure and it was decided that when two-thirds of our group agreed on something, it would hold. Since B., F., and G. weren't pleased with the above ideas we learned that 100% agreement is almost impossible to attain. It did not seem that we gave these three people enough support and understanding concerning their needs in this issue. By using parliamentary procedures we did settle the grade issue. . . .

. . . It was felt that the continued use of parliamentary procedure would change the nature of the group, but with further discussion we felt that we would try to keep the group as it had been. . . .

We felt that a personal, verbal evaluation would be one of the most useful things we could take away from the course. Since we will be constantly dealing with people in our lives it would be beneficial to discover those facets in our personality that may hinder interpersonal relationships. . . .

. . . this writer volunteered to be evaluated, they told me that I had good ability in putting things into short, clear sentences. I seem to possess the ability to summarize the things happening fairly accurately. This was naturally a boost to my ego and is something I've been trying to develop. The discussion then shifted to E.'s speaking ability and a few persons felt that it is difficult to follow him since he includes so many things in his verbalizations. E. seemed to gain some insight and benefited from this.

In summary, it seems that we have ironed out the grading problem and are beginning to use a method of verbal evaluation in the group.

Log 24

Today's meeting began with a discussion of Walt's job possibility overseas and his decision not to accept it. I feel it is fine when the leader shows himself to be a human being with problems of his own. It seems to have led to closer unity in our group.

B. brought up again his concern with the Christian, non-Christian statement he made two or three sessions ago. He tried to clarify his points of view and asked the group's help in order to determine whether or not there are things in his behavior, verbalizations, and mannerisms which would operate against his goals in life. . . .

The discussion of religion seemed to be related to whether or not we are self-sufficient or can we profit from sharing. . . . We don't force anyone to accept our point of view but we offer him our perceptions, in the hope that they may broaden his point of view on an issue or problem. We seemed to be looking for a common ground of communication. . . .

. . . This led A. to describe two areas in his own life in which seeming growth has taken place. It is heartening to know that people do profit from such a form of group activity.

C. got brave enough to ask A. a direct question, for which she received a reply. This may be an indication of growth on her part. . . .

Log 25

. . . This writer mentioned the fact that G. and I felt that those members that get the most from the group are those who present personal problems and those that get involved with each session. I still kind of wonder why G. is so darned silent—perhaps he is afraid or perhaps the group just doesn't measure up to his expectancies. If the group isn't going too well, he could possibly help us out with concrete suggestions. It benefits us nothing if he just sits silently. . . .

F.'s problem opened up the whole area of evaluation and we came to realize that we use our own standards and those of society. . . . I guess the final solution lies within the individual. We also seemed to uncover two other standards—one being growth up to this point, and the other being the ultimate level of attainment. It seems that in this course, we grade ourselves as to where we are now. The ultimate level will be attained in the future, with further study and experience.

So in grading ourselves we measure our growth and compare it with universal or society created standards. . . .

In the past we have revolted against using criteria, for we felt that this might destroy our uniqueness since we would try to conform to the characteristics of a good group leader, or member. . . .

Log 26

After about ten minutes of small talk on rain, hailstorms, tornadoes, popcorn, and foods, B. told us that his thinking had changed in regard to L.'s background and its similarity to American ways of life. . . .

. . . several members tried to pinpoint their hostility toward Walt. They tried to determine what aspects of his behavior made them irritated. E. felt that Walt has been too ambivalent and changes roles too often, or abruptly. He felt that needs can be ambivalent and that the group was too emotionally involved to give Walt assistance last time. It was pointed out that a person can be a leader and a client at the same time. . . . A person can be a leader nominally, by prestige, or by verbal involvement. . . .

It was mentioned that a person who brings in limits is thought of as a leader. I wonder if the group felt as I did—that we attacked Walt last week because he symbolized authority, controls, or society. . . . The group did not want to admit that the unpleasant topic of last time originated within themselves—Walt merely pointed it out more clearly, especially in showing us that it meant a lot of work. . . .

We seemed to be trying to find out who Walt is. Is he a group member or a leader? This writer thinks he has been both and at times we have made him a leader and have refused, at other times, to see him merely as a member. He has also been referred to as the expert and as the resource person. The group is saying that our roles are multiple. We also saw that the group can take over when the leader gets out of line. . . .

Someone mentioned the feeling that it can be painful to be overvalued. . . .

Log 27

Today's meeting saw the group continue to attack issues of concern and was also characterized by a deeper understanding of interpersonal relations in the group.

1. A. began by wondering whether or not drinking is a sin. This discussion was begun when F. mentioned the large amounts of liquor consumption that she had heard about. This topic was not carried long.

2. A. complimented R.'s summarizing ability. This made me become more active as I wanted to show the group that I could summarize and reflect feeling—as I've always wanted to do. I gained some feelings of success in so doing.

3. C. felt secure enough to tell B. that she was hurt by his statement of the previous meeting. B. had anticipated C.'s hurt feeling and related that he had already established good relations with her and therefore wanted to achieve the same thing with G. He realized that his behavior was probably experienced as rejection.

4. B. clarified his role with G. and stated that he wanted to establish better relations with him. He felt that reconciliation was important to him. Although some of the barriers that exist between people cannot be avoided, it is important to make restitution later. We should try to overcome these barriers and get along with others better.

5. Some people get hurt as we try to help others. We therefore searched for a process of helping all concerned at the same time—considering everyone's feelings.

6. The multiplicity of roles was again mentioned, and it was felt that society often expects us to act a certain role most of the time.

7. E. mentioned that our behavior can block communication at times. Therefore, we should try to make our behavior conform to the impression we wish to leave on others. When we forced G. into a certain role he fought back by trying to maintain his individuality. Some members felt that G. has rejected us. Today G. was more verbal than he has been in a long time.

8. When we are emotionally involved in a discussion, we do not always choose the right words, thereby allowing ourselves to be misunderstood. We should try to control our ideas more, especially as these ideas influence others.

9. Should we try to be interested in every topic of concern? It was felt that every member does not have to be interested in each topic but may be able to help others who are confused on an issue. Those things that seem important are brought before the group—the old hierarchy of needs.

10. F. questioned G.'s rejection of member interdependence since this idea tended to make the group secondary to the individual. G. felt that you cannot force interdependence on a group member since it should be a relationship that grows out of felt needs. The group is, however, composed of individuals. In considering a group, we should look at individual needs and behavior as well as group functioning and process.

11. E. seemed to tell G. that it's not as effective to operate alone as it is to receive help from others. Two or three minds are better than one. This led to the feeling that we might fear losing our individuality when we become part of a group. This group, however, has helped us become even more unique and independent. Collective thinking can be more effective than tackling a problem alone.

12. Sometimes silence can be understood as agreement. If a member disagrees with a topic or idea, he should state it or be misunderstood.

13. E. felt cheated when individual needs are placed above group needs.

14. We felt that our thinking has established our group as being therapeutic.

15. G. seemed to be afraid of seeking help in this group for he didn't know the limits of such behavior and questioned our compe-

tency. This feeling seems to have been shared by quite a few others. Unknown limits are fearful.

16. The group can't meet all needs since this is part of life.

17. We have anticipated unpleasantness in self-revelation. Fail to see possible benefits of therapy.

18. What kinds of problems can be handled in such a group? Our feelings of personal security determine the degree to which we reveal to others our personal problems.

19. To know something and understand it, we should experience it. Since we haven't experienced how it would feel to reveal our personal problems, we have left this issue alone.

20. Quite a few members felt that Walt's behavior labeled him as the leader from the beginning. R. defended Walt as a person having needs of his own. The group, however, felt insecure with a leader who had a dual role. The issue of grading and Walt's reaction to it caused him to appear as a leader or a symbol of authority.

21. We again seemed to work on the idea of the qualifications of a good group leader and have begun to spell them out.

Log 28

Very soon after our group was formed today, A. related his feelings on missing E. and he probably voiced what others also felt. Any group member is missed when he fails to attend a meeting and this seems to indicate our cohesiveness.

We determined that only three of our group will be on campus next semester while the rest will be at various jobs in the world. We seem to have begun feeling sad about breaking up and already are seeking the addresses of various members. . . .

This writer asked for the group's help in regard to his anticipated handling of classroom order and was glad to receive help from a few of the members. . . .

. . . This became related to E.'s proposed use of group guidance techniques with freshmen at . . . and then became related to C.'s use of group techniques in her apartment house for girls. . . .

In a sense we seem to be satisfying our own need to define our group more clearly with its limits. Using Walt as a resource person proved very successful. Walt told us that limits can come from the group itself or from the leader. . . .

We then turned to a discussion of therapy and its varied definitions. Part of adjusting lies in integrating what we are with what we want to be. Therapy was broadly defined as a growth process leading to a better adjustment to society and our level of aspiration. When we realize and accept our inadequacies we are in a better position to make improvements. It was pointed out that part of adjusting lies in developing more harmonious relations to society since we do not live in a vacuum. The individual can gain greater satisfaction from adjusting to society. Many of our needs can be met only through others; therefore, we must be able to get along with them.

When group members are secure enough they will correct a leader that manipulates his group too frequently. We can ignore or attack a hostile figure. We become acceptable to others by helping them meet their needs. . . .

. . . B. felt that life goals are part of the individual and should be recognized in order to understand the other person. Motivation may be attained by keeping the goals just a little higher than the achievement level. We finally agreed that "nothing succeeds like success itself." Success is the great provider of motivation. We decided that level of aspiration was a relative term and that part of adjustment lies in keeping this level in line with our capacities. . . .

Near the close, F. asked the group generally: "Have we made progress as a group?" This writer reacted by pointing out that we seem to have gotten closer together, attack problems more objectively—as a group—and certainly know each other better. Since we are now pretty secure with each other we are able to handle heretofore "touchy" subjects with sufficient objectivity and understanding. Many individual members have changed for the better. In fact, I firmly believe that each member has grown for the better—some more so than others. I know that this writer has grown quite a bit and has gained much from being a group member and leader. We felt that one measure of our growth is our ability to tolerate differences. We can become even more unique and individualistic as a group member and still contribute to group progress.

Log 29

. . . We mentioned that therapist can impose his value system on the client and that part of his job is to prevent, to some extent, this type of procedure. If the therapist is aware of his values and beliefs he is in better position to prevent this from interfering with his work. We are responsible for employing our values in therapy. . . .

We tried to determine the place of values in a therapeutic relationship. We concluded that the therapist does not try to change the client's values but helps him to look at the feelings behind the values;

feelings which may have been intentionally ignored. The feelings and abstractions behind an experience determines the kind and degree of learning taking place. . . .

There may be some degree of fear in our attempts to fully understand another, for in so doing our own viewpoint or perspective may be changed. . . .

. . . We seem to need some form of external criteria against which to compare man's behavior.

The meeting closed when this writer asked for a restatement of the grading process. I was given an answer.

The preceding log represents just one kind of group as perceived through the eyes of only one person.

Readers seeking comparable protocols describing groups conducted by other people may find the following sources helpful.

Bach, George. *Intensive Group Psychotherapy*, New York: Ronald, 1954.

Corsini, Raymond. *Methods of Group Psychotherapy*, New York: McGraw-Hill, 1957.

Driver, Helen. *Multiple Counseling*, Wisconsin Monona Publications, 1954.

Hinkley, Robert, and Lydia Hermann. *Group Treatment in Psychotherapy*, Minneapolis: University of Minnesota Press, 1951.

Slavson, Samuel. *The Practice of Group Therapy*, New York: International Universities Press, 1951.

Wilson, Gertrude, and Gladys Ryland. *Social Group Work Practice*, New York: Houghton Mifflin, 1949.

Index

Abrams, Arnold, 176
Algren, Nelson, 39
Allport, G. W., 75, 175
Almada, Albert A., 128
Alpert, A., 24
Alton, Illinois, YWCA, 44
American Personnel and Guidance Association, 42
Arbuckle, Dugald, 38, 40
A.S.C.D., 150, 162
Ash, P., 106, 127
Association for Supervision and Curriculum Development, 7
Axelrod, P. L., 128

Bach, George R., 86, 91, 105, 127, 129, 171, 175, 232
Bales, Robert F., 127, 176
Ballin, Marion Ruth, 176
Barnes, Fred, 148–49, 162
Barnes, M. J., 128
Barr, Lawrence, 176
Baruch, Dorothy W., 24, 39, 175
Beck, Dorothy Fahs, 100, 127
Beers, Clifford, 39
Benne, Kenneth, 16–18, 24
Bennett, Margaret, 7
  Guidance in Groups, 7
Berg, Janice, 92
Bergson, H., 22
Bethel, Maine, Group Dynamics Researches, 144
Bettelheim, Bruno, 39, 127
Bion, W. R., 90, 92
Bisch, Louis E., 39

Blessing, Harold D., 176
Blocksma, Douglas D., 127
B'nai B'rith, 135
Bold, Richard W., 177
Bookman, G., 133, 161
Bordin, Edward, 40
Borgotta, Edgar F., 127, 176
Boring, R. O., 128
Borow, Henry, 162
Bosco, John, Sr., 176
Bradford, Leland, 24
Brammer, Lawrence M., 132, 161
Briskin, Gerald J., 177
Broedel, John, 150–151, 177
Burchard, Edward M. L., 172, 176

Cameron, M. S., 128
Canter, Irving, 177
Canter, Ralph R., Jr., 171, 175
Cantor, Nathaniel, 150, 162
Caplan, Stanley William, 161, 177
Carlson, Bill, 44
Cartwright, Dorwin, 23, 25, 106, 127, 160, 163, 176
  Group Dynamics, 23
Case conference method, 159
Central Michigan State Teachers College, 44
Chang, Thomas, 177
Chenven, Harold, 177
Chicago Council on Foreign Relations, 44
Clampitt, Richard R., 177
Clark, D. H., 92
Client-Centered Therapy, 23

Coffey, H. S., 128
Cole, Natalie R., 150, 163
College orientation, 132–134
Combs, Arthur W., 11, 22, 23, 25
  Individual Behavior, 22
Common Errors in Psychotherapy, 22
Cope, J. Raymond, 128
Copeland, Theodore, 133, 161
Corsini, Raymond, 23, 25, 86, 91, 232
Cotton, John M., 127
Counseling, 12
Coyle, Grace L., 8, 151, 163
Cozzens, James G., 39
Croley, Hugh T., 177
Cronbach, Lee, 173, 176
Curriculum Development as Re-education of the Teacher, 6

Daniels, Marvin, 177
Danville Veterans Administration Hospital, 44
Darley, John G., 171, 175
Davis, Ruth G., 175
Davis, W. A., 39
Deabler, H. L., 128
De Boer, John J., 150, 162
De Grazia, Sebastian, 22, 24
  Common Errors in Psychotherapy, 22
De Huzar, George B., 7
Deutsch, Helen, 39
Dollard, John, 22, 25
Dreikurs, Rudolph, "Group Psychotherapy from the Viewpoint of Adlerian Psychology," 7
Driver, Helen, 151, 161, 163, 232
Dunbar, H. Flanders, 39
Dynamics of Groups at Work, 23
Dysart, James M., 177

Education, definition of, 13
Elkins, Deborah, 150, 163
Engstrand, Stuart, 39
Evans, John T., 175, 177
Evanston Township High School, 150–151
Examinations, 145–147
Eysenck, Hans J., 39

Farris, Dorothy, 44
Fedder, Ruth, 151, 163

Feish, Irving J., 177
Feldman, Leonard, 177
Fiedler, Fred, 172, 176
Fihs, Charles T., 133, 161
Fine, Harold J., 177
Fisher, Bernard, 177
Flemming, Edward L., Jr., 177
Foulkes, S. H., 90, 92
Frank, Jerome D., 92, 105, 127, 172, 176
Freedman, M., 128
Freeman, Lucy, 39
Freud, Sigmund, 15, 24
Freudian philosophy, 10
Fromm, Erich, 39

Gage, N. L., 128
Geller, Max, 177
Gerber, I. J., 39
Gerstenlauer, Charles A., 177
Gestaltists, 11
Gibbs, J. R., 127
Gillies, Emily P., 150, 162
Glatzner, H. T., 127
Goodrich, Thomas A., 133, 161
Gordon, Ira J., 24, 177
Gordon, Thomas, 7, 86, 92, 120, 127, 128
Gorlow, Leon, 127
Grades, 166–170
Grier, Daniel J., 177
Grob, Samuel, 178
Gross, Neal, 171, 175
Group, The, 23
Group-Centered Leadership, 7
Group Dynamics, 23
Group dynamics, definition of, 14–15, 19
Group guidance programs, see Group techniques
Group leader, checkpoints for behavior of, 98
  effects of courses on, 147–148
  functions of, 93–102
  relationship of group with, 100, 115–116, 143, 172, 180–181
  responsibilities of, 27, 93–95, 101, 139–140, 142
  role of, 6, 91, 94, 101, 106, 115–116, 139–140, 158–160, 173–174

Group process, contents in, 87, 88
  definition of, 1–7
  diary report of, 184–232
  problems in, 93–126
  progress in, 87
  techniques for quantifying of, 172
Groups, action demonstration of, 43–86
  admission of new members into, 111–112
  checklist for being effective member in, 182
  comparisons of members within, 166–170
  composition of, 105–107
  decisions in, 119–122
  definition of, 15–16
  evaluation within, 164–170
  growth of maturity in, 100
  growth within, 164–165
  helping techniques used in, 125–126
  identification of goals by, 143–145
  individual in, 20, 165–166
  involuntary membership in, 102–105
  length of life of, 110–111
  limitations in, 122
  maturation of, 101–102
  minority groups in, 120–122
  missing member, 115
  monopolist in, 116–117
  moral values, 156–158
  motivations of, 19–20
  mutual respect for security in, 90
  nature of, 102–105
  need for logs in, 88–89
  needs of members in, 87
  position of silent member in, 112–114
  problem of out-of-group encounters in, 108–110
  protocols of group sessions, 43–86, 95–97, 99, 101–102, 106–107, 112–113, 119
  reaction to catharsis in, 117–118
  reactions to missing leader in, 115–116
  reactions to use of time in, 88–89
  reasons for, 20
  research on, 170–174
  resistance to changing status quo, 117

Groups, responsibilities in, 120, 122–125
  rights of individuals in, 120–122
  role of food in, 126
  role of leader in, *see* Group leader, role of
  role of stereotypes in, 118–119
  role playing in, 125
  roles of, 16–19
  rotation of leadership in, 100, 116
  silence in, 114–115
  size of, 110
  spiritual values in, 156–158
  termination of, 180–182
  themes in, 87–88
  therapeutic effects of, 106
  training of effective members in, 181–182
  uses of, 180–181
  voluntary membership of, 102–105
  voting in, 119–122
Group techniques, application of, 130–160
  group guidance programs, 135–140
  keeping records in, 145–147
  need for definite program in, 158–160
  orientation in, 130–135
  results of a workshop in, 148–150
  studies with underachievers, 150–151
  subject matter classroom uses of, 140–143
  use of home-room for, 139
  use of student council for, 151–156
Group therapy, definition of, 14–15
  effectiveness of, 44
  films about, 86
  interpretation of, 11, 12–15
  problems of older people in, 109–110
Group Work in Education, 7
Guidance, 12
Guidance in Groups, 7
Grunwald, Hanna, 161

Haas, Robert Bartlett, 128, 151, 163
Hadden, Samuel, 127
Haiman, Franklyn S., 126
Hale, Paul, 162

Hall, Calvin, 9, 23
Handbooks, 132–133
Hare, Paul, 127, 176
Harlow, George, 161
Harris, F. E., 150, 162
Havighurst, R. J., 39
Hemphill, John K., 175
Hermann, Lydia, 86, 91
Herrold, Kenneth F., 24
Hewer, Vivan H., 161
Heyns, Roger, 172, 176
High school orientation for college,
    132–134
Hinkley, Robert G., 86, 91, 232
Hobbs, Nicholas, 86, 92
Hoch, Erasmus L., 127
Holden, Ruby M., 178
Hoppock, Robert, 133, 136, 151, 161,
    163
Horwitz, Murray, 176
Horwitz, Selma, 128
Hoyt, Don P., 161
Hunter College Veterans Guidance
    Center, 131
Hymes, James L., 128

Illing, H. A., 24
Illinois, University of, 43, 44
    College of Education, 2
    Office of Teacher Placement, 44
Illinois Association of Student Councils,
    151–156
Illinois Curriculum Program, 141, 148
"Index of Cohesiveness," 171
"Index of Mutuality," 171
Indiana University, 43
Individual, growth of, 1–7
Individual Behavior, 22
*International Journal of Group Psycho-
    therapy*, 7, 22
Interpretation, definition of, 28

Jenkins, David H., 24, 150, 163
Jennings, Helen H., 126, 175
Jersild, Arthur T., 23, 25, 39
    When Teachers Face Themselves, 23
Joel, Walther, 175
Jones, Francis D., 178
Josselyn, Irene, 39

Journal of the National Association of
    Deans and Women, 24
Jung, C. G., 20

Kamm, Robert, 133, 161
Kimball, Jack F., 178
Knopka, Gisela, 127, 128
Knox, Wilma Jones, 178
Kotkov, Benjamin, 127, 172, 176

Landin, Esther, 162
Langworthy, Stanton B., 178
Lawlor, Gerald W., 175
Laycock, Samuel R., 23, 150, 162
Leary, T., 128
Lecky, P., 23
Leino, Walter B., 178
Levy, John, 39
Lewis, Bill, 44
Lewis, Robert T., 178
Lifton, Walter M., 3, 11, 23, 24, 25,
    142–143, 151–156, 164–174, 175,
    176
    "Group Therapy in Educational In-
        stitutions," 11
    "A Reply to a Plague on Both Your
        Houses," 23
Lindner, Robert, 22, 24
    Prescription for Rebellion, 22
Lindsay, Gardner, 9, 23
Lindt, Hendrik, 92
Lippitt, Ronald, 24, 176
Little, Harry M., 127
Loeser, Lewis, 15–16, 24
Logs, 166, 185–232
Lowenstein, Norman, 133, 136, 161
Luck, Juanita M., 8

Maas, H., 150, 162
McCann, Willis H., 128
McCorkle, David B., 139, 162
McFarland, John W., 139, 162
McKown, Harry C., 162
Manteno State Hospital, 44
Martin, John H., 178
Martin, William E., 171, 175
Maslow, Abraham H., 39
May, Rollo, 39
Mazzitelli, Dominick, 44
Mehlman, Benjamin, 178

Menninger, Karl A., 39
Metcalf, Harold H., 150, 163, 176
Michaels, Joseph J., 172, 176
Michigan: Central Michigan State Teachers College, 44
Miller, Lorraine, 127
Miller, Neal E., 22, 25
Minnesota Multiphasic Personality Inventory, 172
Mitchell, Dorothy, 178
Monroe, Ruth, 39
Mooney Problem Check List, 137, 141
Moreno, J. L., 86, 92, 128, 129
Moustakis, Clark, 162
Mullins, Elizabeth, 43–44

Naboisek, Herbert, 178
Neal, Harley, 138
Nelson, Alice D., 175, 178
Newburger, Howard M., 178
Newton, Rita, 44
Noble, Frank G., 176
Northern, Helen, 178

Occupations, 23
O'Dea, David J., 139, 162
Oedipal situation, 10
Ojemann, Ralph H., 24, 141, 162
Orientation: definition of, 131–132, 134
   programs in, 134–135
Ossorio, A., 128

Packard, Vance, 39
Page, Curtis W., 178
Parloff, Morris B., 178
Patterson, Cecil, 40, 41
Pelican, Mary Ann, 44
Pepinsky, Harold B., 24, 175
Peres, Hadassah, 176
Perkins, Hugh V., 150, 162, 175
Personality, changes in, 10, 21
   description of, 10
   theories of, 9–13
Personnel and Guidance Journal, 23
Peters, Arthur A., 39
Petrillo, Luigi, 176
Pivnick, Harold, 178
Platts, Grace, 127
Polansky, Norman, 176
Porter, E. H., 38, 40

Powdermaker, Florence, 92, 105, 127
Practice of Group Therapy, The, 7
Prescot, Daniel, 150, 162
Prescription for Rebellion, 22
Progressive Education, 22
Protocols involving groups, 86
Psychoanalysis and Group Behavior: A Study in Freudian Group Behavior, 7
Psychotherapy, definition of, 10, 11

Rank, Otto, 10, 22
Raths, Louis, 30, 36, 38, 40
Reading for Living, 141
Readings in Group Work, 23
Redl, Fritz, 40, 90, 92, 128, 176
Reflection of content, definition of, 28
Reflection of feeling, definition of, 28
Reik, Theodor, 40
Richardson, Harold, 162
Robert's Rules of Order, 120, 133
Rogers, Carl R., 11, 22, 23, 25, 38, 41, 134, 161
   Client-Centered Therapy, 23
Roman, Melvin, 178
Rook, LeRoy, 178
Rorschach, 172
Rosenberg, Bernard, 161
Rosenburg, Pearl P., 179
Rousseau, Jean Jacques, 22
Ryland, Gladys, 232

Saloshin, Henriette E., 179
Samler, Joseph, 129
Scheidlinger, Saul, 7, 23, 179
   Psychoanalysis and Group Behavior: A Study in Freudian Group Behavior, 7
Schick, Sarah J., 179
Schulberg, Bud Wilson, 40
Schwebel, Milton, 128
Seeley, John R., 141, 162
Seeman, Alice Zerbola, 179
Selye, Hans, 40
Shakespeare, William Makepeace, 27
Shapiro, David, 175
Sharp, George, 6, 7
   Curriculum Development as Re-education of the Teacher, 6
Sharp, Louise, 44

Shartle, Carroll, 144
Shaw, Franklin J., 22, 24
Sheats, P., 16–18, 24
Sherman, Max A., 92
Sheviakov, George V., 128
Shoben, Edward J., 22, 24
Shostram, Everett L., 132, 161
Singer, Stanley L., 162
Sinick, Daniel, 136, 161
Slawson, Samuel R., 7, 23, 92, 127, 128, 232
  The Practice of Group Therapy, 7
Smucker, Orden, 175
Snygg, Donald, 22, 24
  Individual Behavior, 22
Social Group Work, 7
Social Work Yearbook, 7
Sociometric ratings, 167–170
Solomon, J. C., 128
Southern Illinois University, 133
So You Want to Help People, 38
Spotnitz, Hyman, 128
SRA Youth Inventory, 137
Stafford, Curt, 44
Stefflre, B., 162
Steiner, Mrs. Lee, 40
Stendler, Celia, 128
Stieper, Donald, 127
Stiles, Frances A., 141, 162
Stock, Dorothy, 175, 179
Strang, Ruth, 7, 162
  Group Work in Education, 7
Structuring, definition of, 29
Student council, *see* Group techniques, use of student council in
Sullivan, Dorothea F., 23, 25
  Readings in Group Work, 23
Super, Donald E., 24
Swift, Fletcher H., 133, 161
Sylvester, Emmy, 127
Symonds, Percival, 13, 24

Taft, Jessica, 11, 22
Taguiri, Renato, 176
Talland, G. A., 92
Teacher, role of, 6
Teachers College Bureau of Publications, 6
Teaching techniques, clarifying operations in, 30–32

Teaching techniques, description of, 26–39
  security giving operations in, 35–38
  show how operations in, 32–34
Telschow, Earl, 127
Test questions, 145–147
Tests, 145–147
Thelen, Herbert, 23, 25, 92, 106, 109, 127, 128, 175
  Dynamics of Groups at Work, 23
Thematic Apperception Test, 172
Thorne, Frederick, 38, 41
Trapp, Edward P., 179
Trecker, Harleigh, 7, 8
  Social Group Work, 7
Tropp, Emanuel, 127
Trow, William Clark, 24, 150, 162
Turner, Marion E., 128
Twelfth Annual Conference of Orientation Directors, 133
Tyler, Leona, 38, 41

Understanding of people, 39–40
University of Illinois, 2, 43, 44

Welch Convalescent Hospital, 102, 113–114
Wertheimer, Max, 22
Westie, Charles M., 175
When Teachers Face Themselves, 23
White, Robert M., 132, 161
White, Robert W., 40
Wieder, Gerald S., 12, 24, 179
Wilson, Gertrude, 232
Winder, Alvin, 127
Wittenberg, Rudolph M., 38, 41, 92
  So You Want to Help People, 38
Wolfe, Thomas, 40
Wrenn, C. Gilbert, 133, 161
Wright, Richard, 40
Wright, Wayne E., 161, 162
Y.M.C.A., 135
Y.M.H.A., 135
Y.W.C.A., 135
  Alton, Illinois, 44
Y.W.H.A., 135

Zander, Alvin F., 23, 25, 172, 176
  Group Dynamics, 23
Zlatchin, Philip J., 24, 171, 175, 179